Fodor's

E X P L O R I N G
SAN FRANCISCO

FODOR'S TRAVEL PUBLICATIONS, INC.

NEW YORK • TORONTO • LONDON • SYDNEY • AUCKLAND

While every care has been taken to ensure the accuracy of the information in this guide, time brings change, and consequently the publisher cannot accept responsibility for errors that may occur. Prudent travelers will therefore want to call ahead to verify prices and other "perishable" information.

Published in the United States by Fodor's Travel Publications, Inc.
Published in the United Kingdom by AA Publishing.

Fodor's and Fodor's Exploring Guides are registered trademarks of Fodor's Travel Publications, Inc.

ISBN 0–679–03015–8
First Edition

Fodor's Exploring San Francisco

Author: Mick Sinclair
Series Adviser: Christopher Catling
Joint Series Editor: Susi Bailey
Copy Editor: Beth Ingpen
Original Photography: Rob Holmes
Cartography: The Automobile Association
Cover Design: Louise Fili, Fabrizio La Rocca
Front Cover Silhouette: Rob Holmes

Special Sales
Fodor's Travel Publications are available at special discounts for bulk purchases (100 copies or more) for sales promotions or premiums. Special editions, including personalized covers, excerpts of existing guides, and corporate imprints, can be created in large quantities for special needs, For more information, contact your local bookseller or write to Special Markets, Fodor's Travel Publications, 201 East 50th Street, New York, NY 10022.

Printed and bound in Italy by Printers S.R.L., Trento
10 9 8 7 6 5 4 3 2 1

Mick Sinclair is the author of Fodor's *Exploring New York*, Fodor's *Exploring California* and Duncan-Petersen's *Versatile California*. He has also written or co-written three titles—*Florida*, *Scandinavia*, and *California*—in the Rough Guide series. His newspaper and magazine reviews on travel, culture, and the arts have appeared all over the world.

How to use this book

This book is divided into five main sections:

❏ Section 1:
San Francisco Is
Discusses aspects of life and living today, from environmental concerns to politics

❏ Section 2:
San Francisco Was
Places the city in its historical context and explores those past events whose influences are felt to this day

❏ Section 3: *A to Z Section*
Covers places to visit, with suggested walks and excursions, and lists itineraries, tips for those on a tight budget, and sightseeing ideas for children. Within this section fall the Focus-on articles, which consider a variety of topics in greater detail

❏ Section 4: *Travel Facts*
Contains the practical information that is vital for a successful trip

❏ Section 5:
Hotels and Restaurants
Lists recommended establishments in San Francisco, giving a brief description of what they offer

How to use the star rating
Most places described in this book have been given a separate rating:

▶▶▶   **Do not miss**

▶▶   **Highly recommended**

▶   **Worth seeing**

Not essential viewing

Map references
To make the location of a particular place easier to find, every main entry in this book is given a map reference, such as 176B3. The first number (176) indicates the page on which the map can be found; the letter (B) and the second number (3) pinpoint the square in which the main entry is located. The maps on the inside front cover and inside back cover are referred to as IFC and IBC respectively.

Contents

This quick-reference guide high-lights the sections of the book you will use most often: the maps; the introductory features; the Focus-on articles; the walks and the drives.

7

Adair Lara
Since 1989 Adair Lara has been a staff columnist for the *San Francisco Chronicle* and in 1990 won the Associated Press award for best columnist in California. Two collections of her columns have been published, *Welcome to Earth, Mom* and *At Adair's House, More Columns by America's Formerly Single Mom*. Her work has also appeared in numerous magazines.

My San Francisco

by Adair Lara

I have lived here most of my 42 years, and I still find San Francisco a distracting, bewitching place. Although I'm a native, I find myself driving blocks out of my way to see the murals in Balmy Alley in the Mission District or to see how the waterfront looks now the Embarcadero Freeway is down. And, like most residents here, I behave like a tourist, always heading out to see what I can discover on my own. One of my favorite places to explore is Russian Hill, where you discover just how quirky San Francisco is in its layout: walk around Russian Hill and even North Beach today, see Napier Lane and the little alleys, and you realize no city planner ever came along and said, we have to regulate this; no one straightened out the famous curves of Lombard Street—a major artery, after all, that empties into a switchback. And many people are unaware that there's a world beyond Telegraph Hill and Fisherman's Wharf: tiny Glen Park, on the slopes of Twin Peaks, for instance, the 1920s fantasyland of the Sunset fogbelt, the stately, Mediterranean neighborhood of Sea Cliff.

But in the end, what grabs us all, visitors and natives alike, are the views. Living in a city perched on 42 hills means that every day brings something I have never seen before—the Bay Bridge at night from a friend's deck on Dolores Street, Market Street from the 17th floor of Fox Plaza, the Golden Gate Bridge through columns at the Palace of Fine Arts, or the green of Angel Island hanging like a painting at the end of a street on Russian Hill. Maybe this is why problems just never seem urgent in this city. When you can look outside at the marvelous scenery, nothing else is as important.

My San Francisco

by Frank Heaney

As a child, before the Bay Bridge was built, I remember crossing San Francisco Bay on a ferry boat and looking back at the city's beautiful skyline. Since then, multi-shaped skyscrapers have changed that skyline radically—but it's still just as beautiful, just as incredible.

During the years that I worked and lived on Alcatraz as a correctional officer, I used to gaze across the bay at the city, sitting there in all its elegance and splendor. To the prison inmates it was a tantalizing, depressing sight, so close but out of reach. As they watched the sail boats skimming by, they were constantly reminded of all its inaccessible activities and diversions.

Now, each time I walk from Fisherman's Wharf through the Italian North Beach area, into Chinatown and Union Square, and through the downtown sector, I am reminded that San Francisco is one of the best walking cities in the world, one that reveals its majesty every step of the way. The song by Tony Bennett, "I left my heart in San Francisco," says it all: the sight of tiny cable cars climbing to the stars or of the fog coming through the Golden Gate and flowing over Alcatraz Island. The experience is unforgettable.

Frank Heaney
At the age of 15, in 1948, Frank Heaney became the youngest guard to work on Alcatraz Island, the notorious prison in San Francisco Bay. He knew Machine Gun Kelly, the Birdman of Alcatraz, Robert Stroud, and the driver from *Bonnie and Clyde*. He has written of his experiences in *Inside the Walls of Alcatraz* and has appeared on several TV shows.

SAN FRANCISCO IS

■ **A striking mix of nationalities, cultures, languages, and religions has been a feature of San Francisco since the gold-rush days. However, it is still easy to be surprised by the ethnic diversity of the city, with less than half of its 750,000 population born in the U.S. Those described below represent only the most visible—or most unexpected —ethnic groups in the city.....■**

Italians San Francisco holds the largest concentration of Italian-Americans in the U.S., and their impact on the city has been incalculable. Since the first wave of immigration in the 1880s, Italian names have become dominant in city politics and business. Although the Italian population is now spread throughout the city, scores of Italian restaurants and cafés are still found in North Beach, the city's original Italian district.

The Chinese Largely through the legalized racism which forced them into Chinatown during the late 1800s, San Francisco's Chinese have long been one of the largest and most visible elements in the city's ethnic mosaic. Traditionally, almost all have been of Cantonese origin, although the easing of Chinese immigration restrictions by the U.S. in 1965 brought settlers from some of the country's far-flung regions—a fact evinced by the expanding selection of regional Chinese cuisines offered in Chinatown's many restaurants.

Chinatown may provide a spiritual home for San Franciscan-Chinese but many have departed for middle-class

Fish at its best: Japantown sushi bar

lifestyles in the Richmond District, where Clement Street holds some of the city's best Chinese bakeries and restaurants.

Filipinos Strong links between the U.S. and the Philippines enabled Filipinos to study and work in the U.S. in comparatively large numbers. Many arrived during the 1920s to labor on Californian farms, while others acquired the American academic qualifications which led to powerful positions in their homeland. Those in San Francisco are seldom visible as a group except during mass at St. Patrick's Church.

Elbow to elbow, discerning Chinatown shoppers

❏ Of the U.S.'s 7.2 million Asians, 35 percent live in California, with San Francisco holding the largest Asian community outside Asia. ❏

The Japanese Since the end of World War II, when its Japanese-American population returned from internment camps, the Japanese community of San Francisco has consistently numbered just under 2 percent of the city's total population, currently around 12,000. Few of them, however, actually live in Japantown, where Shinto and Buddhist churches, Japanese shops, restaurants and social centers nevertheless provide a focal point for the community and a site for its festivals.

Southeast Asians California's Asian population increased by a startling 127 percent in the 1980s, a significant proportion of the new arrivals coming from the countries of Southeast Asia. Recent waves of Vietnamese, Cambodian, and Laotian immigration have resulted in a proliferation of new businesses—mostly restaurants—in the Tenderloin, carrying the promise of regeneration in this run-down neighborhood.

Latin Americans Spanish is more prevalent than English on the busy streets of the Mission District, which was settled in the 1940s by a Latin American population lured northwards by the prospect of work in shipyards and in other industries stimulated by the war. Latin Americans now comprise 15 percent

A Latin American bakery in Mission La Estrella

of the total population; around 50,000 live in the Mission District.

Russians The livestock of 19th-century Russian peasants who migrated to escape religious persecution became a feature of the Potrero Hill area until the late 1950s. More in evidence today are the cafés and bakeries dispensing Russian specialties in the Richmond District, which gained a significant community of urbanized Russian immigrants during the Soviet era. The neighborhood's magnificent Cathedral of the Holy Virgin is the major Russian Orthodox Church in the western U.S.

Enjoying Golden Gate Park

11

■ **Chain-smoking couch potatoes are firmly in the minority among San Franciscans, who typically sport well-tuned bodies and engage in athletic activities with enough energy to make even spectators feel exhausted. Furthermore, San Francisco has frequently been the birthplace of cult sports which have gone on to become international obsessions.....■**

Foot power As walking and jogging became *de rigueur* across the U.S. in the 1970s, San Franciscans quickly developed a desire for something more challenging. The popularity of walking grew into a mania for "striding" or "race-walking", both popular terms for athletic walking—a brisk 4 miles an hour trot. In 1985, the participants of the first San Francisco Hill Stride (held each August) made mincemeat of a 7-mile route around the city, barely breaking stairs as steep streets—and even flights of stairs—loomed before them.

Another event in which San Franciscans pit themselves against the city's gradients is October's California Infiniti mile: an ascent to the top of Nob Hill contested by walkers, runners, cyclists—and even formally dressed waiters carrying trays of drinks.

Cycling Also undeterred by the city's hills are legions of devoted cyclists. One way San Franciscans beat rush-hour traffic is by taking their bikes to work: more than a few Financial District employees swap their bicycle clips for a business suit in their office restroom.

For pleasure cycling, Golden Gate Park has many miles of bike paths and is included on one of the city's two sign-posted bike routes.

Stereo joggers

❏ "Like a swarm of killer bees"—A *San Francisco Chronicle* journalist describing the approach of a group of rollerblade skaters. ❏

The brush-covered hills and protected wilderness of the Bay Area are also exploited by cyclists, often on well-supported guided bike tours—some of which last for two or three days. Many of these rural routes were made accessible by the advent of the mountain bike, which evolved from ad-hoc hillside races held by locals on the slopes of Marin County, to the north of the San Francisco Bay, during the mid-1970s.

Biking beside the Bay

Rollerblades (opposite) are the smart way to move. Above: Tiburon

While mountain bikes—with their innovative design and countless gears—have swept the world, the hills of Marin have been damaged by cyclists' wheels, and biking across them is only permitted in certain areas and within a 15 miles per hour speed limit—rules upheld by patrols.

Rollerblading The mass-marketing of the rollerblade—a type of roller-skate with four or more wheels set in a line—revolutionized roller-skating in the early 1990s, enabling skaters to reach speeds of up to 40 miles per hour. In San Francisco, the popularity of "in-line" (as it is often known) skating led to the organization of communal "skates". Anyone can join a group skate but the organizers insist that pads and helmets are worn and that the skater—very importantly—knows how to stop. Large numbers of roller-bladers also descend on Golden Gate Park each Sunday, while lone skaters can often be spotted weaving through the traffic almost anywhere.

Snowboarding The winter snows that coat the mountains of the Sierra Nevada draw thousands of skiers from San Francisco. The innovative snow-sports enthusiast, however, is finding regular skiing increasingly *passé* compared to snowboarding: essentially a fast trip across the snow with one's feet attached to a glorified skateboard. The newness of the sport and the tough initiation which beginners endure—many injuries will be encountered before a snowboarder becomes proficient—give the activity growing cult status.

■ **Like any city, San Francisco constantly ferments with political issues and intrigues, although the matters raising the hottest passions are often those which relate to California rather than just the city. Nonetheless, San Francisco is frequently gripped by local issues which few people would imagine coming to the forefront anywhere else.....■**

North versus south Rare is the San Franciscan who has anything good to say about Los Angeles, 400 miles to the south. L.A. is popularly viewed as a flat, smog-affected basin crisscrossed by car-jammed freeways, whose population fears to walk the streets. San Francisco, though, is regarded as a beautiful city of hills and bay views where cultured and sociable residents mingle in cafés, walk the streets without a care, and make frequent use of public transportation. Anything tainted as southern Californian—such as the Transamerica Pyramid (built by an L.A.-based architectural firm)—is met, initially at least, with suspicion.

The antipathy between L.A. and San Francisco echoes a wider north–south division within California. North of San Francisco, the state continues for several hundred miles and holds a sparse population living amid the rivers and forests which provide the state with the bulk of its natural resources. By contrast, heavily populated southern California, behind its sun-and-surf image, has evolved into a vast industrial and suburban sprawl which depends for its water supply on damming and diverting the northern rivers. This tampering with nature brings endless ecological headaches and upsets rural economies.

As the social problems of the south place an increasing burden on state funds, the rising taxes which result are resented in the north. In 1992, immediately following L.A.'s Rodney King riots, a poll found that all the state's northern counties supported a north–south break up, with northern California becoming the U.S.'s

❑ In 1993, as part of a campaign to improve public transportation in the city, a law was passed attempting to compel all city officials to travel to work by public transportation at least twice a week. ❑

51st state—a scenario which one analyst described as "the Balkanization of California."

People power Any San Franciscan who raises sufficient support can put a proposal before the city electorate. While this may seem like democracy in action, the reality finds San Franciscans turning up to vote and facing a bewildering array of choices on issues ranging from the serious to the frivolous. In the elections of November 1993, one item among the usual round of complicated fiscal measures and bond issues, was a proposition from a policeman seeking the public's consent to disregard the rulings of his superior officers and patrol the streets in the company

Top, below: appealing to the voters

of his ventriloquist's dummy. While the cop got his way and the issue might be seen as a triumph for the individual over bureaucracy, many San Franciscans felt the issue—and the enormous amount of publicity it generated—made the city look foolish and took attention away from more important issues.

Neighborhood power Another form of people power—or perhaps more accurately small-business power—has been seen in the troubled Tenderloin area. Lobbying from local store and restaurant owners resulted in the removal of several public telephones which drug dealers and prostitutes were using for business

Lady Liberty reaches out...to SoMa

purposes. In another move to reduce the neighborhood's crime, owners of local tourist hotels proposed the levying of taxes on local businesses to finance a private security force to patrol the streets.

Gay power As in no other city, gay issues are part of the San Franciscan political agenda, but the size and influence of the gay community has, some feel, distorted the political landscape and resulted in gay-supportive politicians being branded homophobic (and thereby losing votes) if their general policies differ from those of the majority of the gay population.

■ **San Francisco may not be able to match New York or Los Angeles as an in-demand film set, but its distinctive architecture, climate, natural setting, and cosmopolitan population have helped the city win a starring role in some memorable movies. The following is a highly selective list of the most thrilling, entertaining, or just plain strange, films to have cast the city in a prominent role.....■**

16

Basic Instinct (1992). Controversial San Francisco-based big-budget feature which found Michael Douglas and Sharon Stone tormenting each other, and the city's gay population hitting the streets to protest the unsympathetic portrayal of lesbians.

Bullitt (1968). Steve McQueen turns in an outstanding performance as a San Franciscan cop embroiled in mafia shenanigans. But what every action-movie fan remembers best is the car-chase climax along some of the city's steepest streets. Real-life re-enactments are not possible, however, as the actual route was pieced together in the editing room.

Chan is Missing (1982). Wayne Wang went on to bigger things with *The Joy Luck Club* (see below) but cut his directorial teeth with this low-budget exploration of contemporary Chinatown and Chinese-San Franciscan society based around a search for an elusive taxi driver.

The Conversation (1974). A brilliant Gene Hackman stars as the cynical private detective who eavesdrops on a Union Square conversation from a gadget-packed room at the St. Francis Hotel; his descent into paranoia as a major conspiracy unfolds around him is played out against various city locations.

Above: The Maltese Falcon

Dark Passage (1947). Humphrey Bogart's second major outing (see *The Maltese Falcon*, below) into the San Franciscan fog comes after he escapes from San Quentin prison and enlists the aid of Lauren Bacall in proving his innocence; the art deco apartment house featured in the film as Bacall's home is on Montgomery Street, just beneath Telegraph Hill.

Dirty Harry (1971). In the first and best of the Dirty Harry series, Clint Eastwood established his superstar credentials as a lone-wolf San Franciscan cop stalking a demented kidnapper to an unforgettable finale at Candlestick Park.

Frisco Kid (1935). The city's notorious Barbary Coast—albeit a highly sanitized Hollywood version—provides a vehicle for James Cagney to brawl his way to the top of the waterfront pecking order.

Harry's day... being made

THE CONVERSATION

directed by Francis Ford Coppola   starring Gene Hackman   DISTRIBUTED BY **CINEGATE**

❏ Seldom mentioned in accounts of cinematic San Francisco, *The Subterraneans* (1960) is an abysmal screen version of Jack Kerouac's novel which, inadvertently, provides plenty of laughs in its attempts to capture the city's late-1950s beatnik scene. ❏

Invasion of the Bodysnatchers (1978). In this clever remake of the 1950s sci-fi classic, it is not small-town Americans who are turned into zombies by strange pods from Outer Space, but the entire population of 1970s San Francisco. The main characters amusingly epitomize the era's alternative lifestyles.

The Joy Luck Club (1993). The director of *Chan is Missing* (see above), Wayne Wang, used major Hollywood funding to great effect in this adaptation of Amy Tan's best-selling novel; opening in modern-day Chinatown, the film evolves into a classy tearjerker about the trials and tribulations of several generations of Asian-American women.

The Maltese Falcon (1941). The third screen version of the Dashiell Hammett story could well be the best—and most influential—private detective film ever made; an electrifying Humphrey Bogart leads the quest for the bird, beginning on the fog-covered steps of the Stockton Tunnel.

Pacific Heights (1990). One of San Francisco's venerable Victorian houses is the centerpiece of this engaging thriller in which a young professional couple inadvertently lease a room to a tenant with severe antisocial tendencies.

Vertigo (1958). Alfred Hitchcock's complex—or perhaps just confusing—psychological thriller draws a San Franciscan private detective (James Stewart) out of retirement and into a doomed affair with Kim Novak.

Vertiginous: Stewart and Novak

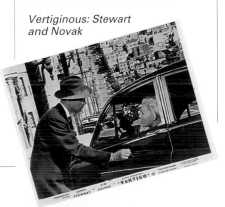

■   **Not only does San Francisco enjoy an exquisite natural setting but its own appearance is immeasurably enhanced by an abundance of distinctive architecture, be it playful Victorian gingerbread homes or uniquely contoured high-rise office buildings.....■**

18

Early structures Protected from earthquake damage by its thick adobe walls, Mission Dolores dates with dignity from the 18th-century Spanish settlement and is easily the city's oldest structure (see page 124). The only other evidence of Spanish-era building is a small section of adobe wall which forms part of the Presidio's Officers' Club (see page 155).

Handsome Victorians Architectural refinement was the last thing on most people's minds in gold-rush San Francisco, but among the great influx of arrivals aiming themselves at the gold fields were a number of highly-trained architects who, when fortune eluded them, took up their trade in the growing city.

As new residential areas sprang up to house the booming city's more affluent population, innovations in

San Francisco bay windows

Top: Levi Plaza, North Beach
Above: the straight-line Stick style

mechanized carpentry were allowing wood to be shaped in ways previously impossible. San Francisco, by now the west coast's major port, received shiploads of mail-order building materials, and pretty wood-built Italianate homes—modeled on Italian villas and commonly marked by extended porches and Corinthian columns—arose during the 1860s as the favored dwellings of the wealthy.

Stick and Queen Anne Through the 1870s and 1880s, the Stick style—which involved the use of flat wooden boards to emphasize the building's vertical lines—was increasingly favored over simple Italianate. Desire for greater ornamentation led to a prevalence of Stick-Eastlake homes, so named for their elaborate decoration inspired by the work of British designer, Charles Eastlake.

By the 1880s, the extravagant towers, turrets and sharply gabled

roofs of the Queen Anne style were popular in high society. Each decorative flourish—stained-glass windows were a definite plus—was seen as an indication of the owner's financial standing.

Approximately 14,000 Victorian houses survived the 1906 earthquake and fire—as well as more recent efforts by developers to raze them—and roughly half have been fully restored by their owners. The main groupings of these wood-built houses are found in Pacific Heights (see pages 148–50), the Western Addition (see page 179), Haight-Ashbury (see pages 106–9), the Mission District (see pages 124–5) and Russian Hill (see page 157).

❑ A notable feature of many Victorian houses are large bay windows. Besides being visually attractive, they make the most of the sunlight in this often foggy city. ❑

Commercial building The fire which followed the 1906 earthquake destroyed much of the city, including the Financial District and the area around it. Forsaking stone walls for terracotta façades and adapting classical themes into what became a new American urban architecture, the rebuilding of the Financial District was characterized by ground-level glass fronts intended for retail purposes and upper stories holding office space. Of numerous remaining examples, some of the best are on the lower sections of Sutter Street and Grant Avenue (see pages 86–8).

In 1925, the completion of the Pacific Telephone Building, its cultured profile still visible just south of Market Street, heralded another new look—one of stepped-back towers and art deco decoration echoing Eliel Saarinen's award-winning Tribune Tower in Chicago. Though stunted by the Depression of the 1930s, this phase of building began studding the Financial District with tall towers which poked above surrounding rooftops to become visible from all over the city.

Two Alamo Square "painted ladies"

Modern towers In the 1970s, the city administration bowed to commercial pressure, and what critics attacked as the "Manhattanization" of the Financial District got underway. The forest of largely unremarkable high-rises which arose (exceptions include the Transamerica Pyramid, see page 177) stimulated tighter building controls and monetary rewards for the preservation and adaptation of existing landmark structures. Levi's Plaza provides a widely acclaimed example of how to convert existing buildings—in this case, 19th-century warehouses—to modern commercial use (see page 115).

The Financial District: then and now

19

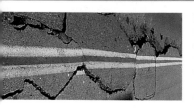

■ **Living on one of the world's most notorious geological fault lines helps instill a sense of the earth and its mighty powers in San Franciscans, but the prospect of the ground opening up and swallowing the city is just one of a host of environmental concerns affecting the area.....**■

Earthquakes Earthquakes are a fact of life all over California (which experiences 15,000 a year) and many occur each week in the San Francisco area. The majority of these measure less than 3 on the Richter scale and are too small to cause damage or even to be noticed in the city. For anyone who grows complacent, however, the Friday edition of the *San Francisco Chronicle* carries details and maps of the past week's earthquakes, while seismologists predict that a major quake will hit the Bay Area within the next 30 years.

For all the trepidation they inspire, earthquakes can have their advantages. The 1906 earthquake destroyed the city's notorious red-light area, while the 1989 Loma Prieta quake (7.1 on the Richter scale) resulted in the razing of the loathed Embarcadero Freeway, which had separated the Ferry Building and eastern waterfront from the rest of the city. One practical concern for San Franciscans is the extraordinarily high cost of insuring

A quake-buckled street

their homes and possessions against earthquake damage.

Forest fires In October 1991, fire swept across the Berkeley and Oakland Hills (above the cities of Berkeley and Oakland, see pages 58–9 and 140–4), destroying 3,000 homes, sending enormous dark clouds of smoke above the bay, and depositing several inches of ash on San Francisco's streets. California living, however, particularly in hillside "dream homes", means living in a high-risk environment. In the tinder-dry conditions of a hot summer, the smallest spark can cause a blaze to rage across an area where there are no natural firebreaks, where the homes are made of wood, and where narrow winding roads make access difficult for firefighters.

The bay Besides providing a scenic backdrop to the city, San Francisco Bay plays a crucial ecological role. In

Above and opposite, below : devastation in the Marina District

the bay's marshes, microscopic marine creatures thrive and provide food for migratory waterfowl or, after being swept out to sea, for large ocean-dwelling creatures such as the California gray whale.

Commercial development has seen 75 percent of the marshlands disappearing beneath new housing districts and industrial sites, while the diversion of the Sacramento and San Joaquin rivers to the farms of California's Central Valley has severely reduced the amount of fresh water tempering the bay's salty environment.

In the mid-1960s, in one of the state's first modern conservation campaigns, lobbyists forced the state government to create the San Francisco Bay Conservation and Development Corporation, which first stopped the pumping of raw sewage into the bay and then introduced laws to restrict landfill. Nevertheless, the decline of the bay was slowed rather than halted, despite marshland reclamation projects and the requirement for any new landfill project to be matched by an equal-sized area being returned to water.

Currently, groups such as Save the Bay and the Bay Institute are focusing

❏ "A vanishing wonder of the world"—a Californian journalist describing San Francisco Bay in 1965. ❏

on the toxic substances building up in the bay, destroying its vital wetlands. Another problem is the thirst of expanding southern California—a region without its own water supply—which places ever-greater demands on the bay's freshwater rivers.

California gray whales (complete with barnacles) often visit in winter

The ocean Much of San Francisco's Pacific shoreline is wild and rugged, and enjoys federal protection as the Golden Gate National Recreation Area (see page 99). Widely supported volunteer efforts help keep the coastline clean, and have contributed to the restoration of the bay area's brown pelican population,

Meanwhile, few San Franciscans ever get tired of keeping a look-out for California gray whales, which migrate between the Arctic and Baja California and can usually be spotted between December and March.

■ **To varying degrees, San Francisco has its share of all the contemporary problems which afflict any modern American city. The most emotive issue and one which polarizes local opinion like no other, however, is homelessness.....■**

On the streets Estimates suggest that around 25,000 people in San Francisco become homeless every year, and that at any given time there are between 6,000 and 10,000 people living on the city's sidewalks.

The Matrix program The most recent of numerous political initiatives intended to ease the homelessness problem is also by far the most controversial: Operation Quality of Life (better known as the

An all too-common scene around the Tenderloin

Matrix program), launched in August 1993 by Mayor Frank Jordan. Under Matrix, police can issue citations to the homeless for activities such as sleeping in public, obstructing the sidewalk, and "littering"—any of which might be performed with impunity by the general public.

Police actions In practice, the police have usually issued an infraction (a level below a misdemeanor in seriousness) to any homeless person guilty of one of the above. An infraction carries an automatic $76 fine to be paid within 21 days. Since few homeless people are able to raise $76, many fail to pay the fine and have warrants issued for their arrest.
 This state of affairs, anti-Matrix groups claim, results in some police officers threatening homeless people with arrest unless they move to a different area. Those homeless who are arrested face a spell in prison which, anti-Matrix groups say, puts a greater strain on city finances than providing more homeless shelters.

Shopping cart wars Under the "littering" aspect of Matrix, police are permitted to remove shopping carts—used by many homeless people to carry their possessions—if they are "abandoned" on the street. A supply of duffle bags was issued to police to give to homeless people as replacements for their carts.
 In November 1993, however, press reports suggested that police had been confiscating carts still filled with homeless persons' possessions, some of them from outside churches where the homeless were receiving free meals.

Protest By January 1994, more than 7,000 arrests and citations under the

Matrix program prompted 600 local religious leaders to issue a statement declaring that the Matrix program has "led to new levels of inhumanity and heartlessness." Meanwhile, four homeless people began a lawsuit claiming Matrix to be unconstitutional.

Since 1988, a direct-action group called Food Not Bombs has regularly handed out soup and bagels to homeless people in front of City Hall. Citing violations of public health codes, city officials have responded by ordering police to arrest those providing the food.

Related problems One City Hall response to criticisms of Matrix was to have social workers accompany police on sweeps of the homeless, although this took social workers away from other cases at a time when social service funding was being cut.

With drug and alcohol addiction common on the streets, Nob Hill's Grace Cathedral was forced to stop allowing the homeless to sleep in its

Passersby can be a godsend to those without a home or a job,

basement when crack cocaine was found being sold on the premises.

As Matrix forces greater numbers of the city's homeless into shelters, the struggle to secure one of the few beds (sometimes allocated on a lottery system) has led to ethnic tension escalating between homeless blacks and Hispanics.

Future solutions? Prolonged economic recession and an increasingly unsympathetic mood at City Hall appear to offer few rays of hope for San Francisco's homeless. One promising development, however, is the handing over of decommissioned military bases, such as the Presidio (see page 155), to organizations helping the homeless. A legal provision enables such groups to have the first option on the sites, although stiff criteria must be met and numerous other groups have their eyes on the potentially lucrative sites.

■ **San Francisco has more festivals than it knows what to do with and barely a weekend passes without a neighborhood street fair, an ethnic celebration, or a display of arts or crafts enlivening some portion of the city. The free weeklies and the Friday editions of daily newspapers carry current festival details, and the Visitor Information Center (tel. 415/391 2000) can provide information on special events taking place during your stay.....■**

January

The Chinese New Year Two weeks of events in and around Chinatown mark the Chinese New Year and climax with a parade—complete with costumed characters, dragons and fire crackers—beginning on Market Street. The New Year is based on the lunar cycle and sometimes falls in early February.

Tet Festival The Chinese community stages the largest, but not the only, Asian New Year celebration; another is the Vietnamese Tet festival, lasting a weekend, held along two blocks of the Tenderloin.

Martin Luther King Birthday Celebration Events across the city recording African-American history and achievements mark the birthday of the Civil Rights leader.

San Francisco Sports & Boat Show San Francisco's weekend sailors descend on this week-long display of the latest in yachts and yachting.

February

Russian Festival At Russian Center, 2450 Sutter Street, the culture and cuisines of Russia's diverse regions are enjoyed and devoured over a weekend.

United States Art Show At Fort Mason Center, works by U.S. artists illustrate the growth of the nation's art and crafts from the late 1700s to the present day.

March

St. Patrick's Day Parade Begins at Market and Second streets. Irish and

Top: Gay Freedom Parade
Below: Mission District Carnaval

would-be Irish San Franciscans dress in green for this brash and noisy parade; the day is also marked by special services at St. Patrick's Church, and events at the Irish Cultural Center (2700 45th Street).
Contemporary Crafts Market Craftspeople from near and far display their handiwork at the western U.S.'s largest crafts show (Fort Mason Center).

April
Cherry Blossom Festival Japan Center, Japantown. Be it sumo wrestling or flower arranging, few aspects of Japanese culture are missing from this weekend fling. The main event is a parade from Civic Center to Japantown, and further activities take place in Golden Gate Park's Japanese Tea Garden (see page 102).
Yachting Season Open Day San Francisco Bay. On the last Saturday of the month, thousands of tiny—and not so tiny—private boats fill San Francisco Bay. The colorful spectacle is best observed from any suitable hill.

May
Cinco de Mayo Mission District. Two-day celebration of the Mexican victory over the French in 1867, featuring Mexican arts, crafts and cooking, and a colorful parade from Mission Street to the Civic Center.
Bay to Breakers A few serious runners and 100,000 exhibitionists participate in this 7.5-mile run from

A regular visitor to Chinese New Year celebrations

the edge of San Francisco Bay to the Pacific Ocean.
International Film Festival Several weeks of the latest films from around the world, premièred at selected cinemas around the city.
Carnaval Mission District. One of the city's most colorful and most crowded events, with floats, costume contests and highly infectious dance music.

June
Lesbian/Gay Freedom Day A massive display of gay and lesbian pride, beginning in the Castro district and winding along Market Street to Civic Center Plaza, where food stalls, live music and other entertainment complete the day.
Stern Grove Midsummer Music Festival The first of six successive Sundays of free music and arts events at Stern Grove, off Sloat Boulevard at 19th Street.

July
Independence Day The focal point of the city's 4th of July festivities at Crissy Field, on the northern waterfront, scene of picnics, fireworks and a 50-cannon salute.
San Francisco Marathon The third-largest and certainly the most scenic marathon in the U.S. takes its participants across the Golden Gate Bridge to a finish line in Golden Gate Park.

Carnaval rhythms on the Mission District streets

August

Cable Car Bell-Ringing Contest Union Square. Clangs resound as expert cable car bell-ringers compete to become this year's champion.

September

San Francisco Fair Fort Mason Center. An urban version of a country fair that—with food, art exhibitions and bizarre contests—celebrates the city and all its eccentricities.
San Francisco Blues Festival Fort Mason Center. A weekend of top blues artists playing in the open air.

October

Columbus Day North Beach. The landing of Christopher Columbus in the New World is celebrated with vigor by San Franciscan Italians and includes a re-enactment of the

❏ The following street fairs offer locals (and anyone else) a chance to eat, drink, and generally celebrate the neighborhood: Castro Street (September); Folsom Street (SoMa, September); Haight Street (June); Nihonmachi (Japantown, August); Potrero Hill (October); Union Street (June); Upper Grant Avenue (North Beach, June). ❏

landing, a Blessing of the Fleet, and numerous street stalls. The city's Latin American population tends to take a different view, however, and Berkeley marks the event with **Indigenous Peoples' Day**.
Halloween Parade Outrageous costumes and riotous behavior along Castro Street are the order of the day in the year's biggest gay party.
Reggae in the Park A weekend of live reggae and world beat rocks Golden Gate Park's Sharon Meadow.

November

Day of the Dead Mission District. The Mexican tribute to the spirits of the dead celebrated with macabre art exhibitions and a parade along Mission Street.
San Francisco Book Festival Concourse Exhibition Center, 8th and Brannan streets. Vast gathering of publishers, authors, and the very latest books, enlivened by readings, signings and other book-related events.
Tree lightings The city prepares for the season's festivities with Christmas tree lightings across the city, the last and biggest of them in Union Square.

December

Santa Claus Parade Mission District. A gift-laden Father Christmas makes a three-hour trip along Mission and 24th streets.

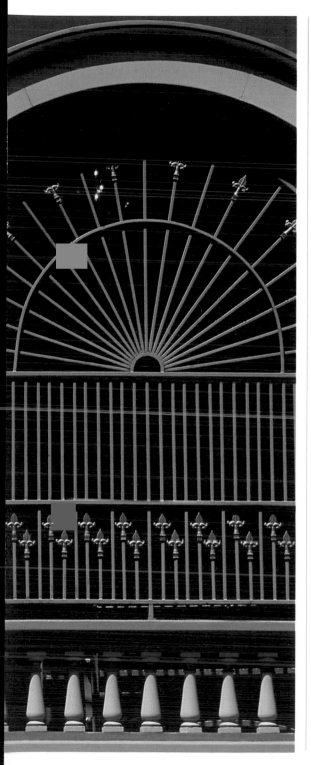

SAN FRANCISCO WAS

SAN FRANCISCO WAS *Formed*

■ The geological upheavals which led to the formation of the San Francisco peninsula—blessing the city with a spectacular natural setting but cursing it with frequent earthquakes—began millions of years ago and show no signs of abating.....■

From the ocean What is now California was beneath the Pacific Ocean when, 200 million years ago, the Pacific plate and the North American plate (two of the 20 tectonic plates which form the earth's crust) began moving, the heavier ocean plate sliding beneath the continental plate and pushing against it. The buckling which ensued created huge undersea mountains, which surfaced 10 million years ago and eventually became the mountains of present-day California. The future site of San Francisco also broke surface at this time, forming part of a vast valley.

The peninsula As storm water from the mountains washed downwards, it took the lowest and most direct course to the ocean. In doing so, deep channels, one of which became the Golden Gate, were created. Successive Ice Ages (the last about 10,000 years ago) caused ocean levels to rise and the Pacific pushed inland, filling what became San Francisco Bay with water. A ridge of

❏ Geologically, San Francisco is not part of North America; as with everything west of the San Andreas Fault, it sits on the Pacific plate, which is pushing steadily northwards at the rate of two inches a year. ❏

high ground—the San Francisco peninsula—was left above water between the bay and the ocean.

Fault lines The existence of hundreds of geological fault lines, two of the major ones being the San Andreas (running beneath San Francisco) and the Hayward (running beneath Berkeley), prove that the two tectonic plates continue to push against each other. Pressure along the faults leads to the earthquakes which occur regularly in the region.

Top: the San Andreas Fault
Below: carved by storm water—San Francisco Bay, seen from Sausalito

■ **A socially and culturally diverse Native American population—descended from Asian tribes who crossed the Bering Strait from Alaska—had been present in the San Francisco Bay area for thousands of years. The arrival of Europeans, however, brought their existence to an abrupt end.....■**

First Californians At the time of European discovery, California held an estimated 300,000 Native Americans, split into many small ethnic groupings (too small to be termed "tribes"), each with a particular way of life and belief system. With its hills and sand dunes, the future site of San Francisco was not attractive to Native Americans although approximately 3,000 Miwok people lived on the north side of the Golden Gate, with some 10,000 Ohlone to the south.

Native lifestyles Miwok and Ohlone people, divided into self-contained village communities, hunted the region's abundant wildlife to supplement their staple diet of acorns. Particularly among women, much time was devoted to basketmaking. Besides their obvious practical purpose, baskets allowed each group to express artistry, and distinct and recognizable styles evolved. Peaceful co-existence was a characteristic of the native Californians; the region

❑ Some 400 shell mounds have been located around San Francisco Bay; these comprized the discarded remains of shellfish and other animals eaten by many generations of Ohlone. ❑

saw none of the great conflicts that occurred between the tribes elsewhere in North America.

European impact When the Spanish began settling in California in the late 1700s, they brought not only Catholicism—which eroded native cultures—but European diseases, such as chickenpox and measles, to which the indigenous people had no immunity. In the Bay Area, surviving natives also bore the brunt of the mid-1800s gold rush, which brought tens of thousands of white settlers with an insatiable desire for land.

Top and below: Miwok Indians

29

■ **The Spanish had become established in South and Central America but the North American continent remained a barely charted territory, where just a few bold seafarers and adventurers carried the flags of European colonial powers, eager to strengthen their empires by locating the fabled "northwest passage" to the spice islands of the East.....■**

California sighted Juan Rodriguez Cabrillo, a Portuguese navigator employed by Spain, sailed along the California coast in 1542, briefly dropping anchor off what is now San Diego. In 1579, the first European known to step ashore in California was a Briton, Sir Francis Drake, who berthed his *Golden Hind* for 36 days at a (much-disputed) point close to Point Reyes, several miles north of San Francisco Bay. Drake claimed the land for Queen Elizabeth I of England.

An early visitor: Sir Francis Drake and (top) his ship, the Golden Hind

❑ Besides being the first Europeans to see San Francisco Bay, the members of the de Portola expedition were also the first Europeans known to have experienced a Californian earthquake. The event took place when they were camped by the Santa Ana River in present-day Orange County, near Los Angeles. ❑

Spanish foothold The British colonies took root on the American east coast rather than the west coast, however, and it was the Spanish who established the first European settlements across California, making Monterey, south of San Francisco, their base. The Spanish founded a chain of missions in California, ostensibly as a crusade to convert the indigenous population to Catholicism, but also to cement their territorial claim and gain native support in any potential colonial conflict.

San Francisco Bay Although San Francisco Bay makes an excellent natural harbor, it cannot be seen from the ocean. Consequently, the first European sighting of the bay was by an overland expedition under Gaspar de Portola in 1769. The first navigation by ship occurred six years later, led by Juan Manuel de Ayala who mapped the bay and bestowed lasting Spanish names on many of its features.

San Francisco born Part of de Ayala's assignment, as his ship became the first to sail through the

Mission Dolores: the city's oldest building and earthquake survivor

Mexican descent), who effectively governed themselves. The wealthy and easy-going Californios left the administration of business to foreign settlers, and from a cove on the eastern side of the peninsula, U.S. ships would be loaded with Californian hides and tallow. Around the cove grew the settlement of Yerba Buena (or "good herb"), which would later become San Francisco—renamed for the bay on which it sits.

U.S. acquisition As the U.S. pushed westward, waging war with Mexico and establishing an accessible overland route into California, it became inevitable that California would fall into U.S. hands. On July 9, 1846, the USS *Portsmouth* berthed at Yerba Buena and a delegation unfurled the Stars and Stripes across the plaza—today's Portsmouth Square (see page 75).

Golden Gate into San Francisco Bay, was to meet an overland party led by Juan Bautista de Anza. In March 1775, de Anza reached the tip of the San Francisco peninsula and planted a cross to mark the site of a future presidio (or garrison, see page 155). Three miles south in a more sheltered location, the mission of San Francisco de Asis (soon better known as Mission Dolores, see page 124) was founded. Neither the mission nor the presidio stimulated growth in this distant outpost of the Spanish empire, however, and the expected threat from rival colonial powers failed to materialize.

The Californios In 1821, newly independent Mexico acquired California from Spain. Uninterested in this distant land, the Mexican government permitted large sections of California to pass into the hands of the *Californios* (Californians of Spanish or

> ❏ "I am afraid we shall see a great deal of trouble in California this year. There are 7 or 8,000 emigrants from the USA expected."—W. D. M. Howard, San Franciscan merchant and landowner, 1846. ❏

Renaissance Faire, Marin County

■ **The discovery of gold in California in 1848 was the making of San Francisco, turning a remote and sleepy trading post with a few hundred inhabitants into a major city—and doing so almost overnight.....■**

The discovery On January 24, 1848, a farm worker discovered gold 50 miles west of present-day Sacramento. Although the find would transform California, word spread slowly because many people did not believe what they heard. Nonetheless, the handful of fortune-seekers who made their way to the site of the alleged discovery found that the rivers did indeed hold easily panned gold, washed down over millions of years from the Sierra Nevada mountains.

In San Francisco, the discovery was not announced until May 12th, when it was theatrically proclaimed by newspaper owner Sam Brannan striding through Portsmouth Square holding a bottle of the precious substance. There was no doubting Brannan's belief in the find. Besides the newspaper, he owned a hardware store which he had recently equipped with everything a prospective gold seeker could wish for—all of it for sale at inflated prices (see also page 37).

A prospector strikes lucky

The 49ers By the end of 1848, news of the discovery had spread across the U.S. and beyond. The following year saw the arrival of the "49ers", mostly single men in pursuit of an instant fortune. While some 49ers made the perilous overland journey from the east, others arrived by ship, and San Francisco Bay became blocked with abandoned vessels as their crews headed inland to the

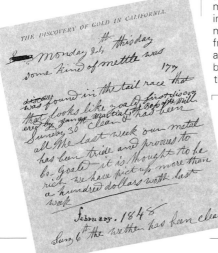

❏ San Francisco's booming population:

1847	500
1848	812
1849	20,000
1852	34,776
1860	56,802
1870	149,473
1880	233,959 ❏

Getting rich—or not—the hard way

gold-bearing areas (known as "the Diggins").

During 1849, the population of San Francisco rocketed from 812 to 20,000. Many of the new arrivals lived in makeshift tents and stayed long enough to equip themselves for a crack at the Diggins, alleviating the boredom at the countless saloons and gambling halls which sprang up in the chaotic shanty town.

Changing fortunes Many who effortlessly plucked gold from California's rivers in the early days believed that it would always be as easy to find, and squandered their riches on riotous bouts of drinking and gambling in San Francisco before returning to the Diggins.

The rivers quickly yielded all the gold they had, however, and mines had to be dug to reach the seams beneath ground. Finding gold quickly became an industry dominated by mining companies and—far from becoming rich overnight—many of the 49ers found themselves providing manual labor in the mines.

The lasting gold-rush riches were made by the merchants who supplied the 49ers with tools, food, shelter, and liquor, often accepting gold dust as currency. Prices in San Francisco had risen as fast as the population, often ten times higher than the equivalent in New York. As they grew wealthy, many merchants also bought plots of San Francisco land, soon to become valuable assets.

Below: hopeful panners, 1849
Opposite, top: gold-washing

■ The gold rush made an instant city out of San Francisco, but only through succeeding years—and not without much anger and anguish—did it acquire an infrastructure commensurate with its size and economic importance.....■

Law and disorder The vast majority of people in 1850s San Francisco had arrived solely to get rich quick, and seldom was concern for the law allowed to interfere with this pursuit. A series of fires razed substantial sections of the largely wood-built city. Some fires were started deliberately by criminal gangs—one such was the Sydney Ducks, a notorious group of former convicts from Australia—who looted unattended shops and warehouses as their owners tackled the blazes.

An ineffectual police force (which, in 1850, numbered just 12 men) and judges who struggled to interpret the law (California's change from Mexican to U.S. rule brought endless legal conundrums), set the scene for vigilante committees, first formed in 1851 by disgruntled merchants and property owners. Several public hangings later, the city's crime rate dropped dramatically.

❏ On land created by the filling-in of the shallow Yerba Buena Cove in the 1850s, the city's Financial District was born in 1866 when the Bank of California moved to a site at the corner of California and Sansome streets. Ships abandoned in the bay were used in the landfill operation, and their remains still lie beneath the district's modern skyscrapers. ❏

Financial insecurities By 1851, San Francisco was the fourth busiest trading port in the U.S. but still lacked a reliable banking system. To replace gold as currency, San Francisco's banks began minting their own coins (a practice then permitted under

San Francisco burns—a regular event in the 1850s

Opposite, top: Nob Hill, where the
Big Four built their opulent homes
Above: a Chinatown street in 1927

❏ The 120ft.-wide Market Street
was laid out in 1847 by an Irish
engineer, Jasper O'Farrell. For no
apparent reason, O'Farrell cut
through the city's existing grid-
pattern streets at a 36-degree
angle, inadvertently contributing
to modern-day San Francisco's
traffic congestion. ❏

federal law) and made considerable
profits by using less gold in the
manufacture of a particular coin than
its face value suggested. The banks
used their profits to finance new
gold-mining operations and later
invested heavily in the silver mines of
Nevada's Comstock Lode.

Comstock boom and bust By the
1860s, San Francisco was reaping
the profits of the Comstock Lode, and
a building boom swept the city. On
Nob Hill, recently made accessible by
the creation of the cable car, the Big
Four—the four merchants-turned-
railroad-barons whose monopolistic
business practices allowed them to
dominate California (see page 37)—
enraged the working classes by
building extravagant mansions.
  The linking of the city's economy to

mining was to prove disastrous, however. The Comstock silver was quickly exhausted, banks closed and a
depression hit the city. It was thought
that the opening in 1869 of the
transcontinental railroad—California's
first link to the eastern U.S.—would
alleviate this. Instead, the cheap
goods the railroad carried from the
east destroyed local markets. As jobs
became scarce, the Chinese were
unjustly blamed and banded together
within the confines of Chinatown.

The Barbary Coast Drinking and
gambling were major activities in
1850s San Francisco and, as soon as
enough women had arrived, so too
was prostitution. Along the
waterfront were brothels of such
unbridled sleaziness that sailors nicknamed the area "the Barbary Coast",
after an infamous part of North
Africa. Quick and casual sex could be
found for as little as 25¢, although
classier "parlors" aimed at "gentle-
men" charged much more.
  Faced with such distractions, finding crews for their next voyage was a
constant problem for ships' captains.
The practice which became known
as "shanghaiing" began in San
Francisco's waterfront bars, and
involved knocking out a customer
with a spiked drink and ferrying his
unconscious body to a ship, on which
he would have to work his passage
to some distant port.

■ **A cast of larger-than-life characters emerged during San Francisco's formative years, some achieving prominence through their suddenly acquired wealth and power, others becoming notorious for their eccentricities or opinions. Loved or loathed, many of them earned lasting places in city folklore.....■**

Emperor Norton (1818?—80)

Joshua Norton was a successful entrepreneur until 1853, when his attempt to corner the rice market caused him the loss not only of his money but also of his mind. Wearing a cockaded hat, epaulettes, and a ceremonial sword, Norton proclaimed himself "Emperor of the United States and Protector of Mexico." He spent the rest of his life wandering the city's streets issuing proclamations and collecting a 50¢-a-month levy (for "court expenses") from businesses, many of which not only paid the levy but also honored Norton's handwritten promissory notes. On his death, flags flew at half-mast and Norton was (albeit not until 1934) buried with the mayor and a military band in attendance.

Eccentric, Emperor Norton

Sugar magnate, Claus Spreckels Top: the transcontinental railroad

Claus Spreckels (1828—1908) A Prussian who settled in San Francisco in 1856, Claus Spreckels founded a sugar refinery to end dependence on the expensive supplies being imported from the East Coast via Cape Horn. Spreckels' sugar monopoly was the root of a vast fortune, which was later increased by his sons. One of the sons, Adolph, erected the French Renaissance mansion (one of several Spreckels-family homes popularly dubbed "sugar palaces") which still overlooks Lafayette Park. With his wife, Adolph founded the California Palace of the Legion of Honor.

❏ Other significant early San Franciscans, described elsewhere:
Lillie Coit (page 174)
John McLaren (page 101)
William C Ralston (page 127)
Adolph Sutro (page 171) ❏

Sam Brannan (1818—89) A convert to the Mormon faith (excommunicated as his greater devotion to money than to God became clear), Sam Brannan arrived in San Francisco in 1856. After opening California's first flour mill and founding its first newspaper, Brannan corruptly bought city plots and deliberately delayed the news of the gold discovery until he had equipped his own hardware store with prospector's tools (see page 32). Brannan spent his wealth on champagne and developing the spa town of Calistoga in the Wine Country (see page 209). Later, investing in the Mexican revolution was Brannan's financial undoing, and he ended his days as a penniless alcoholic in a boardinghouse near San Diego.

Rags to riches to rags, Sam Brannan

Ambrose Bierce (1842–1914?) Sharp wit and cynicism made Ohio-born Ambrose Bierce the city's most frequently read newspaper columnist by the 1880s, when he was given a job on the *San Francisco Examiner*. Nicknamed "Bitter Bierce", the writer was later posted to Washington D.C. and disappeared during a trip to Mexico. Bierce became legendary in his apparent contempt for San Francisco, which he (in)famously described as a "moral penal colony."

The Big Four Charles Crocker (1022–88), Mark Hopkins (1813–78),

The columnist they loved to hate, Ambrose Bierce

Collis P. Huntington (1821—1900) and Leland Stanford (1824—93) joined forces to channel their money (and dubiously obtained federal grants) into the construction of the transcontinental railway. Its completion in 1869 gave the Big Four a monopoly on transportation routes in California, through which they acquired unprecedented political power and amassed monumental wealth—some of which created the first Nob Hill mansions.

The Bonanza Kings The discovery of Nevada's silver-rich Comstock Lode made millionaires of James G. Fair (1831–94), James C. Flood (1826–98), John Mackay (1831–1902) and William S. O'Brien (1826–78). All Irish-born settlers, they became known as the Bonanza Kings and earned $500,000 a month each at the height of the boom. Flood and O'Brien's mining investments began with tips from the stockbrokers who patronized their saloon; Flood built the only Nob Hill mansion to survive the fire of 1906 (now the Pacific Union Club, see page 131). The nearby Fairmont Hotel was named in honor of Fair, and was built by his daughter.

■ **Fires and earthquakes had been a regular feature of San Franciscan life in the 1850s and 1860s, and hardy settlers learned to take such things in their stride. The geological calm enjoyed through subsequent decades ended suddenly on April 18, 1906, when an earthquake (and subsequent fire) reduced the city to ruins.....■**

The quake At 5:12a.m., an earthquake measuring 8.3 on the modern Richter scale and lasting approximately a minute rumbled along a section of the San Andreas Fault in northern California. San Francisco was some distance from the epicenter, but the city (by now the ninth largest in the U.S. with nearly 400,000 inhabitants) was the only major seat of population in the vicinity and suffered the most obvious damage.

The worst-affected areas were the Financial District and North Beach, where many buildings collapsed, as did the recently completed City Hall. Streets and cable-car lines buckled, chimneys fell through roofs, many buildings were left without their exterior walls, and windows and crockery shattered throughout the city.

The fire Although San Franciscans rose (or were thrown) from their beds in a state of shock, the damage the actual quake inflicted on the city was comparatively minor. Beneath

After the earthquake and the three-day fire (above)...

the city's streets, however, many of the gas mains which carried power for lighting and heating were ruptured, as were the water mains. As leaking gas (and electrical short circuits) caused fires to break out, there was insufficient water to contain them. Small fires burned uncontrolled and quickly formed into larger blazes—in a few hours, a single gigantic inferno was creeping steadily westwards across the unprotected city.

The flames spread As the fire came closer to their homes, thousands of San Franciscans gathered their possessions and fled to the open spaces of Golden Gate Park or the Presidio, or escaped on ferries across the bay.

Without official sanction, the Presidio's commander declared martial law and ordered his troops into the city. In the ensuing confusion, soldiers shot or bayoneted innocent citizens who were assumed to be looting as they sought to retrieve their possessions from gutted buildings.

Destroyed

□ The earthquake revealed the corruption behind San Francisco's new City Hall, erected over a 20-year period at a cost of $8 million. Construction costs on what should have been the emergent city's crowning glory had been cut by using cheap materials, with surplus funds diverted to private pockets. □

Efforts to stop the fire with dynamite failed dismally, and succeeded only in creating new fires and destroying some of the city's finest homes. By Friday, two days after the earthquake, the flames had left North Beach and Chinatown in ruins and were threatening to cross the wide Van Ness Avenue and engulf the Western Addition.

It was feared that the fire would sweep through the entire city, stopping only when it reached the ocean. Eventually, though, exhausted firefighters fought back the flames, and late on Saturday the fire burned itself out.

The aftermath The toll from the earthquake and fire was 300 dead and 250,000 rendered homeless. The fire had razed 28,000 buildings on 490 city blocks across an area of almost 3,000 acres, and destroyed all of the city's public records. The problem of housing and feeding refugees became paramount, but a well-organized relief effort, bolstered by $100 million in donated supplies

Scene of destruction in the Financial District

from all over the U.S., eased the difficulties. As life returned to normal, the most energetic San Franciscans set about rebuilding the city in the spirit of the phoenix depicted on the city's crest—a symbol of its recovery from earlier fires.

...city rubblescapes

■ **San Francisco quickly emerged from the devastation of the earthquake and fire, and was ready to enjoy the booming 1920s as much as any other U.S. city. However, it was the tumultuous and unpredictable events of the 1930s and 1940s which were to have a longer-lasting influence on San Francisco's future.....■**

40

A new city With 60,000 construction workers in the city, the rapid rebuilding of San Francisco echoed the lightning-paced development of the gold rush era. By 1909, 20,000 new buildings had arisen, many of them built with the new, earthquake-resistant steel frames. At the same time, a much-publicized court case saw the city attempting to rid itself of the corruption which had tainted its administration in past decades. The magnificent Civic Center complex, and the new City Hall, were completed and symbolized the city's hopes and aspirations for the future.

The Expo of 1915 Ostensibly a celebration of the opening of the Panama Canal, the 10-month Panama-Pacific Exposition opened in 1915 with the real intention of showing the world that San Francisco had fully recovered from the 1906 catastrophe. Across a 600-acre site (now the Marina District), the best architects of the day erected beautiful *beaux-arts* pavilions to house exhibits ranging from classical art to the latest technology. (Although the buildings were intended as temporary, the Palace of Fine Arts survives today.) With exhibits from 35 countries, the Expo was a roaring success.

The Depression San Francisco boomed in the nationally prosperous 1920s and reaped further benefits from California's growing agricultural and industrial economy, stimulated by World War I in Europe and further improved by the discovery of oil at several sites. However, the rise of Los Angeles as California's most economically important city dented the optimism which followed the

Longshoremen's strike, 1934

rebuilding, while the Depression of the 1930s ended it almost completely.

General strike In 1934, a three-month strike over pay and conditions by the city's International Longshoremen's Association paralyzed the city's economy. On July 5th, a date remembered as "Bloody Thursday", police (supported by hired thugs) attempted to end the strike by firing tear gas into picket lines and, in the ensuing battles, shot dead two strikers. Widespread anger at the police action resulted in 150,000 city workers heeding the call for a general strike. As San Francisco ground to a halt, the State Governor put the city under martial law and posted the National Guard to its streets. Although the general strike lasted just four days, it ended with the longshoremen winning many of their demands.

The Bay bridges The major event of the 1930s was the planning and

Opposite, top: the Palace of Fine Arts. Above: Civic Hall interior

completion of two enormous engineering projects: the Bay and Golden Gate bridges. These links to the East Bay and to Marin County gave a massive boost to the city's economy.

World War II To celebrate the completion of the bridges, the Golden

Gate International Exposition opened in 1939, hoping to repeat the success of the 1915 Expo. The outbreak of war in Europe provided a chilling backdrop, however, and the Japanese attack on Pearl Harbor in 1941 (which led to the city's Japanese-Americans being interned) brought huge changes: the city gained a massive ship-building industry and a booming workforce, and became the embarkation point for more than a million troops destined for the war in the Pacific.

Golden Gate Bridge

■ **In the decades following World War II, from which it emerged with a strengthened economy and greatly increased population, San Francisco became a social laboratory where many of the trends which would first shock, and then shape, the modern U.S. first saw light of day.....■**

Birth of the Beats With its long history of nonconformity, San Francisco provided an obvious refuge for those who found themselves at odds with the materialist values of the postwar U.S. By the mid-1950s, a ramshackle group of artists, writers, and existentialists was colonizing the cafés of

❏ It was San Francisco newspaper columnist Herb Caen who, mindful of the recently launched Sputnik satellite, coined the term "beatniks" as a derisory title for the Beats. ❏

42

Berkeley students rally against President Nixon in the 1960s

North Beach. In 1957, the publicity surrounding Allen Ginsberg's narrative poem *Howl* alerted the country to the city's new bohemians and, as the original protagonists moved on, the neighborhood was quickly awash with the sandals and bad poetry of the nation's first mass movement of disaffected youth.

Campus revolts In 1964, Berkeley students instigated the first of the campus protests which, a few years later, would escalate into massive, nationwide anti-Vietnam War revolts. Fronted by the besuited Mario Savio, the Free Speech Movement (FSM) arranged student sit-ins and rallies in response to the university authorities' efforts to ban the distribution of political material on campus. An occupation of an administrative building resulted in the largest mass arrest in California's history as 750 students, offering passive resistance, were dragged out by police.

Student demands for participation in the running of the university were eventually met and the FSM's success encouraged nationwide student activism, which became increasingly confrontational and violent. In Berkeley in 1968, several days of rioting followed the blocking of a student march. At another protest a year later, a bystander was killed and another blinded as the National Guard fired tear gas and buckshot.

Luv conquers all on Haight Street

Black Panthers Dressed in black jackets, black berets and dark glasses, and brandishing automatic weapons as they advocated self-determination for black Americans, the ultra-militant Black Panthers formed in Oakland in 1966. Though described by the F.B.I. as "the gravest threat to domestic peace", as their message spread across the country, the Black Panthers were much smaller in number than their publicity suggested. Following shoot-outs with police and the imprisonment of many of its members, the Oakland Panthers grew less and less militant, and began concentrating on local community projects and canvasing black support for the Democratic Party.

Hippies By far the largest reaction against conventional social attitudes in the 1960s was provided by the hippies. What quickly spread around the world in a mass of tie-dye tee-shirts, rock music, and burning incense, however, began with a disparate group of ex-Beats and others living in the low-rent, ethnically mixed Haight-Ashbury. The hippie era is fully described on pages 110–11.

❏ One way the Black Panthers raised money for guns was by buying 20¢ copies of Mao Tse-tung's "Little Red Book" in Chinatown and reselling them to students for a dollar each. ❏

Gay liberation Although San Francisco had a gay history stretching back to the gold rush, the city's gays had remained very much in the closet until the changing sexual attitudes of the 1960s and the 1970s' gay settlement of the Castro district. The emergence of openly gay city politicians was a national first and helped put San Francisco at the forefront of worldwide gay and lesbian consciousness. See also pages 70–1.

43

Berkeley now: less confrontational

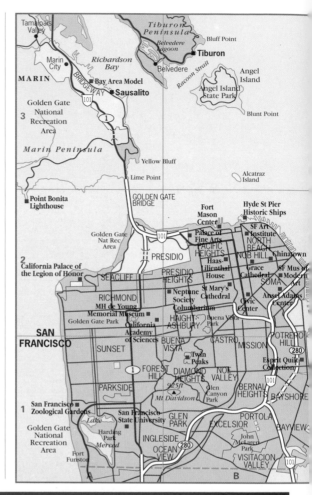

A nighttime view from Twin Peaks—at slightly over 900ft. the highest point in San Francisco—across the city to Alcatraz island

45

Compact and well-suited to walking, San Francisco occupies the tip of a peninsula which juts northwards between San Francisco Bay and the Pacific Ocean. Splitting into a mosaic of clearly defined neighborhoods, the city's streets spread across hills and valleys and give spectacular views—of the bay or the city's skyline—from almost every corner.

Financial District On the city's eastern side, the skyscrapers of the Financial District leave no doubt that this is where the city conducts its business. Here, the instantly recognizable Transamerica Pyramid looms above streets bustling with sharp-suited office workers, and banks dating back to the gold rush line streets which once faced the busiest waterfront in the western U.S.

Chinatown and North Beach Pushing hard against the Financial District, **Chinatown** may have fewer Chinese residents than it once did, but it remains the largest Asian community outside Asia, with 75,000 people crammed into its claustrophobic confines. Temples, herb shops,

Above: close-up of Chinatown, showing a detail from the Tien Hou (Tin How) Temple
Below: lining the broad avenues of Pacific Heights are many eye-catching Victorian architectural curiosities

and fortune-cookie factories (see page 102) all play their part in Chinatown life, but most San Franciscans come here for the restaurants, which are, for the most part, inexpensive and excellent.

The rice and noodles shops of Chinatown are just a few steps away from the fresh pasta dishes being served in the distinctly Italian-flavored **North Beach**. Besides its highly rated restaurants, North Beach has many of the cafés which helped make coffee drinking a favorite San Franciscan pastime.

North Beach was once synonymous not only with Italians but with struggling writers and artists. Many of the seminal figures of the Beat generation occupied low-rent apartments here or along the streets leading steeply upwards to Coit Tower, which sits at the top of **Telegraph Hill**, now surrounded by expensive bay-view homes.

On the other side of North Beach, **Russian Hill** drew its share of literary notables during the 1920s and is of greater contemporary renown for Lombard Street, hailed as the crookedest (and probably the most photogenic) of San Francisco's many crooked streets.

Nob Hill and beyond For property owners, Telegraph and Russian may both be highly desirable hills, but it is **Nob Hill**, rising from the cacophonous streets of Chinatown, which is unrivalled as the city's most prestigious residential address. Nob Hill has enjoyed high social standing since the late 19th century, when mining and rail barons (whose shady business dealings made them millionaires and determined the course of Californian history) chose it as the site of their million-dollar mansion homes.

All but one of the mansions perished in the calamitous 1906 earthquake and fire, and on their plots arose several fine hotels, the majestic Grace Cathedral, and high-rise apartments with the best views in the city.

Bus routes
Throughout the A–Z gazetteer, the most useful bus routes to the location being described are given, usually on the assumption that you are traveling from the Union Square area. With many routes criss-crossing the city, however, there is usually a good choice of alternative routes which will drop you within a few minutes' walk of the destination. Inside the back cover of this book, a map shows the main routes; local telephone books also carry a bus map.

Leafy and literary, Russian Hill is also well stocked with elegant 19th-century homes

Only slightly less expensive homes characterize **Pacific Heights**, which stretches northwest of Nob Hill in a mixture of low-rise dwellings and elegant and expansive Victorian homes with "gingerbread" trim. Packed with antiques, ornaments, and chic European designer fashions, the shops of Union Street reveal the consuming passions of Pacific Heights' wealthy residents.

Northern waterfront North of Pacific Heights, the city's northern waterfront holds the museum-packed **Fort Mason Center** and, to the east, **Fisherman's Wharf**. The one place in San Francisco where tourists outnumber locals, Fisherman's Wharf finds the city at its tackiest and most commercial. Nevertheless, the area can be fun for a short visit, with some genuine history dispersed among the souvenir shops and over-priced seafood stands. Fisherman's Wharf is also the departure point for ferries to **Alcatraz Island**, the notorious former prison easily visible in the bay.

A mile or two west of Fisherman's Wharf, the engineering and aesthetic perfection of the **Golden Gate Bridge** links the city to the strikingly undeveloped hills of Marin County. Near the bridge, on the city side, are the similarly wild woodlands of the **Presidio**, a decommissioned military base with a soldiering connection reaching back to the days of Spanish settlement.

South of Market Street Socially as well as geographically, **Market Street** has long been a dividing line, keeping the well-to-do neighborhoods on its northern side apart from the industrial flatlands to the south, an area known as **SoMa** (SOuth of MArket Street).

San Francisco's steepest street
You might frequently find yourself thinking that San Francisco's steepest street must be the one you are running short of breath trying to climb. You will be correct only if you are laboring up the section of Filbert Street between Hyde and Leavenworth streets, in Russian Hill, which rises at an angle of 31.5 degrees.

AREA OVERVIEW

Dangerous neighborhoods
Compared to many major U.S. cities, San Francisco is remarkably safe and only three small areas might be considered dangerous. One is the Tenderloin (see page 176), between Union Square and Civic Center, where most of the city's poor and homeless congregate. Another is the Western Addition (see page 179), a down-at-heel neighborhood between Haight-Ashbury and Japantown which should be avoided after dark. Parts of the Mission District, too, should only be visited by day (see page 124).

In recent years, many of SoMa's unused warehouses have been converted to spacious apartments and trendy nightclubs. Yerba Buena Gardens—a gleaming modern complex of museums (including the stunningly designed Museum of Modern Art) and performance art venues laid out between green walkways and waterfalls—has cemented the district's rapid improvement.

West of SoMa, the **Mission District** takes its name from a mission founded here by the Spanish in 1776. The mission survives, but the area's ambience is determined not by history—though several side streets hold impressive examples of Victorian residential architecture—but by a sizeable Hispanic population, responsible for Latin American bakeries and restaurants and the vivid murals on many buildings which catch the eye. Low rents and social vitality have also made the Mission District attractive to the city's newest bohemian fringe of artists, writers, and activists.

Continuing west, the **Castro** is probably the world's most famous gay neighborhood. With its businesses predominantly gay run and its balconies draped with rainbow flags of gay solidarity, the Castro might soften the attitude of the meanest homophobe.

Haight-Ashbury Booming gay culture may have been the big news of 1970s San Francisco, but a decade earlier it had been hippies that made the headlines, and it was in Haight-Ashbury, north of the Castro in the geographical heart of the city, that the flowers, beads, and long hair reached their zenith. Reminders of the psychedelic days are easily found, as are Victorian homes tidily restored to become bed-and-breakfast inns. Meanwhile, vintage clothes shops and critically acclaimed restaurants are bringing a buzz to the neighborhood's Haight Street.

Golden Gate Park Between Haight-Ashbury and the ocean, the great green swath of Golden Gate Park stakes its claim to be one of the greatest—and certainly one of

Seen from the Marin headlands, San Francisco looms up behind the cables of the Golden Gate Bridge

the biggest—urban parks anywhere in the world. Encompassing botanical gardens, statuary, a boating lake, a golf course, a herd of buffalo, and a full-sized polo field, the park also finds room for two of the city's major art collections: the M. H. de Young and Asian Art museums.

The Bay Area Visitors quickly become aware that there is much more to San Francisco than the city on the peninsula. What locals call the Bay Area also includes the communities around San Francisco Bay, separated from the city by a bridge or a ferry ride.

On the bay's east side, Berkeley holds the vast University of California campus, which sprawls across the town and up the neighboring hillsides. Several campus museums and the campus itself justify a look, as do the plethora of bookshops and cafés, the haunts of lifelong Berkeley radicals and fresh-faced students alike.

South of Berkeley, Oakland became infamous during the late 1960s as the base of the ultra-militant Black Panthers. While poverty-stricken areas remain, much of Oakland has blossomed into a likeable, friendly town where the tacky shops of the newly developed waterfront do little to detract from the appeal of Oakland's Chinatown or the outstanding art and historical collections of the Oakland Museum.

Sausalito and Tiburon On the north side of the bay, Sausalito climbs vertically from the waterside into tree-coated hills, where many expensive homes and a few expensive hotels offer a bucolic setting and fabulous bay views.

Sausalito makes a great day trip destination, but on busy days the village of Tiburon, also on the north side of the bay, can be a more attractive proposition. Beyond the quaint shops close to the dockside, much of Tiburon is a picture of pastoral tranquillity.

A short sail from Tiburon's harbor, Angel Island served as a fort, military hospital, and immigration processing center, before becoming a state park

San Francisco's twins
Many seasoned travelers share the opinion that San Francisco has few equals anywhere in the world. Nonetheless, the U.S.'s most liberal and beautiful metropolis is officially twinned with 11 cities: Abidjan, Assisi, Caracas, Cork, Haifa, Manila, Usaka, Seoul, Shanghai, Sydney, and Taipei.

Following the U.S. government's lifting of trade restrictions with Vietnam in 1994, there are also plans to twin San Francisco with Ho Chi Minh City, formerly the South Vietnamese capital, Saigon.

Itineraries

Itinerary assumptions
These itineraries assume you are staying close to Union Square. Do not despair if this is not the case, however, as it is easy to travel between San Francisco's neighborhoods, either by bus or—less often—by cable car. If museums are your main interest, check that the ones you intend visiting are open on that particular day. For example, two of the major collections, the M H de Young Memorial and the Asian Art museums, are closed on Mondays and Tuesdays.

San Francisco offers great rewards for those who make judicious use of their time. Even with just a weekend to spare, a surprising amount of this varied but modestly sized city can be enjoyed provided you plan ahead. With a full week available, there is no excuse for leaving without having every major sight and neighborhood—and some minor ones—under your belt. The itineraries below aim to provide a representative impression of San Francisco and its environs, but can easily be adapted to taste.

Weekend itinerary

Day one On foot, explore the landmark buildings of the Financial District (see pages 86–8) and continue through the streets and alleyways of Chinatown (see pages 72–5), choosing one of its many restaurants for lunch. In the afternoon, head north by bus (or cable car through Pacific Heights, see pages 148–50) to spend an hour at Fisherman's Wharf (see pages 90–3). Afterwards, walk into North Beach (see pages 134–7) to sample the Italian cafés, the offbeat shops of Grant Avenue and the neighborhood's many dinner options.

Day two Take a bus to Haight-Ashbury (see pages 106–9) to discover the area's Victorian architecture and the funky shops and restaurants along Haight Street. Have lunch on Haight Street, or carry provisions for a picnic by Stow Lake in nearby Golden Gate Park (see pages 100–3). Spend the rest of the afternoon in the park, exploring the gardens and the Conservatory of Flowers, or the M. H. de Young Memorial and Asian Art museums (see pages 118–23). If you have children, include a visit to the California Academy of Sciences (see pages 64–5).

One week itinerary

Day one Take a bus or cable car to Fisherman's Wharf (see pages 90–3) and catch an early ferry to Alcatraz (see page 55). Returning from Alcatraz, explore Fisherman's Wharf and indulge in an overpriced snack from a seafood stand. Continue to the area's less commercial sights such as Hyde Street Pier Historic Ships (see pages 112–13) and the National Liberty Ship Memorial (see page 128). If time permits, continue from Fisherman's Wharf to the museums of Fort Mason Center (see page 96).

Golden Gate Park

CULTURE PASS

NORTH "DUTCH" WINDMILL—WEST END OF GOLDEN GATE PARK

VISIT
5
GOLDEN GATE PARK ATTRACTIONS
AT 1 DISCOUNT PRICE

Day two In the morning, explore Union Square (see page 178), Maiden Lane (see page 116) and the architecture of the Financial District (see pages 86–8). Take a walk around Jackson Square (see page 113) before continuing into Chinatown (see pages 72–5) for lunch. Spend the afternoon weaving around Chinatown's streets and alleyways.

Day three Walk or take a bus to North Beach (see pages 134–7) and explore the shops and cafés of the Italian commu-

nity and the haunts of the 1950s Beat poets. After lunch, climb Filbert Street to the top of Telegraph Hill for Coit Tower and its murals (see pages 174–5). From the tower walk a short way down the Filbert or Greenwich steps. Leave Telegraph Hill and take a bus from Washington Square to Pacific Heights (see pages 148–50) and the fashionable shops and restaurants of Union Street.

Day four In the morning, travel into SoMa (see pages 166–9) and explore the museums and architecture of the Yerba Buena Gardens complex. Have lunch and continue west by bus into the Mission District for Mission Dolores (see pages 124–5). If time allows, explore some of the Mission District's murals. Take the Bay Area Rapid Transit (BART, see page 252) back to the city center.

Day five Travel by BART to Berkeley (see pages 58–61). Tour the university campus and its museums and have lunch on Telegraph Avenue or in one of the gourmet eateries of Shattuck Avenue. Take BART to Lake Merritt for the Oakland Museum (see pages 142–3). Depending on time, return to San Francisco either by BART or by ferry from Oakland's Jack London Waterfront. For a less active Day five, spend the day in Sausalito or Tiburon (see page 163 or 176).

Day six Same as Day two of weekend itinerary. Find time on your way to Haight-Ashbury to take a souvenir photo of Alamo Square's "painted ladies" (see page 54).

Day seven In the morning, tour City Hall and the Civic Center (see pages 78–9). After lunch, visit the Cable Car Museum (see page 63) and take a cable car along California Street to Nob Hill (see pages 130–1). At Nob Hill, visit Grace Cathedral (see page 105) and relax over afternoon tea at the Stanford Court Hotel.

The bright lights of the Mission District

Golden Gate Park
CULTURE PASS

Conservatory of Flowers

Valid July 1, 1993 to June 30, 1994

San Francisco by car
San Francisco is not ideally seen by car, but if you are traveling beyond the city and have only a short time, you might spend a day following the blue and white seagull signs which mark the 49-mile Scenic Drive. This takes in all the city's major areas and many of its points of interest. A map of the drive is available free from most hotels and tourist information offices.

■ **With countless hills and water on three sides, it should be no surprise that fabulous views are common in San Francisco. Whether a sweeping panorama of the Golden Gate or a postcard-perfect outlook across the city's skyline, memorable views are often discovered by doing nothing more arduous than walking to the end of the street.....■**

San Francisco's fog
Visitors underestimate the view-spoiling capabilities of San Francisco's infamous fog at their peril. Even when the spot you are viewing from is bright and sunny, the expansive panorama you are hoping to enjoy may be obliterated by fog creeping stealthily through the city's valleys. However, fog is usually an early morning phenomenon, which clears as the sun burns it off.

The view over San Francisco from Twin peaks (top) and (below) from the Bank of America

Views from buildings The views from the summit of Coit Tower, at the top of Telegraph Hill, are not very different from those at its base, but both are worth savoring (see pages 174–5). To the north lies Fisherman's Wharf and San Francisco Bay, to the south is Chinatown and the Financial District, and immediately east is a sheer drop to the Embarcadero and the East Bay.

The first-class hotels of Nob Hill (see pages 130–1) have a head start for impressive views. Both the Fairmont and the Mark Hopkins have cocktail lounges with stunning outlooks, and the glass-sided elevator which climbs the outside of the Fairmont to reach the 24th-floor Crown Room will test the mettle of anyone who claims they never suffer from vertigo. Some rooms—but not all—offer views. Alternatively, you might opt for a scenic if expensive stay at the Financial District's Mandarin Oriental, where you can enjoy a view stretching beyond North Beach while luxuriating in your bath.

Do not expect to see the whole city from the Transamerica Pyramid's 27th-floor observation level. The views are restricted to the north.

Floating views A sightseeing trip on San Francisco Bay (see page 89) takes in some of the city's major landmarks—including Coit Tower, the Golden Gate and Bay bridges—from an unusual sea level angle. The ferry to Oakland passes under the Bay Bridge, and the return leg puts San Francisco's high-rise Financial District into sharp relief.

Street views Do not forget to look around whenever you climb one of the city's countless steep streets. The view to the rear will often take away what is left of your breath. Good areas for street views include Russian Hill (see page 157), Pacific Heights (where Lafayette and Alta Plaza parks are designed to make the most of their high perches; see pages 148–50) and Potrero Hill (see page 153).

Juxtapositions As its brigades of shutter-clicking visitors attest, the sight of Alamo Square's "painted ladies" (a row of six well-preserved Victorian homes; see page 54) with the modern towers of the Financial District in the background spans almost a century's worth of San Francisco architecture and makes an excellent photograph. Similar camera-worthy juxtapositions are found around Mission Dolores Park (see page 104), Haight-Ashbury (see pages 106–9), and SoMa (see pages 166–9).

Coastal views The Golden Gate National Recreation Area (see page 99) overlooks the Pacific and encompasses much of San Francisco's remarkably wild coastline. Walk the coastal trail and you will find the waters of the Golden Gate lapping at tiny beaches at the foot of treacherous hillsides, enjoy the uncommonly glimpsed west side of the Golden Gate Bridge from a point where the whole city is almost hidden behind hills.

The California Palace of the Legion of Honor (see pages 67–8) is memorable not only for its art, but also for the stirring ocean views from its Point Lobos Headland site.

Views from afar Some of the best views of San Francisco are found by leaving it. From the UCB campus in Berkeley (see pages 60–1), the city sprouts evocatively from the peninsula with the Golden Gate Bridge clearly visible. The Golden Gate Bridge offers some fine approach views of San Francisco, and the city is at its most photogenic when seen through the cables of the bridge from the Marin County side of the Golden Gate National Recreation Area.

A Mission District view

Aerial views
When the outlook from terra firma fails to please, try looking down on San Francisco from an aerial tour (usually costing $50–$80 per person) operated by one of the following companies: Scenic Air Tours (tel. 1-800/354 7887); San Francisco Helicopter Tours (tel. 1-800/400 2404 or 510/635 4500).

The view from Alcatraz
One of the best overall views of San Francisco is from the former prison on Alcatraz Island (see pages 54–5). While stepping ashore and enjoying the spectacle, spare a thought for the mental agony such a vision brought to the inmates who could often see (and hear) the city—so near and yet so far—from their cellblocks.

AFRICAN AMERICAN HISTORICAL & CULTURAL SOCIETY

The Birdman of Alcatraz
Murderer Robert Stroud was imprisoned in 1909 at the age of 19. In Leavenworth jail, Kansas, he began keeping and studying birds and wrote the highly regarded *Stroud's Digest of the Diseases of Birds*. Not until 1942 was "the Bird Doctor of Leavenworth"—as Stroud was known—transferred to Alcatraz, and not until 1955 did a biography of Stroud first coin the phrase "Birdman of Alcatraz." This gave Stroud a lasting nickname and provided the title for the 1962 film about Stroud, which starred Burt Lancaster.

54

The classic shot of Alamo Square's Victorians backed by the towers of the Financial District

▶ **African American Historical & Cultural Society**   *IFCD6*
Building C, Fort Mason Center and 762 Fulton Street
Bus: 28
A limited number of items from the society's archives are displayed at Fort Mason Center, together with works by notable artists of African descent. The society's energies, however, are primarily devoted to the Library and Collection—documents, videos, audio tapes and much more pertaining to African-American history in northern California—which are housed at a separate site at 762 Fulton Street in the Western Addition. Also at Fulton Street, the Howard Thurman Listening Room holds taped speeches by the influential liberal Baptist minister whose name it bears.

▶▶ **Alamo Square**   *IFCD4*
Bordered by Fulton and Hayes, and Scott and Steiner streets
Bus: 21
When property developer Matthew Kavanaugh raised a terrace of pretty wooden homes overlooking Alamo Square in the mid-1890s, he could not have suspected that a century later they would be nicknamed "the painted ladies," and be among the most photographed houses in San Francisco.

The sight of the elaborate Victorian carpentry contrasting with the sleek towers of the Financial District looming in the distance behind them, is one of the city's most memorable, and most widely reproduced images. For the best camera angle, you will need to stand in Alamo Square itself, a compact patch of tree-fringed greenery set on a steep slope.

*The island of
Alcatraz, a mile and a
half north of
Fisherman's Wharf, is
easily sighted from
any high vantage
point in the city*

▶▶▶   Alcatraz   *IFCE7*

Ferry: from Fisherman's Wharf

The most famous—or most infamous—place in San
Francisco, Alcatraz (whose Spanish name means "pelican") became the most feared place of incarceration in the
U.S. from 1934, after the federal government took control
of the island from the U.S. Army, for whom it had served
as a fort and military prison since 1886. It was turned into
a high-security, strict-discipline penitentiary for "incorrigi-
ble" criminals—those deemed beyond salvation and considered too dangerous to be held at conventional jails.

At Alcatraz, even work was regarded as a privilege and
had to be earned through good behavior. There was one
guard for every three inmates, and any prisoners who did
escape from their cells were then faced with the prospect
of crossing the freezing, swiftly moving waters of the bay
(regarded as unswimmable) to freedom.

Already enduring the toughest prison regime in the U.S.,
the inmates of Alcatraz were further tormented by being
able to see the bright lights of the city, and hear its sounds
drifting across the bay into their miserable cells. Although
stays at Alcatraz averaged nearly 10 years, inmates were
denied access to newspapers, radios, and televisions,
and 80 percent never received a visitor. Of the 1,576 convicts imprisoned here—Al Capone, Machine Gun Kelly,
and Robert Stroud (the so-called "Birdman of Alcatraz";
see panel, page 54) being the most notorious—only 36
ever attempted escape: all but five were recaptured within an hour; of the five, nothing has been heard since.

The costs and difficulties of running an island prison,
and widespread opposition to the severity of the system,
led to Alcatraz's closure in 1963. A year later, a group of
Native Americans claimed the island for the Sioux Indian
nation under an 1868 treaty granting them rights to
"unused government land." They began a two-year occupation in 1969. Alcatraz became part of the Golden Gate
National Recreation Area in 1972, opening its once tightly
guarded doors to the curious public the following year.

Most of the semi-ruined prison buildings—the cellblock,
the mess hall with its tear gas cylinders on the ceiling, and
the prison hospital—can be toured, and there is a small
museum and a documentary film. The audiocassette tour
(see panel), with a terse commentary by former guards
and inmates, is an excellent, atmospheric accompaniment.

55

*Maximum security:
an Alcatraz cellblock*

Ansel Adams' childhood home
Ansel Adams' gift for spotting natural beauty perhaps stems from his childhood. Soon after Ansel's birth, the Adams family moved to an isolated self-built home (subsequently demolished) in what was then the San Francisco peninsula's barely populated northwest tip. From his bedroom, the young Ansel could gaze north across the Golden Gate to the wild hills of Marin; to the west, the outlook encompassed a large area of sand dunes and the choppy waters of the Pacific Ocean.

▶▶▶ **Ansel Adams Center** *IFCF5*
250 Fourth Street
Buses: 30, 45, 76 (Sundays)
Anybody who doubts the power of photography to provide social comment and raise questions about the world is advised to pay a visit to the Ansel Adams Center, an outstanding showplace for serious and creative photography. The center's five galleries stage approximately 15 exhibitions each year, and at any given time the combined displays offer an absorbing and sometimes provocative blend of historical and contemporary work. Whether from the U.S. or overseas, household names or comparative unknowns, the photographers represented make full use of the camera's ability to read faces, exploit juxtapositions and make even landscapes resonate with emotion. Past exhibitions have ranged from Eadweard Muybridge's extraordinary panoramas of 1880s San Francisco to Wendy Ewald's work in urban and rural communities of Mexico, giving local children the opportunity to photograph themselves.

The center is named after the award-winning photographer, born in San Francisco in 1902, whose charged landscapes, particularly those of Yosemite Valley and of the U.S.'s other national parks, became iconographic symbols of the country's natural beauty and encouraged countless other photographers to aim their lenses at the features of nature.

In 1967, together with Brett Weston (the photographer son of a photographer father, the esteemed Edward Weston) and art critic Beaumont Newhall, Adams founded the Friends of Photography in Carmel on the Monterey peninsula (see pages 192–5). The Friends of Photography workshops—which continue today—quickly earned a reputation for encouraging exploration of the camera's creative potential rather than dwelling on its technical aspects, and it is the Friends of Photography who now run the Ansel Adams Center. Adams, who died in 1984, donated 125 of his photographs to the center, and selections from these are shown in the Ansel Adams Gallery.

► **Baker Beach**   IFCB6

Accessed from Lincoln Boulevard
Bus: 29

Fringed by rocky cliffs and stands of cypress and pine trees, the mile-long Baker Beach makes an ideal break from the city's streets and draws anglers, joggers, picnickers, and even a few nude sunbathers undeterred by the steady winds and lack of dependable sunshine (swimming here is dangerous). On weekends, history buffs arrive for talks about Battery Chamberlin, a defensive fortification begun in 1904, when a 95,000-pound cannon was placed behind the beach, and continued during World War II with the digging of still-visible bunkers.

► **Bay Bridge**   IFCG6

The longest steel structure in the world on its completion in 1936, the Bay Bridge (more formally known as the San Francisco–Oakland Bay Bridge) suffered a cruel twist of fate: despite providing a vital transportation link across the bay, it was doomed to be overshadowed by the more photogenic Golden Gate Bridge (see page 98), which opened in 1937. Nonetheless, the Bay Bridge—which, in 1933, consumed 18 percent of all the steel produced in the U.S.—is fondly admired by the owners of the 250,000 vehicles which cross its eight-mile span each day and is one of the few bridges which includes an underground tunnel as part of its length. The island of Yerba Buena, provides a convenient meeting place for the two above-water sections of the bridge.

In 1989, the month-long closure of the bridge following the Loma Prieta earthquake cost the city's businesses millions of dollars in lost revenue. In 1993, press reports suggested that the ability of the bridge to withstand another major quake was questionable, and that its complicated construction was bringing headaches to California's most able engineers.

Quite apart from any loss of life, if the Bay Bridge were to be rendered unusable by another major quake, the economic impact on San Francisco would be colossal.

An essential link between the city and Oakland since 1936, the Bay Bridge was closed for a month after the 1989 Loma Prieta earthquake. Its reopening was a great relief to Bay Area residents

Bay Bridge: the cost
$80 million was spent on the building of the Bay Bridge and 27 workers lost their lives during the three years of its construction. Once completed, one commentator described it as "the greatest expenditure of funds ever used for the construction of a single structure in the history of man."

The rustic entrance (above) to Chez Panisse, the birthplace of California cuisine. The acclaimed main courses are matched by similarly good desserts (below)...

▶▶ **Berkeley**   *45D3*

BART: Berkeley

San Francisco may be regarded as the U.S.'s most liberal city, but for left-wing local government, political activism, and general anything-goes atmosphere, it is Berkeley, set across the hills of the East Bay, a 20-minute BART ride (see page 252) from the big city, which sets the pace.

Berkeley owes much of its famed radicalism to its long-standing role as an academic center, being the site of the University of California at Berkeley (UCB), the first campus of the state university system, which now has several other sites throughout California.

It was at UCB that the Free Speech Movement began in the early 1960s; the earliest anti-Vietnam War protests were organized; and Ronald Reagan (then Governor of California) ordered the National Guard to use tear gas against student demonstrators.

Bizarre as it may seem in retrospect, the origins of the university date back to the efforts of New England's Protestant churches to found a Christian educational center on the West Coast, partly inspired by a wish to contain the spread of Catholicism introduced to native Californians by Spanish missionaries. A Christian College opened in the 1850s but, hindered by limited funds, it agreed to a takeover by the gold-rich state administration, and the University of California opened in 1873.

Arriving by BART brings you to Shattuck Avenue, the main thoroughfare of downtown Berkeley, with little of interest beyond the expensive restaurants of the "Gourmet Ghetto" just north of Shattuck's junction with Cedar Street. Among them, **Chez Panisse** (number 1517) is credited as being the birthplace of California cuisine.

Fine food notwithstanding, it is the university which brings most people to Berkeley, and it is an easy walk

*...and by the attentive
service and an
ambience conducive
to memorable eating*

east of the BART station. Drop by the **Visitor Center**, on the corner of University Avenue and Oxford Street, for a free campus map or to join a student-led walking tour (see panel).

The edge of the campus is directly across Oxford Street from the Visitor Center. The trees and winding footpaths which you will see initially, however, disguise the fact that the facility fills 100 acres with confusingly arranged plazas and pathways, and often indistinguishable buildings. Built to accommodate 5,000, UCB now has 30,000 students, and a map is essential to find your way around.

Several specific points of interest on the campus are detailed on pages 60 and 61, but be sure to take a stroll along **Sproul Plaza**. Many of the 1960s student actions originated here, and Sproul Plaza's stalls continue to distribute information on all manner of ecological, social, and political concerns.

Another site of dissent during the 1960s and 1970s was **Telegraph Avenue**, reached by crossing Bancroft Way. Lined by bookstores, restaurants, bakeries, and cafés, Telegraph Avenue is a great place for feeling the pulse of present-day student life in Berkeley.

Campus tours
Free, student-led walking tours of the campus depart from the Visitor Center on Mondays, Wednesdays, and Fridays at 10a.m. and 1p.m. (tel. 510/642 5215). Science buffs may prefer to concentrate on the Lawrence Berkeley Laboratory, where pioneering research has yielded nine Nobel prizes as well as the atomic bomb. Free tours are conducted on Mondays from 10a.m. to noon. Reservations must be made a week in advance (tel. 510/486 5122).

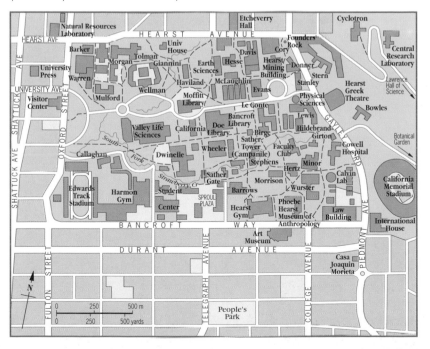

■ **Finding your way around may be a headache but the Berkeley campus has several buildings, historical collections, and a number of museums which are well worth taking the trouble to locate, explore, and enjoy.....■**

Sather Gate
Architect John Galen Howard gave the campus some of its finest features, including the outstanding Hearst Mining Building and Sather Gate. At the southern end of Sproul Plaza opposite Telegraph Avenue, Sather Gate has stood since 1911 and originally marked the main entrance to the campus. The gate has recently re-acquired some of its original decoration: a set of nude figures previously thought improper for a college campus.

60

The study of DNA, Lawrence Hall style

Gold and books You may not be able to borrow a book from the **Bancroft Library** but you can study an 1849 gold nugget, alleged to be the one that launched the gold rush, and admire the paintings of pioneer-era California on the walls. The library also mounts temporary exhibitions drawn from its 44 million books and manuscripts. These include a hoard of Mark Twain's notebooks, letters, and publications, a few of which are likely to be on show.

The university's elegant **Doe Library** is next door, its **Map Room** holding everything cartographers dream about. Off the lobby is the entrance to the **Morrison Library**, where the temptation to grab a newspaper and fall into one of the inviting couches is hard to resist.

Anthropological troves Although it holds the largest stock of anthropological artifacts west of Chicago, the space-starved **Phoebe Hearst Museum of Anthropology** is only able to show off a comparative handful of its 4 million treasures at any one time.

The holdings began with expeditions sponsored by Phoebe Hearst (wife of publisher George; mother of William Randolph) which, from 1899, enabled the leading anthropologists of the day to discover and plunder items of significance from sites of ancient civilization reaching from the Pacific to the Mediterranean.

Although the changing exhibitions focus on diverse anthropological themes and may feature anything from Egyptian deities and Peruvian pots to carved Inuit ivories and Greek urns, the museum's permanent display documents the life of "Ishi", a Native American believed to be the last surviving member of the Yahi tribe. Living at the museum for five years until his death in 1916, Ishi passed on invaluable knowledge about his people's culture and lifestyle.

Art and film Crossing Bancroft Way from the campus and entering the **University Art Museum** is similar to stepping inside an immense concrete bunker. The museum, completed in 1970, has 11 separate galleries and an open-plan style which allows contrasting exhibits—liable to be anything from ancient Japanese paintings to contemporary photography—to hang together with surprising cohesion.

The permanent collection includes 47 paintings by Hans Hoffman, a German-born abstract painter who settled in Berkeley and donated $250,000 (as well as the paintings) to get the museum off the ground.

The building's basement houses the **Pacific Film Archive**, which frequently screens selections from its 6,000-strong collection of cinematic classics, oddities, obscurities, and rarities.

Mining and beaux-arts Arranged around the ground floor of the **Hearst Mining Building** are mineral collections and exhibits on mining in California. More interesting perhaps are the historic photographs lining the walls of the adjacent corridor, showing early Californian mining scenes. Believe it or not, the mining faculty once trained its students in a 200ft. practice mine, its entrance still visible. The building itself merits a close look: an appealing beaux-arts creation, it was designed by John Galen Howard (see panel) and opened in 1907.

Into the hills The traffic circle outside the Mining Building is the pick-up point for the campus bus which climbs into the Berkeley hills, where the university's science laboratories are located. The laboratories are usually not open to the public (although see panel on page 59) but the bus stops at the **Lawrence Hall of Science**, where talking computers and hands-on displays illustrate aspects of the natural world.

Even if you have no desire to put your hand through a laser beam or make a ghost-like appearance on a TV screen, Lawrence Hall is worth a visit for the view from its forecourt. On a fogless day, you can see across Berkeley to San Francisco and the Golden Gate.

Berkeley issues...

The Campanile
Since 1914, the Campanile (officially called Sather Tower) has risen from the heart of the Berkeley campus. At the end of a 50¢ elevator ride, the Campanile's 200ft. high observation tower offers fine views over Berkeley to San Francisco Bay. Each Sunday at 2p.m., a carillon recital resounds from the Campanile across the campus and the neighboring streets.

Deep thinking at the University Art Museum

Buena Vista's fine homes
Better known as the creator of Golden Gate Park (see panel, page 101), John McLaren oversaw the seeding of the barren peak that would become Buena Vista Park in the late 1800s. His efforts, coupled with the development of Haight-Ashbury, encouraged a flow of wealthy residents to the magnificent row of architecturally varied Victorian homes which were erected—and still remain—facing the park along Buena Vista Park West (see page 107).

▶ **Buddha's Universal Church**   *IFCE5*
720 Washington Street
Bus: 15
The popular claim that Buddha's Universal Church, which opened in 1965, was financed by the proceeds of fortune cookie sales (see page 102) is not without foundation, although the cookies were just part of the fund-raising activities. The five-story church makes a striking contrast to Chinatown's compact 19th-century temples, although the finely decorated interior can be seen only on Sundays.

▶ **Buddhist Church of San Francisco**   *IFCE5*
1881 Pine Street
Buses: 2, 3, 4
A few blocks from the heart of Japantown, the Buddhist Church of San Francisco opened in 1938, just a few years before many of its Japanese-American congregation found themselves relocated to internment camps for the duration of World War II. During the war years, the church was maintained by Western converts to Buddhism. While the church offices are always busy, the worship room—at the top of the staircase as you enter—is one of the most peaceful and atmospheric interiors in San Francisco. Services are conducted in English on Sunday mornings, and in Japanese on Sunday afternoons. Guided tours can be arranged by appointment (tel. 415/776 3158).

▶▶ **Buena Vista Park**   *IFCD4*
Junction of Haight and Baker streets
Buses: 6, 7, 66, 71
Branches of pine, redwood, cypress, and eucalyptus trees entwine above the steep slopes of 36-acre Buena Vista Park, creating an enticing pocket of wilderness just a few steps from busy Haight Street. Visitors who weave upwards along the park's footpaths and stairways—some of the walls are made from recycled tombstones—are rewarded with fine views reaching to the Financial District and San Francisco Bay.

The twin spires of St. Ignatius Church poke above the rampant shrubbery of Buena Vista Park

CABLE CAR MUSEUM

The winding machinery that pulls the 56,000ft. of ever-moving cable on which San Francisco's cable cars depend for their movement, can be seen in action in the basement of the Cable Car Museum

▶▶ **Cable Car Museum** IFCE5

1201 Mason Street
Cable car: Powell-Hyde & Powell-Mason lines
After the Transamerica Pyramid and the Golden Gate Bridge, the cable car is the item most people associate with San Francisco. Most visitors are surprised to discover, however, that today's cable cars operate only on three routes and cover a limited area of the city.

Invented by a Scot, Andrew Hallidie, the first cable car ran along Clay Street on August 2, 1873. A safer way of negotiating the city's steep streets than horse-drawn wagons, the cable car also made possible the development of previously inaccessible high areas, most notably Nob Hill (see pages 130–1). By 1906, there were 600 cable cars in operation in San Francisco, but the earthquake and fire of that year, and the subsequent rise of motorized transportation made the cable car obsolete. Public demand encouraged the federal government to award the cable car National Historic Landmark status in 1964, and a proviso written into the San Francisco City Charter preserves the three existing lines.

The museum—housed in the 1907 cable car powerhouse—displays early cable cars, including the first, and provides a largely pictorial account of their development. Also revealed is the clever engineering principle which keeps the cars working: each one is pulled by an underground cable that never stops moving; the "gripman" on each car uses a lever to connect or disconnect the car to or from the cable through a slot in the road.

The heavy whirring sound, audible as you enter the museum, is the noise of the steel cable being pulled over 14ft.-wide winding wheels, the process shown in the museum's lower level.

Andrew S. Hallidie
Legend has it that the sight of a horse falling while trying to drag its load up one of San Francisco's hills inspired Andrew Smith Hallidie—an engineer and manufacturer of wire rope, who arrived in California in 1852—to invent the cable car. Wire rope had previously been used as a means of transporting materials in gold mines, but Hallidie was the first to develop the idea as a means of moving people.

Exploring the tidepool

Botany and Alice Eastwood
The academy's Curator of Botany at the time of the 1906 fire was Alice Eastwood. Realizing that the collections—among the nation's foremost—might be lost, she climbed the exterior ironwork of the building (the interior stairway was destroyed) and carried what she could to safety. Ms. Eastwood, who lost all of her own belongings in the fire, spent 60 years in her job and died in 1953 aged 94.

Dolphin and admirer

▶▶ **California Academy of Sciences** *IFCC4*
Golden Gate Park
Buses: 28, 29, 44

Across the expansive Music Concourse from the M. H. de Young Memorial and Asian Art museums (see pages 118–23), the California Academy of Sciences occupies a grandiose set of buildings which do little to suggest its modest origins. Founded in 1853 by a small group of enthusiastic naturalists who held weekly meetings and published papers on the state's newly discovered species, the academy mounted its first exhibitions of natural history curiosities in any home which would have them.

Subsequently, the academy became established in a six-story building on Market Street, only for the premises to be destroyed by the 1906 fire (see panel). It was decided to move the academy—by then a popular feature among San Franciscans and known throughout the U.S.—to Golden Gate Park, the first section of the new building opening in 1916.

Unfortunately, what may well be the first part you see is also one of the academy's least enthralling sections. The 14 dioramas of **Wild California**▶ use models of Californian creatures in re-created natural habitats to express the state's immense natural diversity: from desert floor to ocean cliffs. Do drop in, however, if only to admire a stuffed great white shark, positioned so you can stare straight into its gaping jaws.

Next door is the **Gem and Mineral Hall**▶▶, where several gleaming lumps of rock, such as a 1,000-pound hunk of quartz crystal, nuggets of Californian gold, and a remarkable amethyst-lined geode, are the star attractions.

By far the academy's most impressive section is the wide-ranging selection of marine life in the **Steinhart Aquarium**▶▶▶, where countless tanks display a vast variety of sea creatures ranging from bloated Amazon Basin predators to the mysterious splitfin flashlight fish, which uses a torch to find its way around the dark waters of the very, very deep.

Walk up the spiral ramp to the **Fish Roundabout**▶▶ and watch multitudes of fast-swimming ocean fish—bay rays, seabass, red snappers, leopard sharks, and assorted others—jostle for position while dashing around a 100,000-gallon tank which encircles the viewing gallery. Be here at feeding time (daily at 2p.m.) for a show of furiously flapping fins and snapping teeth.

Somewhat more sedate is the **California Tidepool**►, which brings close-up views of starfish, sea urchins, and other undemonstrative creatures. **The Swamp**►►, meanwhile, finds frogs, snakes, and lizards making homes amid subtropical shrubbery under the gaze of calmly observant alligators and crocodiles.

One of the academy's newer sections is **Life Through Time**►►, a rewarding walk-through exploration of 3.5 billion years of natural history. Pause to enjoy the fossilized stegosaurus tail spike and a full-sized dinosaur skeleton before taking your place at a computer terminal where you can trace evolutionary links through the recesses of prehistory.

The **Hall of Earth and Space Sciences**►► offers a chance to observe the workings of the solar system, see the rotation of the earth demonstrated by a Foucault's pendulum, and discover why the process known as plate tectonics causes California's foundations to shake at regular intervals. At the **Safequake**►►► exhibit, daring visitors can hop on a vibrating floor, which shakes to the same extent as did the ground when the earthquakes of 1865 and 1906 rocked San Francisco's streets.

The **Wattis Hall of Human Cultures**► may provide stimulation for children, but most adults are likely to find its large-scale tableaux of the world's lives and lifestyles, from Arctic Inuits to Australian aborigines, unengaging.

As a final treat, allow plenty of time to study and enjoy the **Far Side of Science Gallery**►►►, where 159 of Gary Larson's hilarious science-inspired cartoons line the walls. Among them you will discover the real reason dinosaurs became extinct and learn what worms do at parties.

The Morrison Planetarium
Humorously described as "California's largest indoor universe", the academy's Morrison Planetarium offers sit-back-and-stare tours around the star-filled night sky, through black holes, and far beyond. Each evening from Thursday to Sunday, the planetarium's laserium show uses glass lasers to produce a mind-warping show of ever-shifting multicolored patterns to a pumping soundtrack of classical or rock music. For details, call 415/750 7145 (planetarium) or 415/750 7138 (laserium).

65

African habitats re-created at the California Academy of Sciences

► **California Historical Society** *IBCD3*

678 Mission Street
Buses: 15, 30, 45

The state funded California Historical Society dates back to the 1870s, but not until 1922 did it acquire its lasting authority to collect and disseminate information on California's history. Housed at the grand Whittier House (see page 150) from 1956, the society now resides in a handsome wood-framed building which served as an office supply store from 1918 until the early 1990s.

Many of the society's most valuable holdings, such as the historical manuscripts and documents which fill its library, are reserved for the eyes of bona fide researchers. Usually on display, however, are temporary exhibitions of historical artifacts and numerous selections from an excellent collection of 19th-century Californian art, with such late 19th- and early 20th-century luminaries as Edwin Deakin and Grace Hudson capturing scenes from the state's formative years.

An imposing façade: California Palace of the Legion of Honor

▶▶ **California Palace of the
Legion of Honor** *IFCA5*

Lincoln Park
Bus: 18

Auguste Rodin and San Francisco may seem strange bed-fellows, but any fans of the sculptor visiting the city should make the ascent to the windswept hilltop—offering stunning views of the Golden Gate and the Pacific—where the California Palace of the Legion of Honor holds an impressive number of the acclaimed Frenchman's works, as well as a strong general assemblage of European art.

The collection was started in the 1910s by Alma Spreckels, wife of millionaire sugar magnate Adolph. Impressed by the French pavilion at San Francisco's 1915 Panama–Pacific Exhibition and by the Legion d'Honneur on a visit to Paris (where Alma first met Rodin and developed a lasting interest in his work), the Spreckelses commissioned architect George Applegarth to build the California Palace of the Legion of Honor in a style modeled on its Parisian namesake.

While Alma's appreciation of European, and particularly French, art was real enough, the opening of the collection to the public was partly motivated by the Spreckelses' arch rivalry with another prominent San Francisco family, the de Youngs, who were behind the M. H. de Young Memorial Museum in Golden Gate Park. In 1884, Adolph Spreckels had shot and wounded Michael de Young following reports in the de Young-owned *San Francisco Chronicle* that Spreckels had defrauded shareholders in his sugar company.

On Armistice Day 1924, the California Palace of the Legion of Honor was formally donated to the city of San Francisco in memory of the state's dead of World War I.

Since the 1930s, the California Palace of the Legion of Honor and the M. H. de Young Memorial Museum have been under dual directorship, and in the 1970s they formally merged to become the Fine Arts Museums of San Francisco. A ticket at the Legion is also valid on the same day at the de Young (and the Asian Art Museum) and vice versa.

Whatever your liking for other periods of art, it is the pieces by Rodin (1840–1917) which will catch the eye and stick in the mind. *The Shades* stands by the pathway from the parking lot and a *Thinker*—from an 1880 cast and one of the first pieces purchased by Alma Spreckels from the sculptor—sits just outside the columns which mark the building's entrance.Inside, some 70 Rodin works fill two spacious galleries and range from intriguing early experiments such as *Man With a Broken Nose*, to the more confident and accomplished *Victor Hugo*

Where you might feel like spending your time throughout the rest of the collection, arranged in a chronological sequence of galleries from medieval art onwards, naturally depends on personal taste.

The best of the Dutch and Flemish rooms is Rubens' *The Tribute Money*, painted around 1612. Another major piece is El Greco's stirring *Saint*

Closed until autumn 1995
The California Palace of the Legion of Honor is due to re-open in the autumn of 1995, following extensive renovation work. Do check before you go to be sure that the building is open once more (tel. 415/863 3330—recorded message, or 415/750 3600).

The *Holocaust Sculpture*
While an hour or two at the Palace of the Legion of Honor should instill a sense of life's finer things, George Segal's *Holocaust Sculpture*, with its emaciated corpses and solitary figure looking despairingly through barbed wire towards the Golden Gate, intentionally does just the opposite. You will find this emotive work in the grounds of the Legion of Honor, beside the parking lot.

Outside the Legion of Honor and high above the Golden Gate, a Rodin Thinker sits in meditation

John the Baptist (c. 1600). By contrast, seek out a couple of early works (c. 1618–19) by Georges de la Tour, *Old Man* and *Old Woman,* and Seurat's *Eiffel Tower,* which stirred strong passions in 1890s Paris.

Downstairs, the **Achenbach Foundation for Graphic Arts** holds 100,000 prints and 3,000 drawings from artists as diverse as Albrecht Dürer (1471–1528) and Georgia O'Keeffe (1887–1986). Selections are shown in short-term exhibitions.

►   **Cartoon Art Museum**   *IFCE5*
814 Mission Street
Buses: 14, 41, 45

A room above a busy artery of SoMa might be the last place you would expect to discover the secrets behind *Peanuts, Spiderman,* or any of the cartoon strips and characters which have leapt from the printed page—or the movie or TV screen—to become icons of American popular culture. The Cartoon Art Museum, is just such a place, however. The permanent stock of cartoon art— 10,000 pieces of original artwork and drawings, rather than reproductions—reaches back to the 18th century and, along with items loaned from collectors and cartoon artists themselves, forms the core of the museum's changing exhibitions.

Recently, these eclectic shows have featured cartoon art from underground comics, highlighted work by female cartoonists, examined the realistic style of the original *Flash Gordon* strip, glimpsed the future with electronic comics and computer animation, and celebrated the past by displaying the original drawings from cinematic cartoon classics, such as Walt Disney's *Snow White.*

The funny side of San Franciscan sight-secing: above, the Gary Larson Gallery at the California Academy of Sciences; right, a warm welcome to the Cartoon Art Museum

► **The Castro** *IFCD3*

Local landmark:
Castro Theatre

Buses: 8, 24, 35, 37

The area known as the Castro (immediately south of Market Street and named for its main thoroughfare) was once known as Most Holy Redeemer Parish, and its working-class Irish population was dominated by the local Catholic church. But by the late 1970s it had been transformed into the largest and most famous gay and lesbian neighborhood in the world. San Francisco's place in gay history dates back to the gold rush (see page 70), but the Castro was transformed as its existing population decanted to the suburbs and falling property values attracted arrivals from nearby Haight-Ashbury, a traditionally ultra-liberal neighborhood where the sexual freedoms of the hippie era had attracted many gay and lesbian settlers during the 1960s and early 1970s. It was from the Castro that Harvey Milk set out on the road that would make him the country's first out-of-the-closet gay elected to public office. Milk's energy and campaigning genius helped to politicize San Francisco's gay and lesbian community, while his assassination in 1978 inspired greater gay and lesbian assertiveness, and brought support from within the city's heterosexual population.

Financially prosperous, the Castro is a well-groomed neighborhood which takes great pride in its restored Victorian homes, while Castro Street strewn with the landmarks of gay history—from the raised sidewalk outside the Eureka Bank, used by Harvey Milk and others as a public platform, to the Elephant Walk restaurant and bar (see page 71). Be sure to visit the **Names Project**►►► (2362 Market Street) where each grave-sized patch of a gigantic quilt remembers a loss to AIDS. Begun in 1987 to offer the bereaved a chance to grieve and remember their loved ones, the quilt now has 15,000 patches. It has been displayed in Washington D.C. to highlight what the gay community regards as the incumbent administrations' failure to respond adequately to the crisis.

The Castro Theatre
Pre-dating the Castro's transformation into a gay and lesbian neighborhood, the Castro Theatre, with its striking Spanish Baroque façade, was completed in 1923. In terms of programming, the Castro is among the city's most innovative movie venues, with everything from classic to cult movies screened beneath its handsome ceiling.

Castro walking tours
For an excellent introduction to gay and lesbian San Francisco and the rise of the Castro, take the Cruisin' the Castro Tour; details are given on page 94.

■ **In no other city do gays and lesbians enjoy such a high social profile or level of acceptance as they do in San Francisco. Even so, the city's gay roots go much deeper than many people realize, and the freedoms which many now take for granted have been hard won.....■**

Gay and Lesbian Center
Housed at the city's New Main Library, due to open during 1996 (see page 79) the Gay and Lesbian Center holds the world's largest collection of gay and lesbian books, videos, and artwork. Whether for serious research, browsing, or just to express solidarity, visitors are welcome to visit the facility—the only one of its kind in the world.

Top: celebrations at the Gay Freedom Parade

Gay Halloween
Halloween remains an important date in the San Francisco gay calendar, and not just as an excuse to dress up and party. In the 1950s, when police regularly raided gay bars and made every effort to harass their users, October 31 was, bizarrely enough, recognized as a gay celebration and the San Francisco Police Department (very unofficially) observed a truce on that date.

Gold rush days The mid-1800s gold rush transformed San Francisco from a barely populated outpost to a booming city almost overnight, and those who came to seek their fortune were mostly young males. The arrivals seldom struck it rich, but they did find themselves in a community where women and laws were in short supply, and where the social restraints common elsewhere—imposed by church, family and peer pressure—were similarly absent. Legend has it that gold miners demonstrated their sexual preferences to other miners by the color of their bandana—part of their work attire. Meanwhile, the lack of leisure activities in the gold-mining communities encouraged miners to spend their earnings on drink, causing any sexual inhibitions to swiftly disappear.

After the gold rush, the widely publicized prostitution of the Barbary Coast, which brought San Francisco infamy through the late 1800s and disappeared following the earthquake and fire of 1906, deflected attention from the city's continuing role as a haven for gays and lesbians who, while forced to conceal their sexual identity in everyday life, were present in considerable numbers.

World War II and after During World War II, San Francisco became the embarkation point for military operations in the Pacific, giving many secret gays and lesbians their first taste of the city and its freedoms. At the end of the war, many gay men received a dishonorable discharge from service; their papers, necessary for obtaining a civilian job, bore a large red "H" to denote "homosexual." With social stigma awaiting them at home and the likelihood that they would not find work, many opted to stay in San Francisco.

By the 1950s, the city had an underground network of gay and lesbian meeting places: often windowless rooms operated by organized crime mobs who realized that the gay dollar was as valuable as anybody else's, and that gay customers were unlikely to complain to the police about unfair business practices.

Police harassment was constant, and city politicians routinely ordered crackdowns on gay bars just prior to elections, encouraging the press to invent lurid accounts of the goings-on inside.

Gay politics San Francisco had acquired the U.S.'s first gay organization in the late 1940s, but it took the upheavals of the 1960s, unease among the city's liberals about anti-gay discrimination, and the gay settlement of the Castro (see page 69)—where plate-glass windows

made the Elephant Walk the city's first gay bar visible from the street—to pave the way for gay concerns to enter the city's political agenda.

In 1977, a Castro camera store owner, Harvey Milk, ran for public office and became the country's first openly gay city official. While Milk's impact on the city's gay and lesbian communities was considerable, it was to be his assassination that galvanized them into direct action.

A year after his election, Milk, and the city's gay-supportive mayor, George Moscone, were shot and killed by Dan White, a right-wing city politician. The token five-year sentence passed on White so incensed the gay—and large sections of the heterosexual—population, that 50,000 people took part in a protest which culminated in police cars being overturned and City Hall being attacked; this event became known as the "White Night Riot."

By the mid-1990s, years of standing up and being counted have earned San Francisco's gays and lesbians a unique level of integration and representation within the city, and among other things, have enabled a powerful reaction to what the gay community—and many outside it—consider to be an apathetic response to the AIDS crisis on the part of the U.S. government.

Except for the higher than average proportion of males in its population, the Castro seems in every respect like any other affluent city neighborhood: a fact which might be a testament to the achievements of San Francisco's gays since the early 1970s, in two decades becoming a largely accepted and integrated section of the city's community

CHINATOWN

The oldest street
In 1834, the Spanish settlement of Yerba Buena—today's San Francisco—acquired its first street, *Calle de la Fundación* (Foundation Street). When U.S. rule was established, this was renamed Dupont Street to honor a naval captain. Dupont Street, with its many brothels, was razed by the 1906 earthquake and subsequently renamed Grant Avenue, ostensibly to commemorate President Ulysses S. Grant (1822–85), but actually in an effort to bury the street's reputation for debauchery.

The Rickshaw Bar
At 37 Ross Alley, the Rickshaw Bar was the epitome of the dark and hidden-away Chinatown drinking den. Consequently, Frank Sinatra made it one of his San Francisco haunts and, the story goes, the Beatles dropped by for a quiet drink after playing a concert in the city in 1964. Unfortunately for those who might want a drink, the bar has been closed for some years and various businesses have since occupied its site.

The pagoda-style Bank of Canton was once the Chinatown Telephone Exchange

▶▶▶ **Chinatown** *IFCE5*

Buses: 15, 30, 45

Squeezed between the corporate high-rises of the Financial District and the Italian cafés of North Beach, Chinatown is San Francisco's most distinctive and energetic ethnic neighborhood. An estimated 75,000 people—Vietnamese, Laotian, Cambodian and Korean, as well as Chinese—form the largest Asian community outside Asia, crowded into a 24-block area. Explore Chinatown slowly and on foot. The shops of Grant Avenue can be enjoyable but are aimed at visitors rather than locals. Intrepid shoppers, and anyone wishing to catch a glimpse of the real Chinatown, should be sure to explore bustling Stockton Street and the many side streets and alleys. With space at a premium, Chinatown's buildings often have several uses: a restaurant might occupy a basement while, four flights up, a temple occupies the upper level.

For many San Franciscans, however, Chinatown simply means food. Some of the neighborhood's fare is described on page 216, its best restaurants on page 275.

The symbolic entrance to Chinatown is the **Chinatown Gate**, decorated with dragons (representing fertility and power), fish (prosperity), and foo dogs (warding off evil spirits), which leads into Grant Avenue from Bush Street. The gate, designed by Chinese-American architect Clayton Lee, was unveiled in 1970.

A neighborhood landmark which has been around much longer is **Old St. Mary's Church**▶, on the junction of Grant Avenue and California streets. Completed in 1854, St. Mary's was the first Catholic cathedral on the West Coast and later housed the city's first language school, teaching English to local Chinese. The biblical quotation on the clock tower, *(continued on page 74)*

Walk Chinatown

Negotiating the bustling streets of Chinatown, this walk begins at the Chinatown Gate and highlights the neighborhood's sights, sounds, and smells, visits two temples, and ends at the Chinese Historical Museum.

The green-tiled **Chinatown Gate** (see page 72) leads into **Grant Avenue**, Chinatown's main artery and seething with pedestrians, street vendors, and

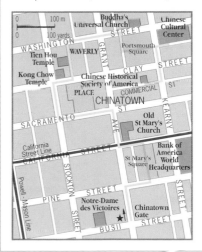

Grant Avenue: tourists' Chinatown

bemused tourists (see panel, page 72).

On the pocket-sized green of **St. Mary's Square** (see page 74) stands an impressive stainless steel and granite statue of Sun Yat-Sen (see page 74). The square takes its name from **Old St. Mary's Church**, California's first cathedral (see pages 72 and 74).

A typical example of Chinatown's mixed-use buildings, the 1857 **Kong Chow Temple** occupies the top floor of the neighborhood's main post office. Another evocative religious site is the 1852 **Tien Hou Temple** on Waverly Place (see page 74).

Portsmouth Square once marked the city's waterfront (see page 75). Facing the square, the **Holiday Inn** is an unsuccessful attempt to blend high-rise architecture into the neighborhood. On the hotel's fourth floor are the exhibitions of the **Chinese Cultural Center** (see page 75). Permanent displays on Chinese life in San Francisco and California are offered by the **Chinese Historical Society Museum**, on Commercial Street (see page 74).

CHINATOWN

Chinese Historical Society

Chinatown Alleys
Once you grow accustomed to Chinatown's ceaseless bustle, take the time to stroll down some of the easy-to-miss alleys which lie between its busier and better-known streets. Exploring Spofford Street (between Sacramento and Washington streets), Hang Ah Place (between Sacramento and Clay streets; the only alley with a bend in it), or Ross Alley (between Washington and Jackson streets), will enable you to discover facets of this intriguing neighborhood which few tourists ever see.

74

Some Chinatown streetlamps have been disguised as Chinese lanterns

(continued from page 72) "Son Observe the Time and Fly from Evil", was directed at the customers who patronized the brothels which stood near by during the first 50 years of the church's existence. It was indeed an act of God—the 1906 earthquake—which left St. Mary's standing, but razed the brothels, providing space for **St. Mary's Square▶**. A neat oblong of greenery which doubles as the roof of an underground parking lot, St. Mary's Square boasts a stainless-steel and granite statue of Sun Yat-Sen. He lived in Chinatown while raising funds and publishing a newspaper espousing his revolutionary ideals, which helped pave the way for the overthrow of China's Manchu dynasty and the founding of the Republic of China in 1911.

A short walk from Grant Avenue, the **Chinese Historical Society of America▶▶** (650 Commercial Street) uses archive newspaper cuttings and numerous artifacts to tell the turbulent story of the Chinese in California and their collective contribution to the state's development. Also detailed are some of the recent individual Chinese-American success stories.

Often called "the Street of Painted Balconies" for its colorfully decorated façades, **Waverly Place▶▶▶** has a few restaurants and numerous family associations, churches, and temples. From the late 1800s, many Chinese-Americans adopted Christianity because the churches offered education—notably English-language classes—which the secular authorities denied them. The Baptists were among the Western religious movements influential in Chinatown, and a sizeable Chinese congregation still attends Sunday service at the pagoda-topped Baptist Church on the corner of Waverly Place and Sacramento Street. However, many present-day Chinese-Americans who consider themselves Christian retain at least some faith in the religions of their ancestral homeland. Also on Waverly Place, Confucian and Buddhist temples occupy the top floors of several buildings and visitors are welcome to look around these small, incense-charged rooms; a donation is appreciated. Most temples are open daily from 10a.m. to 4p.m. and those to see include **Jeng Sen** (number 146), **Norras** (number 109), and Chinatown's oldest temple, **Tien Hou**▶▶ (the sign gives the Anglicized form, "Tin How"), at number 125, which was founded in 1852.

Between Grant Avenue and Stockton Street are a handful of bustling alleys. Far in mood from the tourist-thronged streets, Ross Alley and Spofford Street, and Old Chinatown Lane, are lined by Chinese laundries, fortune cookie bakeries (see panel, page 102), social clubs, barber shops, and a few food stalls. A sharp eye might also discover some of the secret doorways which were used in times past to flee approaching officials, who might be looking for illicit gambling or illegal employment practices.

In 1909 Chinatown acquired its own telephone exchange, raised in traditional style with a three-tier pagoda roof; the building is now used by the **Bank of Canton**▶▶ (743 Washington Street). The Chinese disliked asking for people by number rather than by name, so the telephone operators not only memorized the details of Chinatown's 2,477 subscribers, but also knew where a person could be reached at any particular time of day. The exchange stayed in use until 1950.

Named after the ship which brought Commander John Montgomery ashore in 1846 to proclaim U.S. rule in San Francisco and, two years later, used by Sam Brannan to announce the discovery of Californian gold (see pages 32 and 37), **Portsmouth Square**▶ is now a favorite rendezvous for the hundreds of Chinatown males who enjoy furtively gambling on games of chance (as local police turn a blind eye), or go through slow-motion Tai Chi routines.

From the square, a walkway leads across Kearny Street into the lobby of the **Holiday Inn**. The hotel is a brutal attempt to mimic the architectural themes of Chinatown, but its fourth floor holds the absorbing exhibitions of the **Chinese Cultural Center**▶▶. These are often selected to highlight the arts and culture of China's differing regions.

Chinatown guardian

Robert Louis Stevenson
From late 1879, Scottish writer Robert Louis Stevenson became a frequent visitor to Portsmouth Square, variously relaxing and writing while he waited for his intended bride's divorce to become final. He is remembered with a granite plinth bearing an inscription.

75

Cultural exhibits

■ Recent discoveries on the southern Californian coast suggest that the Chinese reached North America long before Columbus set foot in the New World. Nevertheless, the origins of the city's present Chinese-American community lie with the mid-1800s gold rush.....■

The ubiquitous Chinese script and displays of exotic foods form part of Chinatown's colorful mystique

Mines and railroads Eager to escape their war-torn and famine-stricken homeland, the first large groups of Chinese arrived in San Francisco in the mid-1800s, pursuing the riches promised by what they called *Gum San*, or Gold Mountain. Some became traders, but the majority made their way to California's gold mines. By 1851, one in ten of the state's 250,000 miners was Chinese, and they earned a reputation for being hardworking and dependable. Gold rush California was, however, not a place of racial harmony, and it was the Chinese who were discriminated against by the Foreign Miners License Tax. Imposed in 1851, the tax placed a $20-a-month levy on all non-U.S. miners; in practice, the money was collected only from the Chinese.

As labor-intensive mining declined, the chief source of Chinese employment became the transcontinental railroad, intended to link California with the rest of the U.S. The railroad employed 20,000 Chinese and tested to the full their capacity for long hours of arduous, backbreaking work on difficult terrain and in appalling conditions.

Economic depression Contrary to expectations, the economic recession which followed the gold rush and the end of the Civil War was not alleviated by the railroad's completion in 1869. As jobs became scarce, labor unions blamed the Chinese for the work shortage, and the popular press stirred up "Yellow Peril" hysteria. Anti-Chinese racism was legitimized by the Exclusion Act of 1882, outlawing further Chinese immigration to the U.S. for the purposes of finding work, and by the subsequent Scott Act prohibiting the immigration of Chinese women except as wives of merchants—thereby preventing the expansion of the Chinese-American population.

Chinatown life Barred from many towns and driven out of rural settlements, the Chinese community was forced into the Chinatown districts which became established in many large Californian communities. In San Francisco, 26,000 clustered into a 12-block area within the boundaries of present-day Chinatown. The smells of unusual herbs and vegetables, and the sight of traditionally dressed men with their hair in queues (ordered by China's ruling Manchu dynasty), made Chinatown

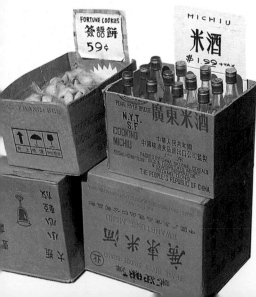

The Tongs
Conflicts between Chinatown's affluent merchants and its downtrodden laborers were many and encouraged the creation of Tongs (an American term for Chinese-American secret societies). Some Tongs claimed long histories to impress recruits, but their main purpose was to organize and control Chinatown's gambling, prostitution, and opium use—regarded as immoral vices by merchants' organizations but seen as necessities by workers. With the Chinese excluded from the American justice system, Tong membership also provided a framework for avenging wrongs and settling disputes.

Chinatown supermarket

a place of great exotica for Anglo-Americans. Denied the comforts of traditional family life, many Chinese men gambled, smoked opium, and visited prostitutes to alleviate the boredom—activities which added to the area's mystique. The Chinese faced violence if they ventured outside Chinatown's tight confines, and while merchants generally prospered, ordinary workers often slept in communal rooms and worked (if they were lucky) 20-hour days.

After the fire By 1900, the population of Chinatown had dropped to 11,000. Following the earthquake and fire of 1906, which destroyed the city's public records, many non-legal Chinatown residents claimed U.S. citizenship and arranged for the arrival of "paper" sons and daughters (see panels, page 176) from China. This boosted Chinatown's population as did, subsequently, a soaring birthrate.

Meanwhile, the founding of the Republic of China by Sun Yat-Sen and others in 1911 ended 268 years of Manchu rule and enabled the Chinese to adopt Western ideas and modes of dress. By the 1920s, the restaurants and shops of Chinatown's Grant Avenue were becoming tourist attractions, and the Chinese were steadily becoming an accepted part of city life.

Immigration became easier from 1940 (although the Exclusion Act was not repealed until 1965), as China and the U.S. became war allies, and the fresh influx pushed Chinatown's boundaries outwards, encouraging established Chinese to settle in other districts.

While Chinatown remains the focal point of Chinese life, Chinese-Americans have become fully integrated into mainstream San Franciscan society, established and successful in virtually every field of endeavor.

Holding the mayor's office and all the cogs of the civic machine, City Hall has been at the heart of San Francisco since 1915

Civic Center guided tours
Each Thursday, the City Guides (tel. 415/557 4266) offer a free guided walking tour of the Civic Center, including City Hall, packed with facts and anecdotes on San Franciscan history and politics. Each Monday between 10a.m. and 2p.m. there are guided tours of the Performing Arts Complex buildings and, on Wednesday and Saturday, tours of the Louise Davies Symphony Hall. For details of these tours, tel. 415/552 8338.

►► **Civic Center** *IFCE5*

Buses: 10, 20, 21, 47, 49, 60, 70, 80

Although they date from the 1910s, the delightful beaux-arts buildings at the core of San Francisco's Civic Center have their origins in the classically inspired City Beautiful movement which began in the 1890s and greatly influenced American urban planning in the early 1900s.

Ironically, or perhaps fittingly for what might be considered the city's major public showplace, the Civic Center also bears evidence of San Francisco's major contemporary headache, with many of its vast homeless population milling listlessly all day around the plazas and gardens.

The centerpiece of the complex is the intricate and inspiring **City Hall►►►** with its huge rotunda topped by a green copper dome, modeled on St. Peter's in Rome and visible across much of the city.

Completed in 1915, City Hall was designed by the architectural firm of Arthur Brown and John Bakewell, both of whom had studied at the École des Beaux-Arts in Paris. A much-disputed story holds that, believing they had no chance of winning the commission, Brown and Bakewell submitted an extravagant design which they budgeted at an astronomical $3.5 million. The authorities were eager for a building to symbolize San Francisco's superiority over fast-growing Los Angeles, and it was Brown and Bakewell's plan—based on the French baroque style—which was accepted in spite of its cost.

Even today, the civic power brokers who scurry about City Hall's corridors seem eclipsed by the building's sheer scale and majesty. Go inside and climb the grand staircase, lined by ornate wrought-iron bannisters and illuminated by free-standing and hanging lamps, and stand by the landings where porticoes and arches, topped by neoclassical sculptured guardians, give access to the labyrinthine complex of offices and official chambers.

City Hall has certainly won greater affection in San Franciscans' hearts than its corruption-tainted predecessor (see page 39), which occupied the site now taken by the **Public Library▶▶**, separated from City Hall by formal gardens and a neatly laid out plaza.

The library building is likely to become the new home of the Asian Art Museum (now in Golden Gate Park) towards the end of the century, when the million or more volumes stored here are relocated to a new $98-million building, a bookmark's throw closer to Market Street. Until the move occurs, you might cast an eye over the mementoes, architectural plans, and photographs filling the **San Francisco History Room▶**, on the library's third floor.

Immediately west of City Hall across Van Ness Avenue, the **War Memorial Opera House** opened in 1935, and was the first of a group of buildings now grandly dubbed the Performing Arts Complex. It was in the Opera House in 1945 that the first United Nations charter was signed. (The event was commemorated by the creation of **United Nations Plaza**, where Hyde Street meets Market Street—only worth visiting for its farmers' market on Wednesdays and Sundays.) Besides operatic performances, for which the city's great and good arrive in all their finery on the season's opening night in September, the Opera House is also the home of the San Francisco Ballet. The streamlined, wrap-around façade of glass and granite facing the Opera House across Grove Street belongs to the city's major classical music venue, the **Louise M. Davies Symphony Hall**. Finally, at 456 McAllister Street, the **Society of California Pioneers▶**, descendants of the earliest Californian settlers, has a modest but interesting collection of gold-mining tools, household knickknacks, and other remnants recalling daily life in late 19th-century California.

The Hibernia Bank building
Described by architect Willis Polk (see panel, page 112) as "the most beautiful building in the city," the Hibernia Bank building on the corner of McAllister and Market streets, close to the Civic Center, was San Francisco's earliest and most successful classically styled "temple of finance." With a copper dome above its porticoed entrance and its columned sides stretching along two streets, the building dates from 1892.

*Louise M. Davies
Symphony Hall,
opened in 1980*

The Cliff House: latest in a line

Side-by-side: the Transamerica Pyramid and Columbus Tower

▶ **Cliff House** *IFCA5*

1066–90 Point Lobos Avenue
Bus: 18

Completed in 1858, the first Cliff House was a restaurant offering dinner and dancing, which perched, as the name suggests, on a headland above the crashing waves of the Pacific Ocean. It hosted three U.S. presidents and the cream of Californian society before being purchased in 1881 by Adolph Sutro, a wealthy philanthropist and a one-time Populist city mayor.

Sutro made the Cliff House, then considered to be far from the city proper, accessible to the ordinary people of San Francisco by laying a railway line. He also began construction on an adjacent site of the remarkable Sutro Baths (for more on the baths, and Sutro himself, see pages 170–1).

After fire destroyed the building in 1894, Sutro pumped $50,000 into the creation of a sumptuous replacement Cliff House. Opened in 1896, the fancy spires and Mediterranean exuberance of the new eight-story Cliff House earned it the apt description of a "French-Château-on-a-rock." Although the second Cliff House survived the 1906 earthquake and fire, it burned to the ground in 1907.

The present Cliff House, built by Sutro's daughter in 1909, and afterwards remodeled, has little charm and offers no suggestion of its predecessors' architectural glamour. It is a good vantage point for sea lion watching (see panel, page 81), however, and for picking up maps and information on the Golden Gate National Recreation Area, of which it forms a part.

▶ **Columbus Tower** *IFCF5*

906 Kearny Street
Buses: 15, 41

Logically enough, the triangular plot of land where Kearny Street meets Columbus Avenue was filled by a triangular building,

Columbus Tower, completed in 1907. Threatened with demolition in the 1970s, the building was bought and restored by San Francisco-based film director Francis Ford Coppola.

The building, with its restored exterior, now dwarfed by the Transamerica Pyramid, wins many new admirers as they approach Columbus Avenue from North Beach.

The Vaillancourt Fountain
Created by artist Armand Vaillancourt, the fountain consists of a series of large, crazily angled concrete tubes through which water (when available) flows and drops to lower levels.

▶ **Embarcadero Center**　　　　　　*IFCF5*

Between the Embarcadero and Battery Street
Buses: Any Market Street bus

A complicated conglomeration of multi-level open-air walkways linking shops, restaurants, terraced cafés, several high-rise office buildings, and new hotels, the Embarcadero Center consumes six city blocks and is part of a determined effort to improve the visitor appeal of the Financial District, while giving thousands of office workers somewhere to spend their lunch breaks.

Begin at **Justin Herman Plaza**, across the busy Embarcadero road from the historic Ferry Building (see page 83). (The Embarcadero Freeway which once dominated this stretch of waterfront was demolished after being damaged by the 1989 earthquake.) Here street musicians and roller skaters add a human dimension to a broad concrete expanse. Select a snack from one of the many food outlets, find a place to sit down, and contemplate the plaza's controversial **Vaillancourt Fountain** (see panel), or its equally opinion-splitting sculptural memorial to the 1934 strike of the International Longshoremen's Association (see page 40).

Before entering the center proper, be sure to pick up a free map, without which locating any of the 100-plus stores—which collectively offer such indispensable items as designer earrings and gourmet chocolates—is almost impossible. For shopping suggestions, see page 227.

Embarcadero Center

▶▶ **Esprit Quilt Collection**　　　　　*IFCF3*

900 Minnesota Street
Bus: 15

Even in San Francisco, few people know that one of the best private collections of Amish quilts (the work of the long-established religious community which shuns modern technology) decorates the open-plan offices of the Esprit company in the Potrero Hill district; they are intended to inspire this clothing company's own designers. For $4, visitors are given a catalog of the quilts and can take a self-guided tour of the best of them. Masterpieces of simple but inventive design, the quilts date from the 1880s to the 1930s; they all have a deliberate mistake in them to demonstrate that only God is perfect.

Seal Rocks
Adolph Sutro was among the first to protect California's seals , sought-after for their skins and oil, by declaring Seal Rocks—beyond the Cliff House—off limits to hunters.

Most of the creatures living around Seal Rocks today are actually Stellars, a species of Californian sea lion which grows up to 14 feet in length and is found along the coast between the Oregon border and Santa Barbara. For more San Franciscan sea lions, see panel on page 92.

The Exploratorium's founder

The visionary founder of the Exploratorium was Frank Oppenheimer, brother of the more famous Robert. Both men worked on the development of the atomic bomb at Los Alamos in the 1940s; because Robert came to be remembered as the "father of the atomic bomb," Frank sometimes referred to himself in jest as the "uncle of the atomic bomb."

Hands-on science at the Exploratorium, where learning can be fun—for everyone

The Tactile Dome

The Exploratorium's most popular exhibit is the Tactile Dome, a completely dark enclosed space which participants can only leave by feeling their way along its walls and crawling out. This memorable experience requires an advance reservation (tel. 415/561 0362) and a separate admission fee.

Art in residence

Since its inception in 1969, the Exploratorium has encouraged examination of the relationship between art and science, and its artist-in-residence program has provided several intriguing pieces. Among these are Ned Kahn's Tornado, a reservoir of fog continually pulled upwards in an inverted vortex, and Paul de Marinis's Alien Voices, allowing two people in separate wooden telephone booths to speak to each other in a choice of 16 computer-altered voices.

▶▶ **Exploratorium** *IFCD6*

3601 Lyon Street
Buses: 28, 30

Described as a "mad scientist's penny arcade," the Exploratorium is undoubtedly the best place in San Francisco to amuse young minds with low boredom thresholds. It is no less pleasurable for adults, who could easily pass an hour or more in its entertaining interior.

Comprising a vast room, a curving hall built as part of the Palace of Fine Arts (see page 152), the Exploratorium is packed with over 650 hands-on, interactive exhibits designed to illustrate and explain the fundamentals of natural science and human perception.

The first set of exhibits describes the processes involved in tracking the weather, and offers the opportunity to experiment with a weather-watching radar and plot the orbit for a satellite. Near by, the Golden Gate Videodisc has aerial views of a 100-square-mile section of

San Francisco and allows the user to pilot a course along a geometric grid, undertaking a literal flying visit to the city and the islands of the bay which appear on a giant screen.

One section of the hall is filled with the sounds of clanking machinery and crackles of electricity, as the action of a Tesla coil and the principles of thermodynamics are demonstrated. Near by, the Sound and Hearing quarter includes a chance to manipulate pre-programmed pieces of music, moving around segments of the tune, altering its tempo and choosing from a selection of digitally sampled instruments on which to play it.

▶ **Federal Reserve Bank Building** *IBCE3*

101 Market Street
Bus: Any Market Street bus

From the other side of Market Street, the Federal Reserve Bank's stepped façade makes a diverting sight in this section of the Financial District. Displays on economic themes and entertaining finance-orientated computer games are arranged on the ground floor (see panel, page 87).

▶▶ Ferry Building   *IFCF5*

East end of Market Street

Bus. Any Market Street bus

Despite the neighboring skyscraping towers and the loss of its once-elegant interior to drab office space, the Ferry Building is perhaps the most enduring and romantic symbol of old San Francisco. Partly modeled on the Giralda Tower in Seville, Spain, by Bay Area architect Arthur Page Brown, the Ferry Building was completed in 1903 and 50 million people annually passed through its portals—mostly commuters from across the bay. With the opening of the Bay Bridge in 1937 and the shift to motorized transportation, use of the Ferry Building gradually declined. At 235 feet it was the tallest building in the city for many years, miraculously remaining relatively unscathed by the earthquake and fire of 1906. An indication of the Ferry Building's seemingly charmed existence, was the demolition in 1992 (following damage caused by the 1989 earthquake) of the Embarcadero Freeway, which had effectively partitioned the structure from the rest of the city. Nowadays, there is a good view of the Ferry Building from Justin Herman Plaza (see page 81).

San Franciscans relax beside the Ferry Building and its much-loved clock tower

Ferry Building ferries
For old times' sake, you might be tempted to board one of the few ferries which these days depart from the Ferry Building's rear landing stage, bound for Larkspur, Sausalito, Tiburon, or Oakland. While you wait, cast an eye over one of the city's lesser-known sculptures: a 1980s likeness of Mahatma Gandhi.

Bars

■ **Caffeine may be the preferred fuel of most San Franciscans, but the city has no shortage of bars ready to pour drinks with an alcoholic kick to them. Whether you want to sip pints of locally brewed beer, drink with a view, imbibe beneath elegant chandeliers, spot the rich and famous, or discover the latest hangout of the terminally hip, the city can deliver exactly what you need.....■**

84

Chinatown bars
It might go against the grain to drink rather than eat in restaurant-filled Chinatown, but doing so can have its rewards. A cave-like entrance is one interesting feature of LiPo's (916 Grant Avenue), a long-serving local watering hole and one packed with tacky Chinese ornaments. Directly across Grant Avenue, the Buddha Bar rarely has more than a handful of customers but—on a good night—those who do enter its spartan interior are liable to be larger-than-life Chinatown characters.

Stone Age entrance to LiPo's, a noted Chinatown bar

Good beer bars The city boasts numerous micro-breweries, establishments which make their own beer on the premises and have it consumed by a clientele increasingly knowledgeable about an ale's finer points. The best is North Beach's unpretentious **San Francisco Brewing Company** (155 Columbus Avenue), where four quality homemade beers are always on tap and attract capacity crowds on Friday and Saturday nights. Across the city, **Twenty Tank Brewery** (316 11th Street) captures the fast-living SoMa nightlife regulars before they hit the clubs, with a strong range of homemade ales and theatrical decor.

Bars with views Even at ground level, San Francisco is laden with fine views but get a (more expensive than usual) drink in your hand at one of the city's high-elevation cocktail lounges and the place can suddenly look much better than it ever has.

On the 19th floor of Nob Hill's Mark Hopkins Hotel, the **Top of the Mark** combines great views with elegant surroundings. For the highest look-out over the city, however, you have to travel down the hill to the Financial District and the **Carnelian Room** (555 California Street); decorated with tapestries and antiques, the bar perches on the 52nd story of the Bank of America building.

For good views in whimsical surroundings, make for the Holiday Inn (480 Sutter Street) where the 34th-floor **S. Holmes Esq. Public House and Drinking Salon** serves drinks and invites its guests to examine its collection of memorabilia relating to Sir Arthur Conan Doyle's fictional London sleuth.

Upscale bars to be seen in Once the afternoon tea crowd (see pages 132–3) moves on, the **Compass Rose** bar at the historic St. Francis Hotel, on Union Square, is the perfect place to sip champagne and assume a sophisticated expression as the sounds of the resident jazz combo reverberate from the chandeliers. For a more intimate ambience amid original art-deco fittings, head for the **Redwood Room**, which opened at the Four Seasons Hotel (495 Geary Street) following the repeal of prohibition and has been on the stylish San Franciscan drinkers' circuit ever since.

Heralded as the city's greatest singles bar, **Perry's** (1944 Union Street) is long past its prime as a pick-up spot, but its good service and cozy wood paneling tempt a regular entourage of fashionable Pacific Heights faces.

To see rather than be seen, plant yourself in a good vantage point at **Act IV**, the comfortable bar of the Inn at the Opera (333 Fulton Street). The hotel's clientele includes not only world-famous opera stars engaged at the nearby Opera House, but also big names from the film and art worlds who savor the low-key atmosphere.

Downscale bars to be seen in Apparently little changed since being patronized by the bright lights of the Beat generation in the 1950s, **Vesuvio's** (255 Columbus Avenue) is still a favored meeting spot for embryonic writers and artists, and those who would like to be.

Across the city, many of Haight-Ashbury's bars offer budget-priced drinking and differ in ambience from the boisterous to the ultracool. Get the flavor by trying **Toronado** (547 Haight Street), which is dark and dingy but offers great beers and a usually convivial crowd.

Serving a limited range of alcohol but packed nightly with students, artists, posers, clotheshorses, and fashion victims, **Café Flore** (2298 Market Street) is worth a call, if only to find out why it has been informally nicknamed "Café Haircut."

Opposite, top, and above: Perry's

The oldest bar
Dating from 1861 and surviving major earthquakes, prohibition, and a period spent as a brothel, The Saloon (1232 Grant Avenue) can justly claim to be the oldest bar in California. The bar makes light of its historical pedigree, however, allowing its wooden floorboards to be shaken almost every night by live rock and blues bands, which attract a beer-drinking clientele in plaid shirts and jeans.

Brainwash: bar cum laundromat

Forgotten streets
Intrepid strollers can weave through almost the whole of the Financial District using only the short side streets, of which few people—even those who work in the neighborhood—are aware. Look for Trinity, Belden, and Spring streets, or walk the three-block Liedesdorff Street, between Pine and Clay streets. This crosses the gold-rush-era Commercial Street, which once extended into a 2,000ft.-long wharf and now gives a splendid view of the Ferry Building.

Reaching for the sky

▶▶ ■ **Financial District**   *IFCF5*

Buses: Any Market Street bus

It may lack hard and sharp boundaries but you can never forget where San Francisco keeps its Financial District: the forest of high-rise office buildings, located close to the eastern waterfront, is visible from all over the city. However, the pace of development has been tightly controlled, and the Financial District's modern architecture, has in some cases—such as the **Transamerica Pyramid** (600 Montgomery Street, see page 177)—greatly enriched the skyline. A walk through the Financial District also reveals some longer-serving buildings. A few predate the calamitous 1906 earthquake and fire, many more survive from the subsequent construction frenzy, and still more date from the building boom of the buoyant 1920s.

Until the 1850s, the present Financial District's main north–south artery, Montgomery Street, marked the city's eastern shoreline, with the east–west streets terminating in wharves. The streets which now run east from Montgomery Street were created from landfill, and the city's earliest financial buildings spread steadily southwards from the foot of Telegraph Hill to line them. Once

Power play
Should you feel like emulating the power-dressed brokers you will see marching along Market Street, the safest way to do so is with the enjoyable computer simulations in the lobby of the Federal Reserve Bank Building (101 Market Street, see page 82). The options among the economics-themed games include becoming U.S. president and trying not to lead the country to bankruptcy.

A medieval skyscraper?
For a final sample of Financial District architecture, step into the lobby of the Russ Building (235 Montgomery Street) to admire an inspired attempt to make a 1920s skyscraper—the city's tallest building until 1964—resemble a medieval castle.

87

Essential information

Where not to be when the next big earthquake hits: the Financial District

the pacesetting Bank of California opened its new headquarters at the junction of California and Sansome streets in 1866, the location of the city's new commercial quarter was confirmed. It was the gold rush which made San Francisco, and made it rich, but following the opening of the transcontinental railroad in 1869 (see page 37), the city also became the unchallenged center of trans-Pacific trade. A look-out would be posted on the roof of the **Merchant Exchange Building**►►► (465 California Street) to announce arriving ships to the traders and businessmen gathered below in the building's Grain Exchange Hall. Designed by Willis Polk (see panel, page 112) and completed in 1903, the Merchant Exchange is now occupied by the **First Interstate Bank**.

By contrast, one of the city's most-acclaimed contemporary towers also stands on California Street, by the junction with Kearny Street. The clever, imposing **Bank of America World Headquarters**► rises for 52 stories above a plaza decorated with a marble sculpture entitled *Transcendence*, but informally dubbed "Banker's Heart."

Contributions from Philip Johnson and John Burgee have sharply divided opinion in San Francisco. Their most intriguing San Franciscan offering is **101 California Street**►►, a soaring silo with a garden theme.

Another bone of contention is Skidmore Owings & Merrill's **First Interstate Center**► (345 California Street), completed in 1987 and circumventing restrictions by incorporating two older buildings as well as a luxury hotel and shopping complex in its 48-story mass.

Walk Financial District

Covering only a few blocks, this walk includes the most distinctive examples of the city's old and new commercial architecture, as well as two museums of Financial District history.

Bank of America World HQ, sold in 1985 for $660 million, the largest sum paid for any building in the U.S.

The **Bank of America World Headquarters** (see page 87) symbolizes the economic boom of the 1970s and is one of the few developments of the period to be warmly received. Close by, the **Wells Fargo History Museum** commemorates the company founded in 1852 to carry people and communications across the American frontier.

In the **Merchant Exchange Building** (see page 87) San Francisco's turn-of-the-century importance as a center of maritime trade is expressed by vast maritime paintings on the walls of the First Interstate Bank.

Art-deco sculptures and classical columns form a curious partnership on the exterior of the 1930 **Pacific Stock Exchange**.

At the Bank of California, the **Museum of Money of the American West** (see page 127) holds some of the gold nuggets which helped make San Francisco's Financial District what it is today.

Boat trips

■ With water on three sides, it is inevitable that San Francisco and boat trips are a winning combination, whether for a scenically memorable hop across the bay or a leisurely dinner cruise..... ■

Around the bay Two cruise companies offer enjoyable, narrated tours daily around San Francisco Bay. The **Red & White Fleet's** 45-minute cruise circles Alcatraz and Angel islands and passes beneath the Golden Gate Bridge. Lasting 75 minutes, the **Blue & Gold Fleet's** bay cruise covers much of the same, but also passes under the Bay Bridge.

To Alcatraz The former prison of Alcatraz (see page 55) should be on everybody's San Franciscan itinerary. The only way to reach Alcatraz Island is with the Red & White Fleet's half-hourly departures from morning to mid-afternoon. In summer, catch an early ferry (the first is at 9:30a.m.) to avoid the crowds and buy your ticket at least a day in advance. The fare includes the loan of a prison-tour cassette and player.

Dining and dancing Several companies offer the chance to combine cruising with eating. On Fridays and Saturdays from May to December, the Blue & Gold Fleet operates three-hour dinner cruises which allow passengers to dance to a live band after eating all they can from an abundant buffet table. Dining and dancing also take place nightly aboard the replica turn-of-the-century bay steamer of **Hornblower Dining Yachts,** also the scene of lunch and Sunday brunch cruises.

Ferry travel One of the best—and least expensive—ways to enjoy the bay is simply to hop aboard a ferry. **Golden Gate Ferries** sail several times a day between the city and Sausalito and Larkspur. The Blue & Gold Fleet has a daily ferry link with Oakland's Jack London Waterfront.

Boat trip details
Blue & Gold Fleet (tel. 415/705 5444) departures from Pier 39, Fisherman's Wharf, and the Ferry Building (for Oakland). Golden Gate Ferries (tel. 415/332 6600), departures from the Ferry Building. Hornblower Dining Yachts (tel. 415/788 8866), departures from Pier 33, Embarcadero. Red & White Fleet (tel. 1–800/229 2784) departures from Piers 41 and 43, Fisherman's Wharf.

89

All aboard for Tiburon, Sausalito, Alcatraz

Assembled from scrap, Pier 39 is now a money-making tourist attraction

San Francisco's ghost ship
On chilly nights when the waters of the bay are eerily shrouded in fog, watch out for a phantom clipper, the *Tennessee*, gliding effortlessly through the waves. The two-masted vessel sank in the bay 100 years ago but is regularly "sighted", most famously by several of the crew of a naval destroyer in 1942.

► **Fisherman's Wharf**   *IFCE6*

Bus: 32
Cable car: Powell–Mason line

The only San Francisco neighborhood where locals are less prevalent than tourists, Fisherman's Wharf attracts 12 million visitors annually and consumes a lengthy segment of the city's northern waterfront, immediately north of North Beach and east of Fort Mason Center.

Today, the only sign of commercial fishing is the modest catch unloaded in the early hours (usually 6–9 a.m.) at Pier 49. Earlier this century, though, it was a very different story, with 300 or more vessels daily disgorging tons of freshly caught sardine and crab along the bay. By the late 1950s, the fishing fleet was in decline, and it took a major urban renewal program to revitalize the area.

While much of present-day Fisherman's Wharf—be it street entertainers, bay cruises, tacky museums, or the endless opportunities to eat clam chowder from a bowl-shaped hunk of sourdough bread (see panels, pages 93 and 218)—is unapologetically geared towards tourists, few visitors leave completely disappointed. Do not expect to learn much about the real San Francisco, however, and bear in mind that the souvenirs sold are almost always considerably higher than those sold elsewhere around the city.

Several of Fisherman's Wharf's genuinely historic sights are given their own accounts elsewhere: Hyde Street Pier Historic Ships (page 112), the National Maritime Museum, National Liberty Ship Memorial and USS *Pampanito* (all page 128), as is Alcatraz (page 55), to which ferries depart from Pier 41. You might combine a tour of Fisherman's Wharf with the museums of the Fort Mason Center (see page 96).

With more energy, you could also tackle the bayside **Golden Gate Promenade** which covers the 3 miles from Fisherman's Wharf to Fort Point (see page 96), located beneath the Golden Gate Bridge. *(Continued on page 92)*

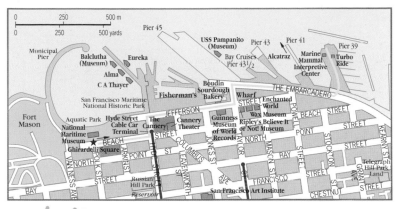

Walk Fisherman's Wharf

This simple walk covers all the major free tourist attractions of Fisherman's Wharf, beginning at Ghirardelli Square and finishing at Pier 39.

Ghirardelli Square (see page 93) has been transformed from a chocolate factory into a strollable grouping of stores and restaurants without sacrificing its architectural integrity.

Another historic site converted to stave off demolition, **The Cannery** (see page 93) was once the world's largest fruit and vegetable canning center.

Frenchman Isadore Boudin was the first San Franciscan baker to produce sourdough bread (see panel, page

218). Fisherman's Wharf has many outlets for this city specialty but the best is a branch of the **Boudin Sourdough French Bread Bakery** (see panel, page 93) which allows a peek at the baking process.

Built of timber from abandoned piers and boats, **Pier 39** (see page 92) is another conglomeration of retail outlets, eating places, and tourist amusements. Completed in 1978 and intended to be a re-creation of a San Franciscan street, Pier 39 is more successful as a place to indulge in a snack and enjoy regular free entertainment.

Making Ghirardelli chocolate

FISHERMAN'S WHARF

Fisherman's Wharf draws all kinds of visitors

Pier 39's sea lions
From an original group of 10 attracted by an abundant supply of herring, some 600 Californian sea lions are now believed to have made their homes beside Pier 39. The creatures can be observed from a viewing area. On Saturday and Sunday afternoons during the peak season (October to April) a sea lion expert leads a question and answer session. You will need to listen closely: a distinguishing feature of the Californian sea lion is its very loud bark. The mammal center is open all year, with displays, amusements, and staff on hand to answer questions. For more sea lions, see page 81.

(Continued from page 90)
   Built in the 1970s on the site of an abandoned cargo wharf, split-level **Pier 39▶** is packed with shops, restaurants and amusement arcades. If buying, eating, or fighting for your life at a computer keyboard holds no appeal, a walk along the wooden boardwalk can be enjoyable. Structure your walk to include the west side of the pier and you will spot the colony of Californian sea lions which took up residence here in 1990 (see panel). On the pier's top deck, the **Marine Mammal Interpretive Center▶▶** provides information on the fish-crazed creatures and the adjoining **National Park Store** has books and pamphlets on other aspects of natural California.
   Near the pier's entrance, the **San Francisco Experience▶** condenses the city's history into a half-hour multimedia show. It may be short on detail, but the special effects—seats rumble in sympathy with the earthquake of 1906; a dragon pops out of the wall to celebrate Chinese New Year—can be entertaining. More thrills and spills can be found at the **Turbo Ride▶**, a bumpy flight-simulated ride through time and space.
   Also on Pier 39, the **Eagle Café** is the antidote to Fisherman's Wharf's over-priced restaurants. The self-service café was lifted on stilts from its original location nearby and placed here in 1978, 50 years after it opened.
   None of the three major tourist attractions which interrupt the souvenir shops lining Jefferson Street offer great intellectual stimulation, but you might welcome them on a rainy day, or if you have restless children to entertain. The **Wax Museum** (number 145) has plenty of what you

92

Sculptured sea lions on Pier 39

would expect: waxen images of stage, screen, and sports stars, and a Chamber of Horrors featuring Dracula, Al Capone, and the founder of the Church of Satan. More entertaining is **Ripley's Believe It or Not▶** (number 175) where the exhibits include an 8ft.-long cable car made of matchsticks and a room devoted to Californian earthquakes that includes a very disorienting moving wall.

Similarly well-endowed with bizarre facts, the **Guinness Museum of World Records▶** (number 235) details the longest, biggest, smallest, shortest, fastest, and slowest achievements in every imaginable field of endeavor.

The Del Monte fruit company once canned their peaches at what, in 1968, was imaginatively and expensively (the cost estimated at $5.5 million) transformed into **The Cannery▶**, on Leavenworth Street between Beach and Jefferson streets. An amiable assortment of shops, eating places, and galleries is now secreted throughout the brick-built factory, while the pretty, tree-lined courtyard is the scene of free entertainment most lunchtimes and early evenings. On the third level, the **Museum of the City of San Francisco▶▶** offers a small but entertaining gathering of knickknacks from the city's back pages.

It was the success of an earlier conversion that inspired the creation of The Cannery and contributed greatly to Fisherman's Wharf's emergence as a tourist center. The redbrick Ghirardelli chocolate factory (9800 North Point Street) had been a city landmark since its opening in 1893. As **Ghirardelli Square▶▶**, the factory's former work spaces became filled with speciality shops and restaurants, and drew scores of visitors to its generously sized plaza (its waterfall is by the artist and street landscaper, Ruth Asawa). The much-loved Ghirardelli chocolate, produced in San Francisco since the gold rush, can be sampled at the Chocolate Manufactory and Soda Fountain inside the Clock Tower building on the Plaza Level.

Boudin's bakery

Sourdough bread
The Boudin Sourdough French Bread Bakery (156 Jefferson Street) is one of 10 descended from Isadore Boudin's original sourdough bakery, opened in San Francisco by the Frenchman in 1849. The crusty, no-yeast sourdough loaf became popular with gold-miners and, subsequently, became synonymous with the city. One of the more bizarre aspects of San Franciscan folklore holds that the quality of a sourdough loaf is dependent upon the local fog.

The fishing fleet

■ **Unlike most U.S. cities, San Francisco is best explored by walking. To get the most from an hour or two of footwork, however, you should join one or more of the city's guided walking tours. Whether they follow Sam Spade's trail, explore gay history, locate hippie hotspots, or provide a beginner's guide to dim sum, these tours reveal aspects of local life which are otherwise hidden. The following are a small selection from the author's favorites; most guided walks cost $20–$30 per person.....■**

Above: Chinatown

Free and inexpensive walks
A tight budget is no obstacle to joining a guided walking tour. Every day of the week, the City Guides (tel. 415/557 4266) operate free tours—including City Hall, Victorian-era Haight-Ashbury, Nob Hill, Sutro Heights Park, and the mansions of Pacific Heights. City Guides also offer a tour of the Mission District's murals, as (for a small charge) does the Precita Eyes Mural Arts Center (see panel, page 126).

Thorough research The enjoyment of a walk naturally depends on the quality of the guide's background research; the most conscientious among them will have pored for hours over dusty archives for the real stories behind the historic headlines.

For accurate, amusing, and sometimes astonishing, background information, no walking tour surpasses those of **Frisco Productions** (tel. 415/681 5555), usually led by local author Mark Gordon. Some of these walks offer a combination of history, architecture, and folklore—others are more specialized. The Crime Tour, for example, scours the dives of the Barbary Coast and Prohibition eras, and the movie walks focus on locations from classic San Francisco films such as *The Maltese Falcon* and Alfred Hitchcock's *Vertigo*.

Another exceptionally well-researched walk is **Cruisin' the Castro** (by reservation only; tel. 415/550 8110). Visitors of every sexual persuasion often wonder why San Francisco has such a large and visible gay and lesbian population, and many of the answers are provided on this three-and-a-half-hour tour. Covering only a few blocks of Castro Street, the walk involves very little legwork but provides fascinating insights into the city's under-publicized gay and lesbian history, which stretches back to the gold rush. The tour comes up-to-date by explaining the importance of the Castro neighborhood and visiting the Names Project quilt (see page 69). The price includes lunch in the gay-landmark Elephant Walk restaurant.

Neighborhood walks The tucked-away temples and narrow alleyways of Chinatown may well seem daunting to first-time visitors, who might also lack the time to gain full enjoyment from one of the city's most vibrant ethnic enclaves.

A crash course in Chinatown's history, culture, and cuisine is provided by the **Wok Wiz** walk (tel. 415/355 9657), which spends three hours weaving through the sidestreets, visiting a fortune cookie factory (see panel, page 102), a wok shop, an herb shop (at last, a chance to find out what bird's-nest soup is all about), a traditional Chinese brush-and-ink artist, and a tea emporium. An optional lunch provides adventurous but shy diners with a demystification of dim sum.

The Wok Wiz is among the city's most popular walking tours (often several Wok Wiz walks are run simultaneously), and an early reservation is advised.

Many walking tours focus on the geographically close-knit Financial District, Chinatown, and North Beach, but the twice-weekly **Flower Power** (tel. 415/221 8442) examines the historical strands that make Haight-Ashbury one of San Francisco's most interesting districts. The walk uses vintage photographs and examples of local Victorian architecture to chart the neighborhood's origins as a weekend resort, and describes its 1960s transformation into the heart of the hippie movement while pausing at significant sites of the psychedelic era.

Enthusiastic guides While research is essential, a guide's personal enthusiasm can also make for a winning walking tour. No San Franciscan walk guide can compete with Helen of **Helen's Walk Tour** (tel. 510/524 4544) for sheer exuberance. Full of infectious passion for the city and her favorite restaurants, shops, landmarks, and curiosities, Helen can structure her walks to suit particular interests. But usually they last two hours and offer a choice of North Beach and Coit Tower, Victorian Mansions, or Chinatown. The price includes a bag of souvenirs and suggestions and directions for further sightseeing in the city.

95

Unusual walks
Among the city's many walks are a few which diverge from the normal themes. One of the walks offered by Roger's Custom Tours (tel. 415/742 9611) is a fact-filled history of the Golden Gate Bridge enlivened by bridge workers' tales. Meanwhile, chocolate lovers and other eat-between-meals enthusiasts will be tempted by The Strolling Nosh of San Francisco (tel. 415/441 4221) which, between pauses for snacks, unravels some of the neglected history of Fisherman's Wharf.

In the Castro district

FORT MASON CENTER

*Culture by the bay:
Fort Mason Center*

Fort Point's cannons
Fort Point was decommissioned in 1914, although to all intents and purposes it was made obsolete a year after its completion with the advent of wall-piercing artillery. None of Fort Point's cannons was ever fired in anger but one of them is kept in a fire-ready state and is used by park rangers to give cannon-loading demonstrations—a far more interesting and complex task than you might imagine.

*Beneath Golden Gate
Bridge: Fort Point*

►► **Fort Mason Center** IFCD6
Between Fisherman's Wharf and the Golden Gate Bridge
Bus: 28
From the time of San Francisco's 18th-century Spanish presidio (or garrison) to the U.S.–Korean war of the 1950s, Fort Mason served a military role. In 1972, however, the fort became part of the Golden Gate National Recreation Area, with its rambling hilltop Victorian office building (near the corner of Van Ness and Laguna streets) housing the park's headquarters and the unused barracks on the waterfront earmarked to become a cultural center.

Today, some 50 non profit organizations, including art, music, and broadcasting workshops, several theaters, and museums such as the African American Historical & Cultural Society (page 54), the Mexican Museum (page 117), the Museo Italo-Americano (page 127), and the San Francisco Craft & Folk Art Museum (page 159), occupy the former barrack buildings.

Fort Mason also houses an offshoot of the San Francisco Museum of Modern Art: the **Rental Gallery** (Building A), which enables prospective patrons of emerging northern Californian artists to rent a piece before making a commitment to purchasing it. A better stop for people of moderate budgets might be **Book Bay**, operated by the Friends of the San Francisco Public Library (Building C), which has copiously stocked shelves of secondhand books at giveaway prices.

Also here, and unique among Fort Mason occupants for paying a percentage of its substantial profits as rent (others pay a token 15¢ per square foot), is the award-winning vegetarian restaurant, **Greens** (Building A).

► **Fort Point National Historic Site** IFCB6
Beneath southern end of Golden Gate Bridge
Bus: 29
As the traffic on the Golden Gate Bridge rumbles overhead, it is hard to imagine how diminutive Fort Point, completed in 1861, was ever expected to deter enemy incursions into San Francisco Bay. Some assistance in doing so, however, is provided by the displays of artillery housed in the rooms off the restored courtyard, alongside temporary exhibits covering diverse aspects of U.S. military history.

■ **The Irish have contributed as much as any ethnic group to the growth of San Francisco, but unlike the very visible Italian or Chinese communities, their impact on the city is not always obvious.....■**

Early Irish A handful of Irish settlers had arrived in pre-U.S. California. One of them, John Read, settled in 1826 as a land-owning *ranchero* in Marin County. Another, Timothy Murphy (known as "Don Timoteo") took charge of the secularized Mission San Rafael. In 1844, Irish priest Eugene McNamara received an enormous land grant from California's Mexican governor intending to bring 10,000 Irish *emigrós* to settle it. However, the gold rush—combined with Ireland's potato famine—prompted the mass Irish migration into California. By the 1870s, they accounted for 30 percent of the state's population.

Irish established In San Francisco, the Irish became pre-eminent in city affairs by the late 19th century, dominating the transportation and construction trades, and the police force. The Irish-formed trade unions had a major impact on the city, and organized popular protests against the elitist millionaires of Nob Hill and the monopolistic business practices of the railroad companies.

Irishman Dennis Kearney became president of the influential Workingmen's Party of California in 1877 and led 3,000 protesters up Nob Hill to show their contempt for Charles Crocker's "spite fence" (see panel, page 130). However, it was Kearney, and other Irish organizations, who stirred up the anti-Chinese feeling which contributed to the ghettoisation of the Chinese community.

Later, Irish-American mayor James Phelan led an anti-corruption drive and championed the City Beautiful movement, which eventually created the Civic Center.

Irish organizations
The St. Patrick's Day Parade (see pages 24–25), a tide of green which sweeps along Market Street each March, is one unmistakable sign of the Irish presence. Less obvious markers can usually be found at the Irish Cultural Center (2700 45th Avenue) and at the Irish Heritage Foundation (2123 Market Street).

97

Irish neighborhoods
Before the earthquake of 1806, SoMa was the city's Irish neighborhood. Subsequently, the Irish moved west to the Mission District (now Hispanic), and the Castro (now gay), before spreading throughout the city.

Legend has it that America's first Irish coffee was served in San Francisco in 1952

GOLDEN GATE BRIDGE

► ► ► **Golden Gate Bridge**   *IFCB6*

Buses: 28, 29, 76 (Sundays and holidays)
Of all the 575,000 bridges in the U.S., probably none is more instantly recognizable than San Francisco's Golden Gate Bridge, linking the city to Marin County.

Eager to create work in the gloom of the Depression, the federal government gave the go-ahead for the bridge in 1930 and authorized a bond issue of $35 million to finance its construction. The Golden Gate Bridge was not created without opposition, however, and there was a particularly angry outcry against an early design offered by the project's chief engineer, Joseph B. Strauss, which was likened to "two grotesque steel beetles emerging from either bank." The authorship of the design which eventually became the bridge has been much disputed but is thought to have been largely the work of Strauss's locally appointed assistant, Irving Morrow.

Seven miles long (including approaches) with towers as high as a 48-story building, the bridge was completed in 1937 and is still among the world's largest suspension bridges. It can be crossed not only by car, but also on foot and by bicycle, though the steady rumble of traffic tends to upset contemplation of the extraordinary views—as do the often ferocious winds zapping across the span.

▶▶ **Golden Gate National Recreation Area**   *IFCB5*

From the cliffs of Fort Funston in the south to the rugged hills of Marin County in the north, the Golden Gate National Recreation Area (GGNRA) bestows federal protection to a long, slender chunk of the San Franciscan coastline. Most of GGNRA's 74,000 acres, which often lack marked boundaries, can be explored on foot (and some parts by bike) and a large section is former military-owned land: abandoned forts are a common sight. Information and maps are distributed at several sites, the main headquarters being at Fort Mason Center (see page 96).

Between the ocean and Sunset District's Lake Merced, the tall cliffs of **Fort Funston**▶ make a popular lift-off point for hang gliders, and footpaths weave around the area's sand dunes, once used to practice coastal assaults. GGNRA's wildest and most hike-worthy section (on the city side), is the **coastal trail**▶▶ which winds through the coarsely vegetated hillsides rising steeply above the tiny beach of **Land's End**▶. From the trail, often subject to blustery winds and frequently offering vortiginous views, you will also spot the pocket-sized **China Beach**▶▶, named after the gold-rush-era Chinese fishermen who lived in shacks beside it. Apart from a foolhardy clamber down the hillside, China Beach is accessible only from the affluent residential area around Seacliff Avenue. The coastal trail continues to **Baker Beach** (see page 57) and through a section of the Presidio before reaching the approach to the Golden Gate Bridge. GGNRA extends to parts of the northern waterfront, and continues on the north side of the Golden Gate.

The undulating hillsides which face the city from the Golden Gate form part of the **Marin Headlands**▶. The Marin Headlands Visitor Center, off Highway 101, is a worthwhile first stop before exploring this enticing mix of ridges, valleys, and beaches.

One part of Golden Gate National Recreation Area

Swimming at China Beach
After a long hike on a warm day, China Beach has special appeal. It is one of the few beaches in San Francisco where swimming is regarded as safe. The lifeguard post is manned from mid-April to mid-October.

Point Bonita Lighthouse
Explore the Marin Headlands on a summer weekend and you will be able to visit Point Bonita Lighthouse, completed in 1855 and the oldest fixed beacon on the West Coast. The lighthouse is the prize at the end of an eventful half-mile trail from Point Bonita.

GOLDEN GATE PARK

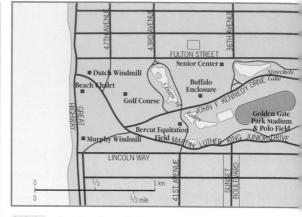

▶ ▶ ▶ **Golden Gate Park**   *IFCB4*

Buses: 5, 7 (daytime), 18, 21, 28, 29, 44, 71

Three miles long and half-a-mile wide, Golden Gate Park stretches between Haight-Ashbury and the ocean, providing San Francisco with one of the world's largest urban parks. Hidden among these 1,000 green acres are a polo field, a golf course, an archery range, a botanical garden, two major museums, countless lakes, ponds, and waterfalls, and even a few windmills. Yet Golden Gate Park still has sufficient space to enable anyone to become hopelessly lost—and quickly found again—around its tree-lined lanes and walkways.

The park has given San Francisco a stage from which to show itself to the world (with events as diverse as the Midwinter International Exposition of 1894 and the hippie

The Conservatory, shipped to California from England in 1879

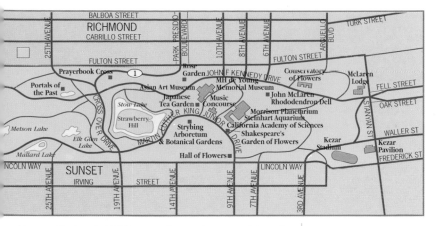

Human Be-In of 1967) as well as a large and bucolic retreat for those who enjoy jogging, skateboarding, roller-skating and kiteflying.

Many San Franciscans were amused in 1869 when the city authorities announced that a wind-bitten area of sand dunes then known as the Outer Lands was to be the site of a new public park, a decision partly influenced by a desire to clear the area of its squatters' camps.

The ecological headache of transforming sand dunes into lushly landscaped parks caused the project to take shape slowly. Not until the appointment of John McLaren as park supervisor in 1890 did Golden Gate Park begin to assume the appearance it still largely retains.

The gifted and single-minded McLaren was to spend the rest of his life creating and shaping Golden Gate Park.

One of the park's many refreshing fountains

GOLDEN GATE PARK

You really can drink tea at the Japanese Tea Garden, which sits in Golden Gate Park close to the M. H. de Young Memorial Museum. The garden's tea pavilion (below) is designed in traditional Japanese style, and its jasmine and green teas are served with fortune cookies

Several entrances lead into Golden Gate Park, but the best approach is from Haight-Ashbury's Panhandle, a slender green strip which faces the red sandstone **McLaren Lodge**, former home and office of John McLaren and where the park maps can be obtained.

Lined by numerous walkways, John F. Kennedy Drive goes west into the park and quickly reaches the **Conservatory of Flowers▶**. Fronted by flower gardens and surrounded by groves of camellias, fuchsias, and dahlias, the conservatory is the park's oldest building, completed in 1878 and inspired by London's Kew Gardens.

Further on, the **John McLaren Rhododendron Dell▶** is the first of the park's many secluded gardens and groves and the only place in the park where you will find a likeness of John McLaren: a statue depicts him holding a pine cone. McLaren's gaze may be a serene one, but he fought tooth and nail against the decision to stage the 1894 Midwinter International Exposition in the park, after which one of the structures built to house it became the first home of the M. H. de Young Memorial Museum (see pages 118–21). The success of the museum encouraged Golden Gate Park's selection as the site of the California Academy of Sciences (pages 64–5), which opened across the Music Concourse from the de Young Museum in 1916.

Also created for the Expo, but perhaps more in keeping with the park's ideology, the **Japanese Tea Garden▶▶▶** is an elegant garden with azaleas, cherry trees, and a carp-filled pond, all linked by winding pathways. Laid out in traditional Japanese style with a bronze Buddha dating from 1790 at its center, the garden was the work of Makoto Hagiwara. A Japanese San Franciscan, Hagiwara remained in charge of the garden until he was interned following the Japanese attack on Pearl Harbor in 1941.

GOLDEN GATE PARK

One of the park's two restored windmills

Touring the park
Golden Gate Park is far too big to be fully toured on foot, though determined pedestrians can visit its major points of interest by coupling their leg work with judicious use of buses along its exterior. Another option, and one encouraged by the park's many miles of cycle trails, is to rent a bike from one of the outlets on Haight-Ashbury's Stanyan Street.

West of the Japanese Tea Garden, a road circles **Stow Lake►** and two bridges—or a boat rented from the boathouse—give access to the tree-lined **Strawberry Hill►** in the lake's center. Several steadily ascending footpaths wind up to the small reservoir and waterfall which mark the hill's 400ft. summit.

Garden lovers should head south to the **Strybing Arboretum and Botanical Gardens►►**, where 6,000 species of outdoor plants fill 70 carefully tended acres. The many volumes of the **Library of Horticulture** are devoted to plant-related subjects and visitors are welcome to browse. Also here is the **Redwood Trail**, a pleasant walk beside some examples of California's mighty redwood trees which connects with the **John Muir Nature Trail.**

The traffic-bearing Cross Over Drive makes an unwelcome intrusion into the park, cutting north–south across it between the Richmond and Sunset districts. The 2 miles of park located west of the drive contain recreational areas, such as the equestrian section, a dog-training field, four side-by-side soccer fields, and Spreckels Lake, exclusively used by model sail- and motor-boat enthusiasts.

Anyone drawn to San Francisco by its associations with 1960s flower power will want to gaze over the **Polo Field►**, scene of many later-mythologized rock concerts and communal LSD trips during the halcyon days of hippies.

A sewage treatment plant is the unappealing occupant of the park's southwest corner, but close by stands one of the two windmills originally used to pump water to Strawberry Hill's reservoir. This one, the **Murphy Windmill**, dates from 1905. Its slightly older partner, the **Dutch Windmill►**, pleasingly restored in 1981, can be found in the park's northwest corner.

Enigmatic statuary—a park specialty

Parks

■ **The great expanse of Golden Gate Park and the vast acreage of the Golden Gate National Recreation Area should be enough to satisfy the most ardent green-space enthusiast, but San Francisco also has a surprising number of small parks, some renowned throughout the city for their views or landscaping, others only known to neighborhood dog walkers.....■**

Park checklist
Other San Franciscan parks worth a visit include the following, described elsewhere:
Buena Vista Park (page 62)
Golden Gate Park (pages 100–3)
Golden Gate National Recreation Area (page 99)
Ina Coolbrith Park (panel, page 157)
Sutro Heights Park (page 170)
Washington Square Park (page 137)

Washington Square Park: taking exercise seriously

Mission Dolores Park Walk south from Mission Dolores (see page 124) and you pass several streets lined with elegant, well-preserved examples of Victorian architecture before reaching Mission Dolores Park. Once a Jewish cemetery, the large, palm-studded park rises to a summit in its southwestern corner where the views reach to the high-rise towers of the Financial District.

Huntington Park No better place for a breather after climbing Nob Hill (see pages 130–1), neat and tidy Huntington Park sits beside Grace Cathedral and is surrounded by historic hotels and expensive apartment buildings. Come here to pass a lazy Sunday morning watching the local Chinese doing Tai Chi exercises while a very affluent congregation goes to the cathedral for morning service.

Lafayette Park The highest point in Pacific Heights (see pages 148–50), Lafayette Park is surrounded by mansions—indeed, until 1936, it had one in its center—with handsome trees, well-tended lawns and attractive flower beds, all struggling valiantly to wrest attention from a glorious look-out over the city.

Alta Plaza Park Four blocks west of Lafayette Park and occupying a similarly impressive Pacific Heights high point, Alta Plaza Park rises in stepped terraces from Clay Street.

South Park Oval-shaped South Park, in SoMa (see pages 166–9), was once a place of recreation for the wealthy occupants of the elegant homes which lined it, but as the area declined, so too did the park. Nowadays, despite the noisy elevated freeway which looms beside it, South Park's sycamores and weeping willows are enjoying a renaissance thanks to the steady gentrification of the surrounding neighborhood.

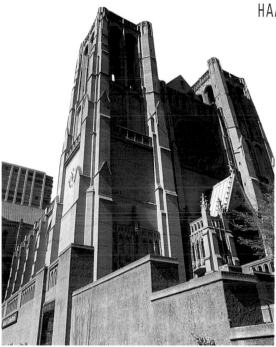

*The Episcopalian
Grace Cathedral,
which sits at the brow
of Nob Hill, was
finished in 1964. It
took more than 50
years to build*

105

▶▶▶ Grace Cathedral   IFCE5
1051 Taylor Street
Bus: 1

Grace Cathedral is a quietly stylish neo-Gothic structure,
modeled on Notre Dame in Paris and consecrated in
1964, which sits confidently on top of Nob Hill, on the site
of the Crocker Mansion (see pages 130–1). The cathedral
has not been helped, however, by the building of the
Cathedral House on its southeastern corner, which
detracts from the most impressive exterior feature: a pair
of gilded bronze doors from a Lorenzo Ghiberti cast used
for the Baptistry in Florence.

  Inside, a 15th-century French altarpiece and exquisite
Flemish reredos can be seen in the Chapel of Grace (open
only for services; otherwise view through a wrought-iron
gate), while the stained-glass windows of the main building depict biblical scenes and such diverse human achiev-
ers as Albert Einstein, Henry Ford, and Frank Lloyd Wright.

*A treasure trove of
Victoriana: the Haas-
Lilienthal House*

▶▶ Haas-Lilienthal House   IFCE5
2007 Franklin Street
Bus: 83

The only fully period-furnished Victorian house in San
Francisco open to the public, the Haas-Lilienthal House
also serves as a base for the Foundation for San
Francisco's Architectural Heritage, devoted to spreading
the word about the city's architectural legacy and, where
possible, preserving choice examples of it.

  Guided tours of the house (see panel) tell the intriguing
story of the Haas and Lilienthal families, several generations of whom occupied this three-story home over an
86-year period, enabling it to survive as its neighborhood
contemporaries were demolished. Countless fine details
highlight changing tastes over the last 100 years.

Cult shopping on Haight Street

University of San Francisco
Not to be confused with San Francisco State University (see page 162), the University of San Francisco lies five blocks north of Haight Street on the borders of the Richmond District, easily spotted by the towering twin spires of the 1914 St. Ignatius Church, which sits in mock Italian Renaissance splendor amid the campus buildings. Other than the church, the university, founded by Jesuits in 1855, holds nothing of note.

In the heart of the Haight

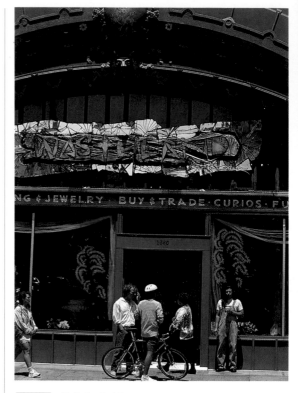

▶▶ **Haight-Ashbury** *IFCD4*

Buses: 6, 7, 66, 71

In 1967, Haight-Ashbury (between the Western Addition and Golden Gate Park) was described as "the vibrant epicenter of America's hippie movement." For the full story on Haight-Ashbury's flower-power era, see pages 110–11.

It was no accident that Haight-Ashbury became the home of hippies. Even by San Francisco's liberal standards, Haight-Ashbury has a long history of tolerance—a trait which continues into the present. Along Haight Street, the district's main artery, long-haired skateboarders in tie-dye T-shirts skim along the sidewalks, homeless old hippies ask passersby for spare change, and street musicians twang their guitar strings from a prone position. Yet the street also holds increasingly classy restaurants, and exceptional used-book stores and vintage clothing outlets which draw shoppers from all over the city. Haight-Ashbury also has countless impressive examples of Victorian architecture (commonly known as "Victorians," see page 18).

What became Haight-Ashbury was dairy farmland dotted by squatters' camps when the grand plans for the creation of Golden Gate Park were unveiled in the 1870s. To carry visitors to the new park, a cable car line was introduced along Market and Haight streets in 1883, and Haight-Ashbury (named for the junction of two of its busier streets) became ripe for development. Though increasingly accessible, (continued on page 108)

Walk Haight-Ashbury

Capturing the flavor of Haight-Ashbury, this walk begins beside Buena Vista Park and continues to the shops and restaurants along Haight Street.

One of a series of fine Victorian homes facing Buena Vista Park, the **Spreckels Mansion** was completed in 1898 for a member of the rich and powerful Spreckels family.

Along Haight Street, retail outlets ranging from the wacky to the worthy sell vintage clothes, records, books, and alternative-lifestyle paraphernalia. Some have the price tags which indicate the area's increasing trendiness and appeal to fashion-conscious consumers. Others, such as **Pipe Dreams**, with its 1960s posters, patchouli oil and king-sized cigarette papers, and **Bound Together**, a co-operatively run anarchist bookshop, are more redolent of the district's counter-culture leanings.

Haight Street's restaurants, too, are steadily becoming upscale while seeking to maintain their "alternative" appeal. One worthwhile simply for the food is **Cha Cha Cha** (1805 Haight Street), which offers Cuban and Caribbean specialities.

Counterculture for sale—credit cards accepted

Haight-Ashbury's Spreckels Mansion, built for Richard Spreckels, part of the Spreckels sugar dynasty, in 1898. Once a bed and breakfast inn, the mansion is now a private home

(*continued from page 106*) Haight-Ashbury was still considered to be some distance from the city. Its first opulent homes were intended as weekend retreats for wealthy families. Although Haight-Ashbury was untouched by the 1906 fire, many of its expansive homes were converted to multi-family dwellings to ease the subsequent housing shortage. The transient population caused Haight-Ashbury's social standing to fall, while the Depression saw the opulent Victorian houses fall into disrepair.

During World War II, many African-Americans, who had arrived in San Francisco to work in war-time industries,

spilled into Haight-Ashbury from the Western Addition, contributing to the ethnic diversity which the neighborhood still retains.

By the early 1960s, low rents lured students from the nearby University of San Francisco and would-be Beats escaping the upwardly mobile North Beach. Not since the gold rush had San Francisco received as many new arrivals as it did during the summer of 1967, all of them headed for Haight-Ashbury. While the events of the time passed into legend, the neighborhood was unable to cope with the 200,000 young people who arrived in pursuit of peace, love, and a life without material possessions. By the early 1970s, Haight-Ashbury had degenerated into a seriously seedy area, filled with poverty and hard drug use.

In time, however, the falling prices of the Victorian houses encouraged the influx of a new and relatively affluent population. Eager to restore their homes and to foster Haight-Ashbury's unique sense of community, many new settlers became active in plans to aid the area's homeless and hungry, and to force drug dealers off its streets. While Haight-Ashbury is still far from problem-free, Haight Street has become an offbeat addition to the city's shopping circuit, more and more Victorian houses are opening as bed-and-breakfast inns, and the many new bars and restaurants are targeting an upscale clientele. Exploring Haight-Ashbury means 1960s landmarks and architecturally interesting Victorian buildings—which in some instances are one and the same. Psychedelic rock music progenitors, The Grateful Dead, occupied various Haight-Ashbury addresses but are most closely associated with **710 Ashbury Street►**, where they were busted for marijuana possession in October 1967. The house is one of a row of pretty Queen Anne-style residences built around 1890 by architect Robert Cranston.

Cranston's many contributions to Haight-Ashbury included a home for himself on **Page Street**. The owl-decorated number 1777 was Cranston's, but look too for the wedding cake Queen Anne at number 1901, a one-time home of 1920s novelist Kathleen Norris, and number 1899, which demonstrates the turn-of-the-century shift in fashion from Queen Anne to Colonial Revival.

On the corner of Clayton and Haight streets, the **Haight-Ashbury Free Clinic►** was founded in 1967 by an idealistic young doctor dismayed by the medical establishment's failure to respond to hippie health problems. The main workload of the volunteer doctors involved venereal disease, drug abuse, and foot ailments (caused by going barefoot). The free clinic still plays an important role in the community, offering free health care for Haight-Ashbury's poor, despite repeated efforts by the authorities to close it down.

The Diggers (see pages 110–11) opened their legendary free store at 1775 Haight Street, while number 1660 was the short-lived **Straight Theater**, where the management got around their lack of a music license by claiming that the concerts staged there were dancing lessons.

One further relic of the 1960s is the **Evolution Rainbow►►** mural, adorning a wall on the corner of Haight and Cole streets.

A mannequin unmoved by Haight Street scenes

Striking stairways
Sections of San Francisco's steepest streets are often traversed by stairways, and two of the most enjoyable—one for its lush foliage, the other for its views—are the Vulcan and Saturn stairways, on the hillsides dividing Haight-Ashbury from the Castro. The stairways can be accessed from Roosevelt Way, which runs between Buena Vista Park (see page 62) and Corona Heights Park.

Lower Haight
Leave Haight-Ashbury heading towards Market Street and you soon reach the loosely defined area called Lower Haight. Free of Haight-Ashbury's commercial trappings and (to some extent) its escalating rents, Lower Haight holds an alternative-minded community of avant-garde artists, musicians, poets, and student subversives who can be found frequenting the boldly decorated cafés on and around the 500 block of Haight Street.

■ In 1967, when Scott McKenzie sang about going to San Francisco with flowers in your hair, Haight-Ashbury was in the incense-scented throes of what was to become known as the Summer of Love: the climax of the American hippie movement. What had begun several years earlier when a disparate assemblage of alternative-lifestyle seekers moved into the neighborhood and began developing an idealistic community sense, now seemed ready to unstitch the very fabric of American society..... ■

Park frolics
Journalist Ralph Gleason describing 1967's Human Be-In in Golden Gate Park: "A beautiful girl in an Indian headdress handed me a long stick of slow-burning incense and another handed out sprigs of bay leaves. Women and men alike carried flowers and wore ribbons in their hair. There were more clean long-haired males assembled in one place than at any time since the Crusades."

Below: strolling down Haight Street in 1967 Top: in Haight-Ashbury today—the influence of the hippie movement lives on

Social ferment By the early 1960s, Haight-Ashbury was an ethnically mixed, low-rent neighborhood with shabby but spacious Victorian homes which made ideal shared homes for students from the nearby University of San Francisco and for anyone at odds with conventional society. For such people, the protest movement, radical campus politics, and the previous decade's Beat genera-tion were important influences.

Among the settlers were The Diggers, a revolutionary offshoot of an avant-garde theater group whose idealistic ideas could be put into practice in the socially tolerant Haight-Ashbury. One project was the Free Store: a shop where everything was free—"customers" took what they needed and gave what they could spare.

The Grateful Dead and other local rock bands played music that veered from rhythm and blues to free-form improvisation, and often did so for free "and for hours at a time" in the streets and parks. When indoor venues could be found, the concerts became multimedia experiences with light shows and body painting. Alcohol was seldom consumed but fruit was provided for free.

Psychedelic drugs The hippies (derisively so-named by the Beats who regarded them as junior hipsters) also took a then-legal drug called LSD. The government had been testing the mind-altering drug on volunteers at Stanford University (one of whom, author Ken Kesey, began "bor-rowing" large amounts to enliven Haight-Ashbury's multi-media events and his own "acid tests"). In Berkeley, the unlikely named Augustus Owsley Stanley III manufactured LSD in a makeshift laboratory.

Revolution soon Many Haight-Ashbury hippies truly believed that a peaceful social revolution would occur just as soon as everyone discovered the joys of LSD. As the media discovered the strange activities in Haight-Ashbury, however, their sensationalist reporting encour-aged a nationwide panic: LSD was made illegal in 1966, and the San Francisco police and other conservative elements missed no opportunity to harass the long-haired of Haight Street, where hippie-run businesses—dispens-ing headbands, talismans, incense, and other prerequi-sites of the lifestyle—were increasingly common.

Summer of love By the summer of 1967, Haight-Ashbury was national news and young people headed west for their share of the free love and drugs which they had heard about. Instead of earthly paradise, though, they found a neighborhood at bursting point: Haight-Ashbury's hippie population swelled from 7,000 to 75,000 in six months.

Barefoot and beaded, the hippies of Haight Street quickly became a tourist attraction. The Gray Line bus company began running "Hippie tours" just as they had "Beatnik tours" of North Beach a decade earlier.

While free concerts became regular events in the Panhandle, many of the original psychedelic bands—most spectacularly Jefferson Airplane—had become financially successful and were quickly sucked into the mainstream music business they professed to despise: only The Grateful Dead remained fully true to their idealistic roots. By October 1967, The Diggers were sufficiently disenchanted to organize a Death of the Hippie march, complete with replica hippie in cardboard coffin.

Haight-Ashbury's decline As the original hippies left the increasingly unstable neighborhood for the rural peace of northern California and beyond, Haight-Ashbury degenerated. Addictive hard drugs replaced LSD in popularity, and sinister figures such as Charles Manson—who recruited some of his "family" among the runaways of Haight-Ashbury—emerged.

In 1969, the year of the most notorious Manson family murders, a Rolling Stones concert at the Altamont racetrack, near Oakland, culminated in a fatal stabbing and for many symbolized the end of the American hippie dream.

A scene from daily life in a 60s commune

Hippiedom's ripples
However shortlived its heyday may have been, the impact of the hippie movement was profound. It encouraged many of the social freedoms now accepted as the norm and—inadvertently—created a mass market for rock music which was enjoyed and exploited by a new generation of musicians and music business entrepreneurs. Currently, as the hippie-influenced Baby Boom generation rises to positions of power, the movement's impact (albeit in diluted form) seems likely to continue far into the future.

Willis Polk
The groundbreaking
Hallidie Building enhanced
Willis Polk's already major
reputation as one of San
Francisco's most capable
architects. His many con-
tributions to the city
include the Merchant
Exchange Building (see
page 87) and the remodel-
ing of the Flood mansion
into the Pacific Union Club
(see page 131). Earlier,
Polk—who as a young man
had reveled in San
Francisco's 1890s
bohemia—built himself a
characterful brown shingle
home which still stands
near the top of Russian Hill,
at 1013–19 Vallejo Street.

► **Hallidie Building** IBCD3

130–50 Sutter Street
Buses: 2, 3, 4
Many architects consider the Hallidie Building to be the
most significant structure in San Francisco, being the first
building in the world to utilize a "glass curtain" (actually a
wall of glass and metal suspended in front of the concrete
façade). Designed by the esteemed Willis Polk (see panel)
and completed in 1917, the Hallidie Building—named for
the inventor of the cable car—also utilizes wrought-iron
fire escapes to add to its aesthetic appeal.

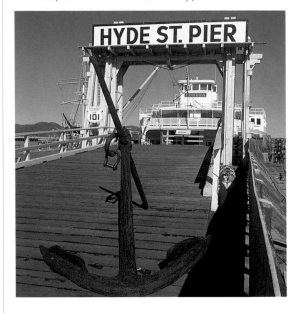

*An anchor shows the
way to Hyde Street
Pier's Historic Ships*

A Cape Horn veteran

►► **Hyde Street Pier Historic Ships** IFCE6

Hyde Street Pier, Fisherman's Wharf
Bus: 32
In the days when Fisherman's Wharf was filled with
fishermen rather than tourists, ferries to Berkeley and
Sausalito sailed from the northern waterfront's Hyde
Street Pier. One such ferry was the *Eureka*, built in 1890
and now one of several lovingly restored vessels moored
permanently at the pier.

The entertaining collection of vintage cars assembled
around its lower decks gives only an inkling of the
Eureka's capabilities; in her day, she was the world's
largest passenger ferry, able to haul more than 2,000
people and 100 vehicles across the bay in a single trip.

The most intriguing of the historic ships, however, is the
Balclutha, a steel-hulled, square-rigged ship launched in
Scotland in 1886. The *Balclutha* rounded Cape Horn
several times before ending its days transporting Alaskan
salmon along the West Coast of the U.S. Clamber down
the narrow ladders and around the claustrophobic decks
to look at the restored cabins and scrutinize the
informative explanatory texts.

Among the other ships (over coming years, it is
planned that many more will be added to the collection)

are the *C A Thayer*, built in 1895 to move the lumber with which many early Californian cities were built, and the comparatively dainty *Alma*. A scow schooner, the *Alma*'s flat bottom enabled her to navigate the shallow waters on the periphery of San Francisco Bay.

► Jackson Square IFCF5
Buses: 41, 42
The 1850s brick buildings of Jackson Square (a district rather than an actual square, between Washington and Pacific street and Sansome and Columbus streets) saw all the wild excesses of the Barbary Coast (see page 35) before the 1906 earthquake and fire terminated such nefarious activities. As the fire razed neighboring streets, a mile-long hose brought water from Fisherman's Wharf and helped save Jackson Square, though lack of commercial interest through subsequent decades saw its characterful buildings fall into disrepair.

Things changed in the 1950s when an inspired group of furniture wholesalers launched a restoration initiative, leading to Jackson Square becoming the city's first designated Historic District in 1971.

Ironically, rising rents drove the wholesalers out and in their place came law firms, architectural practices, advertising agencies—who have offices on the upper levels—and exclusive antiques dealers, who display their expensive wares at ground level.

► Japantown IFCD5
Buses: 38, 50
Concealed behind Japantown's unexciting exteriors are the shops, temples, and social centers serving the city's Japanese community, only a small percentage of whom actually live here. In 1941, however, almost all of San Francisco's 7,000 Japanese-American population had homes and businesses here, within the Western Addition.

The entry of the U.S. into World War II following the Japanese attack on Pearl Harbor resulted in the mass internment of the U.S.'s Japanese citizens. After the war, while some re-established their lives in the area, many

Taking a rest in Nihonmachi mall

Japanese-American generations
The Japanese population of San Francisco divides itself into distinct generations, each with a different name. The first wave of settlers who arrived in the early 1900s were the *issei*, their American-born children were the generation known as *nisei*. Subsequent generations have been *sansei*, *yonsei* and *shin issei*, respectively.

Distinctive Japantown architecture

JAPANTOWN

Fire-fighting relics

Fire Department Museum
Eight blocks west of Japantown at 655 Presidio Avenue, the Fire Department Museum fills a barn-like room with a colossal jumble of mementoes recording San Franciscan fire-fighting from its earliest days onwards. The array includes helmets, badges, buckets, axes, a dainty 1810 fire truck imported from New York, and photographs and press cuttings detailing the city's most famous fires and the men and horses who helped put them out.

moved on, and the Japanese-American population quickly became dispersed across the city and the entire Bay Area.

Visitors to contemporary Japantown are first struck by its smallness—a few blocks enclosed by Octavia and Fillmore streets, and Geary Boulevard and Pine Street—and secondly by the proliferation of concrete. The commercial core is **Japan Center▶**, a 3-acre indoor mall packed with good Japanese restaurants and mixed quality stores but entirely lacking in character. Immediately outside, a broad concrete plaza holds the 100ft. **Peace Pagoda▶**, erected in 1968.

More pleasing is the open-air **Nihonmachi Mall▶** (also called "Buchanan Mall"), a short pedestrian-only strip with street landscaping—benches, fountains, and more—by the noted Japanese-American designer Ruth Asawa.

Away from the shops and restaurants, and the colorful **Cherry Blossom Festival** which is celebrated with vigor each April, Japantown's main points of ethnic interest are religious. The **Buddhist Church of San Francisco** (see page 62) warrants a look; others worthy of a visit are the **Konko Church of San Francisco▶** (1909 Bush Street), built in the 1970s and employing traditional Shinto themes, and the **Soto Zen Mission Sokoji▶** (1691 Laguna Street), where the wood-beamed roof brings a traditional flavor to a recent building.

A few remnants of pre-concrete Japantown can also be seen. Dating from 1910 and bearing a marked Japanese influence on its terracotta-tiled façade, is the **Binet-Montessori School▶** (1715 Octavia Street). Meanwhile, among a handful of tasteful Victorian homes intact along **Webster Street▶**, is the vertically thrusting number 1737, built in the Stick style popular in the 1880s.

Windsocks filling out in the breeze outside the Japan Center

▶ **The Jewish Museum** *IBCE3*

121 Steuart Street
Bus: 1
Founded in 1984, the Jewish Museum claims to be the only such institution with a multicultural and artistic perspective, its exhibitions intended to bring diverse aspects of Jewish life and culture to non-Jewish as well as Jewish audiences.

Certainly, the museum has seldom been shy of staging stimulating and provocative shows. Past exhibitions have included *Art and the Rosenberg Era*, which focused on the McCarthyism of the 1950s and the art inspired by the 1953 execution of the Rosenbergs as communist spies, and *Bridges and Boundaries*, which used art, photography, and other media to explore the shared experiences of American Jews and African-Americans.

Admission to all but the most major exhibitions is free; free guided tours are also offered.

▶ **Levi's Plaza** *IFCF6*

Sansome and Battery streets, between Union and Greenwich streets
Buses: 42, 69, 83
The 1906 Levi Strauss factory in the Mission District (see panel, page 124) continues to manufacture the world-famous Levi jeans, but since 1982 the company's international headquarters has been within this creatively-designed low-rise office complex. Utilizing a group of unused warehouses and a one-time ice house, Levi's Plaza is an admired example of modern corporate architecture and uses the sharp incline of Telegraph Hill, directly across Union Street, as a stunning scenic backdrop.

Pass by the fountains, shops, and food stands around the plaza and enter the spacious lobby of the main building to discover a modest historical display on Levi jeans, including some of the earliest pairs—colored brown and manufactured for California's gold miners in the 1870s.

Levi's Plaza's buildings
Many of the buildings which make up Levi's Plaza are brick-built warehouses, which fell into disuse once the nearby Embarcadero became better-known for its ugly freeway (demolished in 1992, with help from the 1989 Loma Prieta earthquake) than for the rows of ocean-going freighters which regularly unloaded their cargo along it, filling the warehouses with coffee, coconuts, bananas, canned fish, clothing, and other commodities carried across the high seas.

At the foot of Telegraph Hill, Levi's Plaza is modern corporate architecture with a human face

MAIDEN LANE

There's no mistaking Maiden Lane's Circle Gallery, designed by Frank Lloyd Wright

"Mexicano" and other terms
The Mexican Museum defines the term "Mexicano" as describing Mexican, Mexican-American and Chicano. The term "Chicano," derived from the Aztec word for Mexico, was adopted by U.S. citizens of Mexican descent in a radical political movement of the 1970s. "Latino" is used to describe people of Latin American origin or descent, as is "Hispanic" although this, meaning "descended from the Spanish," could be considered insulting if used to describe a person of pure Latin American Indian stock.

The French church
A short distance from Maiden Lane, two blocks north of Union Square at 566 Bush Street, the Church of Notre-Dame des Victoires was raised in 1913 by French architect Louis Brouchard to serve as a religious center and general meeting place for the city's French Catholic population (mass is said in French each Sunday morning). It occupies the site of the city's earliest French church, built in 1856 and destroyed by the 1906 earthquake.

▶▶ **Maiden Lane** *IFCE5*

Opposite Union Square, between Stockton and Kearny streets
Buses: 30, 45
Prior to being gutted by the 1906 earthquake and fire, Maiden Lane was known as Morton Street and was the scene of some of the worst excesses of the Barbary Coast (see page 35). Along this two-block street, topless women would solicit passing males from behind open windows and some of them claimed to service 100 customers per day. Present-day Maiden Lane is a complete contrast: a well-scrubbed alley entered through pretty wooden gates and lined by designer-clothes stores and upscale furniture outlets. Window-shop along the narrow thoroughfare and pause for a snack at one of the cafés which place their tables outside during the day, when Maiden Lane is closed to traffic. At number 140, be sure to admire the brickwork façade and arched entrance of Frank Lloyd Wright's **Circle Gallery**. Inside, the steadily ascending spiral ramp which carries browsers past the artworks for sale was a prototype of Wright's more elaborate design for the Guggenheim Museum in New York.

▶ **Marina District** *IFCD6*
Buses: 22, 30
Dominated by comfortable family homes and spacious, tastefully designed low-rise apartments, the Marina District—occupying the waterfront directly north of Pacific Heights—has a personality closer to that of an affluent suburb than a city neighborhood. Its residents lead their well-groomed dogs on windy walks through Marina Park, take lone contemplative strolls through the wondrous Palace of Fine Arts (see page 152), which borders the district to the west, or rendezvous with their neighborhood friends in the chic restaurants lining Chestnut Street.

The area's abiding sense of stability is deceptive, however. Built on landfill, the homes of the Marina District are particularly vulnerable to earthquakes, and the area was one of the most seriously affected during the Loma Prieta quake which hit the city in 1989.

▶▶ **Mexican Museum**   *IFCE6*

Building D, Fort Mason Center
Bus: 28

Founded in the predominantly Latino Mission District (see page 124) in 1975, the Mexican Museum has evolved into Fort Mason Center's most successful museum. Its fast-growing collections and critical acclaim have resulted in a new $20-million facility being built to house the museum close to SoMa's Yerba Buena Arts Center (see pages 166–8); the move is expected in the late 1990s.

The museum certainly needs more space. At Fort Mason, only a tiny selection from the permanent holdings of more than 9,000 pieces can be exhibited at any one time. These are grouped into five periods: pre-Hispanic Art, Colonial Art, Folk Art, and Mexican Fine Art and Mexican-American and Chicano Fine Art.

It is with short-term shows, however, that the Mexican museum has forged a unique niche. Many Mexican and Chicano artists who would otherwise not be represented in a museum are exhibited here, a process which encourages more conservative establishments to take an interest in them. Simultaneously, the museum is able to present known Mexican and Latin American art and artists in a sympathetic setting: an exhibition of paintings and works on paper by Frida Kahlo, for example, drew 20,000 people here in 1987.

Among the recent exhibitions has been a retrospective of two decades of work by Gronk, a category-defying performance artist who emerged from Latino East Los Angeles in the early 1970s. His early "pieces" included an "erasure" of the U.S.–Mexico border and the No Movie Awards, a comment on Hollywood film-industry back-slapping which presented an awards ceremony for movies shot with no film in the camera. His emphasis later switched to painting and producing large-scale site-specific installations.

By contrast, *Visiones del Pueblo* presented folk-art objects from 17 Latin American countries, while *Chicano Codices* offered contemporary Latino artists' interpretations of the Spanish conquest of Mexico.

A piece of Mexican folk art on display in the Mexican Museum

117

Marina District

M. H. DE YOUNG MEMORIAL MUSEUM

Admission and tours
The M. H. de Young
Memorial Museum is
closed on Mondays and
Tuesdays but is otherwise
open daily from 10a.m. to
5p.m. (and until 8:45p.m. on
the first Wednesday of the
month). Admission is free
on the first Wednesday
and first Saturday morning
of the month. Free tours,
focusing on particular
aspects of the collections,
are conducted most days.
For details, tel. 415/750
3600 or 415/863 3330
(recording).

The admission fee
includes entry to the Asian
Art Museum (pages 122–3).

*Above right and
below: the M. H. de
Young Memorial
Museum, set in
Golden Gate Park and
housing major works
of art*

▶ ▶ ▶ **M. H. de Young Memorial Museum**   *IFCC4*
Golden Gate Park
Buses: 28, 29, 44
Holding San Francisco's major collection of American art,
the M. H. de Young Memorial Museum also enjoys a
picturesque rural setting in Golden Gate Park (see pages
100–3) where it is one of a trio of commendable
attractions—the Asian Art Museum (see pages 122–3)
and the California Academy of Sciences (see pages 64–5)
are the others—within a few steps of one another.

Anyone who has experienced San Francisco in midwinter knows that the Californian idyll of year-round sunshine
and palm trees applies only to the south of the state.

Despite this, in 1894 the publisher of the
San Francisco Chronicle, Michael de Young,
organized the California Midwinter
International Exposition on a 200-acre site in
Golden Gate Park. He intended to convince
the world that the city had a balmy climate
while raising some much-needed revenue
after a year of economic depression.

To the chagrin of the park's creator, John
McLaren (see panel, page 101), the idea of a
permanent museum in the park to remember the successful Expo gained popularity.
The Egyptian-style Fine Arts Building, which
had drawn more than its share of Expo visitors, had been intended as a temporary
structure but was re-opened in 1895 as the Memorial
Museum. Although unskilled as a collector, de Young
began avidly acquiring pieces for the new museum, and
art-starved San Franciscans visited in the thousands.

Within a few years, the collections had outgrown the
building and de Young commissioned Louis Christian
Mulgardt—an architect involved in the city's 1915
Panama–Pacific Exposition—to design a new home for

them. Mulgardt's rather undistinguished Spanish-style structure was completed in 1919, the expanded museum renamed following de Young's death in 1925.

The de Young Memorial Museum's collection of European paintings and sculpture was moved to the California Palace of the Legion of Honor (see pages 67–8) when the museums were formally merged in the 1970s.

The de Young's collection of American paintings begins with the work of John Singleton Copley, and his 18th-century contemporaries such as John Smibert. A self-taught artist who emerged as the country's foremost painter with his finely executed society portraits, Copley's 1763 *Mrs. Daniel Sargent* highlights his many skills.

One of the museum's earliest acquisitions and still among its most striking works, John Vanderlyn's *Marius Amidst the Ruins of Carthage* was painted in 1807 and won a gold medal at the following year's Paris Salon. Through its mighty scale and scope, and its successful tackling of a historical subject, the painting came to epitomize the growing self-confidence of American artists of the time. Refusing offers for the work in France, Vanderlyn returned the painting to the U.S. for exhibition but it failed to excite collectors in the way he anticipated.

In fact, by the first half of the 19th century, as many American painters were beginning to combine assuredness in their own abilities with the young nation's sense of self-discovery, the interest in European-influenced American art was steadily declining. In the early 1800s, Thomas Cole's landscapes—spearheading the Hudson River School, the nation's first homegrown art movement—highlighted American painters' turning away from European traditions and towards the untamed North American continent

Some minor examples of Cole's work can be seen here, although much more imposing is a canvas by one of his former pupils: Frederic Church's 1866 *Rainy Season in the Tropics*. Like many of Church's paintings, this piece offers a detailed study of nature's handiwork, and is

Textiles

It may play second fiddle to the art, but the museum's textile collection has many devoted admirers. From Anatolian prayer rugs and Polish chasubles to Amish quilts and the dresses of Yves Saint-Laurent, the textiles displayed are diverse and intriguing. The selections can be viewed in the Caroline & H. McCoy Jones galleries.

African art

A side room devoted to African art is often overlooked by visitors to the de Young Museum; it contains the unsettling *Nail and Blade Oath Making Image* from 19th-centuryZaire, a fearsome figure used in settling legal disputes.

Snacking among the statues in the Museum Café's garden

Federal-period furniture

Ancient art
Just off Hearst Court, through which you pass to enter the main galleries, are several rooms of ancient art from Egypt, Rome, and the Near East. You might spend time contemplating the 2nd-century Roman *Torso of Hermes*, or the group of 8th-century B.C. Nimrud plaques, but you will probably find the oldest exhibit to be the most absorbing: a Cycladic figure from 2500B.C.

Modern art
The museum's 20th-century holdings are generally less impressive than the older material. Take a look, though, at George Bellows's paintings and cast an eye over the two rooms devoted to mixed-media works by Bay Area artists.

crowned by a double rainbow. Curiously, Church's paintings of far-off, exotic lands were sometimes exhibited in galleries decorated with appropriate vegetation. In this painting, however, the far-off, exotic land seems to be an imagined combination of the Andes and the Caribbean.

High-intensity natural drama is also evident in the landscapes of Albert Bierstadt, who focused his attention on the American West. Among Bierstadt's pieces are *Sunlight and Shadow, California Spring,* and the colossal *Storm in the Rocky Mountains.* Interestingly, a Bierstadt painting of the early 1870s, *View of Donner Lake, California,* was commissioned by rail-baron Collis P. Huntington to mark the building of the highest and most difficult section of the transcontinental railroad. While the painting shows the railroad's taming of nature and the conquering of the Donner Pass—infamous as the spot at which the Donner Party met its doom in the 1840s (see page 188)—it also depicts a romantically charged Sierra Nevada landscape, typical of the artist's mythologizing of western scenes.

Another painting by Bierstadt, *Indian Hunting Buffalo,* gives a misleading impression of Native American life and contributed to the inaccurate opinions formed of Native Americans on the East Coast. It was a natural progression, nevertheless, for American art to celebrate the colonization of the American West. The most significant figure to do so was Frederick Remington; many of his sculptured tributes to the cowboy are collected here.

As western images proliferated during the 19th century, a small band of artists took the increasing industrialization of society as their main subject. Several works of Thomas Anshutz are powerful examples of this school; they are displayed in the same room as a number of studies by his former teacher, Thomas Eakins, noted for his carefully observed portraits and sporting scenes.

Other emerging talents still sought inspiration in Europe. Among them was John Singer Sargent, who produced the subtle and distinguished *A Dinner Table at Night* during a period in England in the 1880s.

Finally among its 19th-century paintings, the museum offers an entertaining room of *trompe-l'œil* works, where attention tends to fall on William Michael Harnett's *After the Hunt*, a canvas turned into a door hung with freshly slaughtered birds and a rabbit.

If you have concentrated on the paintings, you will need to retrace your steps through the galleries to admire the many impressive examples of American decorative art, from the colonial period onward, which share many of the rooms. Among the earliest exhibits are New England armchairs from English and Dutch settlements of 1670, and two rooms re-created with original furnishings: an Adamstyle George III dining room, and a Federal parlor from 1805 Massachusetts. Keep in mind that California was still a thinly populated outpost of Mexico when these furnishings were in use by the most refined East Coast society.

Among the silver knives, forks, spoons, teapots, and kneebuckles in the display cases, look for the work of Paul Revere. Although more famous for his patriotic alerting of the American troops to the approach of the British, Revere also made his mark as a gold- and silversmith.

In furniture, the flowing curves of the Queen Anne style were popular during the colonial period, but by the time of the revolution, American craftsmen had acquired the skills and creativity to evolve a new and distinctive look, using recognizable Queen Anne features but adding unique rococo touches. Philadelphia emerged above Boston and New York as the center of the craft, and a grand 1780 Philadelphia High Chest provides an excellent example of the period.

By contrast, a roomful of Shaker furniture—tools, rocking chairs, and other domestic items, from the millenarian sect founded in 1747 as an offshoot of the Quakers—holds its own with its plain and simple style, now recognized as among the nation's finest folk art.

The elegant dining room typical of an early upper-class American family (above) contrasts with the simple furniture made by the religious sect known as the Shakers (below)

■ **Be it Chinese jade, Thai ceramics, Japanese *netsuke,* or a Tibetan thigh-bone trumpet, the Asian Art Museum of San Francisco is the largest collection of its kind in the U.S. and is certain to have something among its wealth of treasures from the East to catch your eye.....■**

Opening times
The Asian Art Museum, currently in Golden Gate Park but planning a move to the Public Library building at Civic Center, is closed on Mondays and Tuesdays but otherwise open daily from 10a.m. to 5p.m. (and until 8:45p.m. on the first Wednesday of the month). Admission is free on the first Wednesday and first Saturday morning of the month.

122

Avery Brundage Remembered by most people only as a long-serving president of the International Olympic Committee, Avery Brundage amassed a fortune as an engineering company mogul and sank some of his millions into a world-class collection of Asian art. By the late 1950s, Brundage was ready to donate this incredible treasure trove and looked around for a suitable home. On account of its long-standing social links with Asia, San Francisco was chosen as the beneficiary with the proviso that the city erect a suitable home for the collection.

Some pieces went on exhibit in 1960, but the Asian Art Museum of San Francisco—built alongside the de Young Memorial Museum in Golden Gate Park—opened in 1966. Even this purpose-built museum is not large enough to display the entire collection, however, which numbers more than 15,000 pieces and is growing all the time.

Touring the galleries Comprehending the 6,000 years-worth of diverse cultures and religions which have inspired the museum's contents is not easy. For non-experts, there is a lot to be said for simply wandering through the galleries pausing at whatever catches your attention.

Chinese collections The scale and scope of the Chinese collections reflect the fact that China was Brundage's main interest. Among the treasures is the oldest dated example of Chinese Buddhist art (A.D.338) and elegant ceramics from the 10th to the 14th centuries, a period when Chinese craftsmen scaled new heights in the balancing of form and glaze: look for the flower-shaped dishes bearing impossibly delicate outlines of dragons, and the leaf-shaped cup stands.

There are numerous examples, too, of Xuande Era blue-and-white porcelain (1426–35), regarded as the finest period for this particular craft, intriguing and important examples of Ming Dynasty calligraphy and fan painting (1368–1644), and the amazing scroll paintings—including some breathtaking landscapes—housed in the Tang Family Gallery. Save the Magnin Jade Gallery for last; its stunning jewelry and decorations span several thousand years.

Japanese collections Consuming a large portion of the upper floor, the Japanese collections include many excellent Edo-period screen paintings

(1615–1868). Marked by its isolationist policies and prolonged peace, the Edo period saw a great flourishing of arts and culture as artists began exploring new directions. The Japanese galleries culminate in a tremendous display of *netsuke*—wooden, bone, or ivory toggles exquisitely carved and used to fasten purses and pouches, which were fashionable during the 18th and 19th centuries—and of *inro*, lacquer boxes used to carry medicines.

Tibet and Himalayas A thigh-bone trumpet, bone aprons, and a human skull ewer from Tibet are among the museum's more curious artifacts. More significant, however, are the 13th–15th-century religious paintings, or *thangkas*, from the country's leading monasteries. Do not miss the three-headed Bon figure, a symbol of Tibet's indigenous religion which co-existed alongside Buddhism. Take the trouble, too, to scrutinize the modest assemblage of Bhutanese wood carvings, silverwork and textiles, which offer a rare insight into this obscure country.

Southeast Asia Among the relatively small Southeast Asia collections are several worthwhile examples of Thai sculpture from the former capitals, Sukhothai and Ayutthaya. As Buddhism arrived from India, these centers produced the earliest Buddha images bearing the curling eyelids and arched eyebrows which came to define the Thai Buddha image. The Connell Collection offers a major ceramics collection (2000B.C. to the 17th century) from Thailand.

Asian Art spans centuries, nations, and religions

Indian collections
A large upper-floor gallery is devoted to the museum's extensive Indian holdings. Useful maps aid comprehension of this vast land. They show the geographical spread of its three main religions—Buddhism, Hinduism, and Jainism—and the incredible range and richness of the art which they have inspired.

Overlooked by Bernal Heights, the Mission District is the main home of San Francisco's Hispanic population

▶▶ **Mission District**   IFCE4

Buses: 14, 26, 49
BART: 24th Street

Mission Dolores is what brings most visitors to the Mission District, slotted between the Castro, SoMa, and Potrero Hill, and extending southwards. Surprisingly few, however, take the time to explore more of San Francisco's most vibrant ethnic enclave, the home of a Spanish-speaking population drawn from all over Central and South America. Founded by the colonizing Spanish in 1776, **Mission Dolores▶▶** (320 Dolores Street) was completed in 1791 and still retains the thick adobe walls which enabled it to survive frequent earthquakes and become the city's oldest building. The mission's fresco-decorated chapel contains numerous artifacts carried by mule from Mexico at the time of construction; a modest assortment of other historic pieces is gathered in a small museum. In the mission's cemetery, a few Spanish- and Mexican-era pioneers are buried alongside the remains of an estimated 5,000 Native Americans. While the chapel is used for special services, the **Basilica**—built next door in 1913—serves the everyday spiritual needs of the Mission District's current Catholic population.

The quiet streets around the mission give little indication of the hustle and bustle which more accurately characterizes the Mission District. To find the local pulse, head for **Mission Street** and its crowded Mexican bakeries, secondhand furniture outlets, and grocery stores. At the junction of 24th Street you will see a few of the district's many **murals**, described in detail on page 126.

The Mission District's earthiness and low rents have attracted some of the city's avant-garde writers and artists, and encouraged the art galleries and cafés now found around Valencia and 16th streets. Valencia Street has also become the unofficial base of the city's lesbian population and has numerous women-oriented bookstores, such as the well-stocked Old Wives Tales (number 1009).

The Levi Strauss Factory
Arriving in San Francisco in 1853, Levi Strauss created what he called a "waist-high overall" for the miners of the gold rush, a garment which later became much better-known as a pair of "jeans". Following the earthquake of 1906, Strauss built a new factory in the Mission District at 250 Valencia Street. The building still stands, and its workers still produce the world-famous jeans. Once a month, an appointment-only tour (tel. 415/565 9153) winds around the premises and outlines the company's history (see also page 115).

Walk **Mission District**

This walks starts at Mission Dolores and highlights the history and social diversity of the Mission District, before it concludes at the original mission site.

The oldest building in San Francisco, **Mission Dolores** (see page 124) was completed in 1/91. The tiny adobe chapel, small museum, and its graveyard are all reminders of the city's early Spanish settlement.

The relaxing greenery of **Mission Dolores Park** rises steadily upward, culminating in a spectacular outlook across the city. The south side of Mission Dolores Park is fringed by splendidly restored Victorian houses, and more can be seen along **Liberty Street**.

Feminist bookshops are a feature of **Valencia Street** (see page 124), while Mission Street has the bakeries, cafés, and businesses which serve the neighborhood's predominantly Hispanic community.

An unmarked spot near the corner of Albion and Camp streets was chosen by the 18th-century Spanish

settlers as the original site of what became Mission Dolores. After erecting a chapel here, however, they found the ground to be unsuitable for construction.

Mission Dolores: the reredos (above) and in its cemetery (below) the oldest tombs in the city

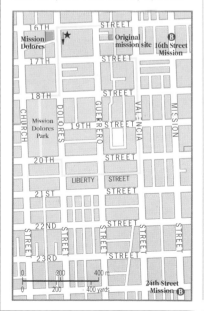

■ **Unlike Los Angeles, which has a large and long-established Mexican community, San Francisco began acquiring a significant and visible Hispanic population from the 1950s, when Central American immigrants were attracted northwards by the factory and shipyard jobs created during World War II and which boomed in the post-war years. For geographical convenience and to save money, they settled in the low-rent Mission District.....■**

Mural tours
A free guided walking tour of some of the Mission District's murals begins at 11a.m. on the second and fourth Saturdays of each month, led by City Guides (tel. 415/557 4266). Another guided tour (for a small charge), which includes a slide show on the history of murals, operates each Saturday at 1:30p.m. from the Precita Eyes Mural Arts Center, 348 Precita Avenue (tel. 415/285 2287).

126

A Latin American tradition, street murals bring color, fun, and comment to Mission District streets

Hispanic influx The Mission's Hispanic population doubled each decade between 1950 and 1970, and by the time another major influx came—to escape the Central American turmoil and strife of the 1980s—they were easily the area's dominant ethnic group, the former Irish and Italian Mission District dwellers having moved on. The community includes Mexicans, Guatamalans, Costa Ricans, Nicaraguans, and Salvadoreans, with lesser numbers from Bolivia, Columbia, Peru, and Chile. With radical central American political groups and support centers for refugees, the Mission is a self-supportive and politically aware community. While some Hispanics have risen to the city's professional ranks, the traditional Anglo-American perception of the Spanish-speaker as an under-educated manual worker is hard to break. The effects of economic recession have been strongly felt in the Mission, where gang violence and drug abuse have appeared.

Mission murals Bold and colorful murals adorning public spaces and buildings are common sights in the Mission, and continue the muralist tradition established in Latin America. Some murals are simple pieces of street art, others are far more complex affairs involving several artists, and some are funded by the city in recognition of their artistic and cultural value.

▶ **Museo Italo-Americano**   IFCE6

Building C, Fort Mason Center
Bus: 28

After beginning, appropriately perhaps, in a room above a North Beach café in 1978, the Museo Italo-Americano has evolved into a respected showplace for the work of Italian and Italian-American artists. There are a few permanent exhibits of painting, sculpture, and photography, but the core of the gallery space is devoted to temporary shows mostly drawn from new artists living in the Bay Area. Besides the galleries, a library and gift shop stock items relating to past and present Italian Americans

▶▶ **Museum of Money of the American West**   IBCD4

Bank of California, 400 California Street
Cable car: California Street line

When the West was still wild, the 1848 discovery of gold in California did nothing to encourage civilized behavior among the fortune-seeking settlers and neither did the lack of a dependable currency.

Housed in a vault in the Bank of California's basement, this one-room museum holds a small but surprisingly interesting collection, ranging from chunks of gold and silver to the various coins and banknotes which changed hands before the advent of a unified currency across the U.S. Among many enjoyable single exhibits are $20 coins minted in gold, and several special coins produced to mark the Panama–Pacific Exposition of 1915.

Also here are the dueling pistols used in 1859 in a celebrated dispute between the Chief Justice of the California Supreme Court, David S. Terry, and a U.S. Senator, David Broderick. The duel, whose immediate cause was an alleged slander, ended in the death of Broderick after his pistol fired prematurely. It was claimed that Terry knew one pistol had a sensitive trigger, and he chose the other.

The Bank of California was one of the first to become established in the state, and the city's financial district grew up around the original (1866) building on this site.

Italian-American handicraft

William C. Ralston
Through shrewd investment in silver-mines, Ohio-born William C. Ralston made the Bank of California the American West's most respected financial institution by the 1860s and became one of San Francisco's most prominent figures. In August 1875, however, with the silver-mines exhausted, the bank was forced to close its doors and plunged the city into economic uncertainty. On the day the bank failed, Ralston took his usual daily swim in the bay—and was later found drowned.

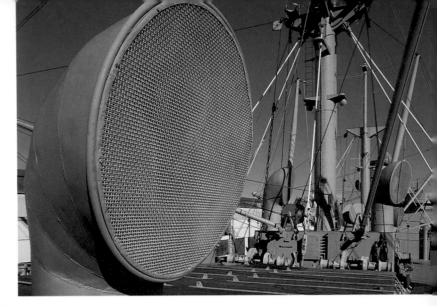

On board the S.S. Jeremiah O'Brien, *the National Liberty Ship Memorial*

U.S.S. *Pampanito*
After touring the National Liberty Ship Memorial, the World War II maritime theme can be continued by exploring the claustrophobic innards of the U.S.S. *Pampanito*, moored at Pier 45. Launched in 1943, the submarine saw action in the Pacific and sank 27,000 tons of enemy shipping. The cramped crews' and officers' quarters, the engine rooms, and the torpedo room are included on the self-guided tour. The only thing missing is a chance to peer through the periscope.

► **National Liberty Ship Memorial**   *IFCE6*
Pier 3, Fort Mason Center
Bus: 28
Preserved as the National Liberty Ship Memorial, the *Jeremiah O'Brien* is the sole still-afloat survivor of the 2,751 "Liberty Ships" launched between 1941 and 1945, part of the merchant fleet designed to carry wartime supplies and troops across the Atlantic.

Anti-aircraft guns provide some interest on deck, but the absorbing matter lies below. Weave around the maze-like corridors and you will find the entire ship maintained in its 1940s appearance: the crew's quarters, the radio operator's room, the bridge, and much more.

Descend to the lower level of the vessel to find the boiler room and the enormous engines, in working order: the *Jeremiah O'Brien* makes regular runs in the Bay Area and in 1994 crossed the Atlantic to participate in the 50th anniversary of the D-Day assault.

One curious fact worth pondering as you tour the craft is that this huge vessel took just 57 days to build.

► **National Maritime Museum**   *IFCE6*
Aquatic Park, north end of Polk Street
Bus: 19
Even as you saunter among the tourist attractions of Fisherman's Wharf, there is no escaping the fact that San Francisco has strong links with the sea, and the National Maritime Museum chronicles the city's seafaring history.

Unfortunately, compared to the preserved vessels of Hyde Street Pier Historic Ships (see page 112), the U.S.S. *Pampanito* (see panel), or the National Liberty Ship Memorial (see above), the exhibits in this museum seem somewhat commonplace. The countless model ships are unlikely to appeal to anyone other than the most salty of sea dogs.

Do come here, though, if only to admire the building itself: an impressive ship-shaped slab of 1930s art deco with a great many of its original features intact.

▶▶ **Neptune Society Columbarium**   *IFCC5*

1 Loraine Court
Buses: 38, 50

Few San Franciscans are aware of the Neptune Society Columbarium, tucked away in a tidy residential neighborhood on the fringes of the Richmond District. And this is despite the fact that the cremated remains of many of the city's most illustrious early citizens lie within—and that the Columbarium itself is a fine example of Victorian architecture.

An elegant rotunda decorated with stained glass, the Columbarium was designed by British architect Bernard

Cahill and opened in 1898. By 1937, it stood at the heart of a 3-acre cemetery in which an estimated 10,000 people were buried. That year, however, concerns about public health resulted in cemeteries being declared illegal in San Francisco.

The graves were exhumed and their contents moved to Colma (a now-cemetery-filled town on the San Francisco peninsula) while the cemetery's walls, and allegedly some of its tombstones, were used to build the sea wall at Aquatic Park, near Fisherman's Wharf. Houses were built over the vacated plot and few property developers informed prospective homebuyers that shortage of funds had resulted in many of the graves not being moved at all—the homes had simply been built on top of them.

Officially declared a memorial, the Columbarium was spared demolition, but with cremations being outlawed, soon found itself without a purpose and was left to decay by its successive owners. Not until 1980, when the Neptune Society acquired the Columbarium, did restoration work on the handsome structure begin and its niches (the places where urns are placed) were again put on sale.

In the three-story interior, you will find the final family resting places of the Eddys and the Turks, and others who gave their names to city streets, and more recent arrivals such as the man who shares his niche with dolls based on TV's *Munster* family, and another placed here with a miniature set of golf clubs.

Columbarium tours
Free guided tours of the Columbarium are conducted on Saturdays (at 10a.m. and 11:30a.m.). The building is also open daily from 9a.m. to 1p.m. for self-guided visits.

A pricey niche
Only 20,000 of the Columbarium's 30,000 niches are occupied and, if a visit encourages you to consider a long-term stay, you might ask at the adjacent office for the latest niche price list. Currently the cheapest niches, unelaborate affairs which resemble mailboxes, cost $700. The choicest spot, however, will set you back $56,000.

A well-kept secret: Neptune Society Columbarium (above) and (below) its interior: the higher the niche, the higher the price

NOB HILL

The Crocker "spite fence"
Determined to call a whole block of Nob Hill his own, Charles Crocker bought up all the homes which stood on his desired plot except one: a German-born undertaker called Nicholas Yung refused to sell. The enraged Crocker promptly erected a 40ft.-high "spite-fence" around three sides of Yung's home, blocking out the sunlight. Yung still refused to sell, however, and only after his death did the Crocker family purchase the house.

The sole Nob Hill survivor of the 1906 fire, the Flood Mansion now houses the exclusive Pacific Union Club

Lobby of the Fairmont Hotel

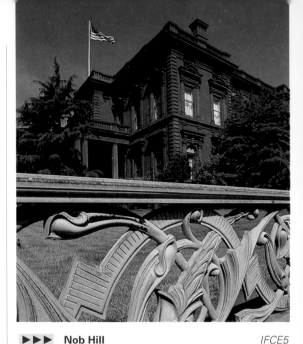

▶▶▶ **Nob Hill**   *IFCE5*

Buses: 1, 27
Cable car: California Street line
Rising steeply above Chinatown and the Financial District, Nob Hill has been the city's most prestigious address since the late 1800s when the Big Four—railway magnates Charles Crocker, Mark Hopkins, Collis P. Huntington, and Leland Stanford (see page 37)—and several Comstock Lode silver barons, chose it as the site of the most expensive homes California had ever seen.

Previously known as California Street Hill and dotted by the plain houses of modest city merchants, Nob Hill acquired its lasting title (derived from "nabob", a term used in colonial India to denote a man of wealth or importance) following the moneyed invasion inspired by the creation of the cable car in 1873. As this new mode of transportation made the city's steep slopes negotiable, Leland Stanford helped finance a new cable-car line along California Street, linking the sandy hilltop site to the Financial District.

As Nob Hill's existing homes were bought and razed to make room for new construction, each incoming millionaire vied to outspend his neighbor. Charles Crocker's home cost $2.3 million and was decorated with a million-dollar art collection; William Sharon's mansion boasted the first hydraulic elevator in the western U.S.; Mark Hopkins topped them all with a $3-million home designed, in a bizarre hodge-podge of styles, by his wife.

Although their cost was stunning, the Nob Hill mansions were seldom aesthetically satisfying. Architect Willis Polk (see panel, page 112) described the Crocker mansion as "wood carver's delirium," while a newspaper of the day derided them as "gingerbread, ignorance and bad taste." Meanwhile, such blatant displays of wealth and privilege, from the men whose fortunes enabled them to control the city, bred resentment among ordinary San Franciscans.

Few tears were shed when all but one of the Nob Hill homes—sandstone walls saved the James Flood Mansion—were destroyed by the fire which followed the 1906 earthquake. Apartment buildings now cover much of Nob Hill and lend it an air of dignified wealth. Nevertheless, evidence of the more flamboyant past is plentiful.

Grace Cathedral (see page 105) sits on the plot of land formerly occupied by the Crocker Mansion, while the neighboring **Huntington Park►**, often filled with Chinese-Americans going through the routines of Tai Chi, marks the site of the home of David Colton, a junior partner of the Big Four. In a sensational late-1800s court case, Colton's widow used her late husband's correspondence with Collis Huntington to expose the railway barons' corrupt business practices. Across Cusman Street, the sturdy brownstone Flood Mansion, paid for with $1.5 million of silver-mining profits (see page 37), was greatly remodeled by Willis Polk following the 1906 fire and has been occupied since 1911 by the **Pacific Union Club**, an exclusive all-male social club for the rich and prominent.

Nob Hill's luxury hotels also have their share of history. The **Fairmont Hotel►►** (950 Mason Street) was founded in 1902 by the daughter of silver-mine benefciary, James G. Fair (see page 37). During the 1906 fire, the decision to dynamite parts of the city to stop the spread of the flames was made in the unfinished hotel's ballroom. Architect Julia Morgan contributed many of the beaux-arts features which still grace the hotel's lobby; a valuable art collection lines the corridors. Opened in 1926, the **Mark Hopkins Hotel►►** occupies the corner of California and Mason streets, former site of the Hopkins Mansion. At the summit of the 20-story tower, the Top of the Mark offers stunning views for the price of a cocktail. The quiet and elegant **Huntington Hotel►** (905 California Street) sits on the site of Leland Stanford's mansion. With the Big Four restaurant, the hotel boasts the city's most illustrious establishment dining room.

Nob Hill's first settler
The first house on what became Nob Hill is believed to have been that of Arthur Hayne, whom history records as hacking his way through the chaparral-covered hillside to erect a wood-and-clay home for himself and his bride in 1856. ("Chaparral" is dense brush and undergrowth.) The Hayne house stood on the site of the present Fairmont Hotel.

Mark Hopkins Hotel

■ **Increasingly in San Francisco, everything stops for tea. Intended as a health-conscious alternative to the alcohol-soaked business lunch, growing numbers of deals are now being sealed over cucumber sandwiches and scones, thus enabling high-class hotels to fill the idle hours between lunch and dinner.....■**

Tea with a view
During afternoon tea, your attention should be devoted to the table and your companion seated across it. However, from a window seat in the Rotunda restaurant of Neiman Marcus (150 Stockton Street), where afternoon tea revives jaded shoppers, a bird's-eye view of Union Square vies for your gaze. At the Marriott Hotel (55 Fourth Street), the tea, sandwiches, and scones are presented in the 40th-floor View Lounge.

Other afternoon-tea hotspots
Campton Place, 340 Stockton Street.
Four Seasons Clift Hotel, 495 Geary Street.
Ritz-Carlton, 600 Stockton Street.
Mandarin Oriental, 222 Sansome Street.

Tea, gossip...

For visitors, afternoon tea (served from 2:30 to 5p.m.) offers a relaxing hour or two's break from sightseeing and a chance to observe San Franciscan high society, some of whom have adopted teatime as part of their daily routine.

Teatime etiquette Social inepts who normally drink tea by large, steaming mugfuls should tread carefully through the ultra-civilized environs of the afternoon tea lounge. Even at the most elegant location you are unlikely to be expelled for not holding your cup correctly, but upsetting the calm atmosphere or showing yourself bereft of manners is considered the mark of the barbarian.

The full tea When ordering afternoon tea, the first task is to select the actual tea. Most establishments offer a choice which includes some or all of the following: Earl Grey, orange pekoe, darjeeling, jasmine, lapsang souchong, oolong, peppermint, Russian caravan, and camomile. The tea will arrive in individual teapots and a strainer will be provided.

Shortly after the tea arrives, a waiter or waitress will arrive at your table with a large, split-level tray holding any or all of the following: delicate sandwiches (filled with bacon, cucumber, smoked salmon, ham, egg and parsley, or English cheddar cheese), scones, and assorted fancy pastries. You might also find a bowl of seasonal berries. Imported Devonshire cream and a selection of fine jams await your scone—but the

first item to be eaten should be the palate-cleansing cucumber sandwiches.

Select locations The choice of tea and nibbles aside, the most important aspect of afternoon tea is simply where you have it: the event puts some of the most luxurious public rooms in the city at your disposal, and the surroundings and ambience can be surprisingly varied.

San Franciscan interiors seldom come any finer than the **Garden Court** of the Palace Hotel (633–65 Market Street) which, with its high glass ceiling, palm trees, and ornate chandeliers, successfully recaptures the aura of unbridled opulence which the hotel, built in 1873, epitomized during San Francisco's early years. Teas include gunpowder green, and the price includes a glass of champagne.

At the marginally less elegant **Compass Rose** room of the St. Francis Hotel (Union Square), afternoon tea is popular enough for well-dressed socialites to be seen lining up for a table. Once seated, connoisseurs will detect something special about the Compass Rose's sandwiches: the cucumber in them is delicately flavored with fresh dill and salt.

The top-notch hotels of Nob Hill all provide afternoon tea, but while the farmhouse fruitcake served on Wedgwood china in the **Lower Bar** at the Mark Hopkins (999 California Street) has many admirers, the setting lacks atmosphere. The in-the-know choice for Nob Hill afternoon tea is the **Stanford Court Hotel** (905 California Street), where the goodies are served in the hushed surroundings of the lobby lounge and include smoked salmon with *crème fraîche* on pumpernickel. Round things off with a glass of fine port (though purists would disapprove of such a suggestion).

Finally, if the thought of having tea surrounded by San Franciscan high society gives you the shivers, you might seek solace at the **Bread & Honey Tearoom** of the King George Hotel (334 Mason Street), where the mood is egalitarian and a pianist tinkles gently as you munch the *à la carte* pasties, pastries, and cakes.

...and music

Tea etiquette classes
Anyone with a burning desire to know whether to bend the little finger when holding a tea cup, or to discover the most appalling *faux pas* to commit with a napkin, should make a reservation (tel. 415/296 7465) for the tea etiquette class (two hours) conducted by tea and protocol expert Dana May Casperson at the Ritz-Carlton hotel (600 Stockton Street).

Church of St. Francis of Assisi
The well-scrubbed façade of North Beach's Church of St. Francis of Assisi (610 Vallejo Street) does little to advertise that this was the first Catholic church founded in California since the time of the Spanish missions. None of the original 1856 church remains, but part of its 1860s successor is incorporated into the present structure, which dates from 1913.

Welcome to the historic San Remo Hotel

Molinari's Deli

▶▶▶ **North Beach** *IFCE6*

Buses: 15, 30, 41

The spiritual home of San Francisco's Italian population, North Beach—between Chinatown and Fisherman's Wharf—has dozens of community landmarks and is packed with highly regarded Italian restaurants. It was North Beach, too, that helped cafés and coffee become part of San Franciscan life. Whether to gorge on melt-in-your-mouth pastries or sip a cappuccino while watching the world go by, a North Beach café is the place to be.

There was a time when North Beach really did have a beach, but the stretch of sand disappeared when 1860s landfill extended the city's northern shoreline to what is now Fisherman's Wharf.

North Beach had long been home to an ethnically diverse, working-class population, but gained its first substantial influx of Italians during the 1890s. Many arrived from Italy's depressed south and sought a living from fishing. The Italian-American community quickly thrived and, by the 1930s, five Italian-language newspapers were operating in North Beach and 60,000 Italian-Americans were calling the district home. Meanwhile, San Franciscans of all ethnic backgrounds were discovering the pleasures of pasta and pesto.

Although the Italian businesses stayed, the neighborhood began losing its established population during the 1950s as immigration from Italy fell and many established North Beach families became wealthy enough to move to quieter, more comfortable parts.

Attracted by low rents, cheap wine, the radical sounds of bebop jazz emanating from its numerous jazz clubs, and the prospect of caffeine-fueled conversation in the cafés, 1950s North Beach became a stamping ground for the seminal figures of the Beat generation, whose followers were derisively dubbed "beatniks" (continued on page 136)

Walk North Beach

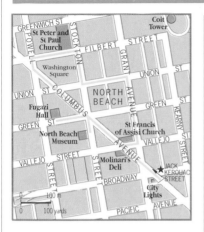

Starting at City Lights, this walk traces the Italian roots and the Beat-era associations of North Beach, and includes Washington Square and the funky shops of Grant Avenue before concluding at the site of one of California's oldest churches.

Opened in 1953, **City Lights** was the U.S.'s first paperback book store (see pages 136–7). **Molinari's Deli** has been popular among North Beach's Italian population since the store opened in 1896 (see page 137).

On the mezzanine level of the Eureka Savings Bank, the **North Beach Museum** does a fine job of preserving neighborhood history (see page 137). Around the corner, **Fugazi Hall** was donated to North Beach Italians in 1912 by John Fugazi (see page 137).

The twin-spired **St. Peter and St. Paul Church** was built over a 15-year period from 1922 (see page 137). The church, gracefully illuminated at night, overlooks **Washington Square** (see page 137).

As Grant Avenue leads back towards Broadway, it is lined by off-beat stores and cafés, such as **Caffè Trieste** (see page 137).

Built in 1913, the Church of **St. Francis of Assisi** occupies the site of an 1856 church (see panel, page 134), the first Catholic church to be founded in California since the Spanish missions.

North Beach street scene

135

NORTH BEACH

Grant Avenue

Aim to spend at least part your time in North Beach taking a leisurely walk along the section of Grant Avenue which climbs gently north from Broadway towards Telegraph Hill. The street is lined by numerous wacky art and bric-à-brac shops. Look for the thousands of vintage and bizarre postcards at Quality Postcards (number 1402), amid Chinese laundries and long-established Italian businesses such as Figoni Hardware (number 1351), open since 1907.

Opened in the 1940s, Beat-era landmark Vesuvio's still has its bohemian atmosphere—and its original graffiti

The home of "Howl"

Allen Ginsberg's epic poem, *Howl*, not only brought what became known as the Beats to national prominence, but also helped establish the author as the world's foremost counter-culture poet during the 1960s. The long, breathless poem, its cadences reminiscent of jazz rhythms, was written when Ginsberg was living at 1010 Montgomery Street, between North Beach and Telegraph Hill. Not a San Francisco native, Ginsberg had arrived in the city from New York ostensibly to work in advertising.

(*continued from page 134*) by San Franciscan newspaper columnist Herb Caen (see page 42). By the late 1950s, North Beach had garnered national headlines as the center of a counter-culture explosion and literary renaissance that rocked the establishment and paved the way for the mass protest movements, and the psychedelia, of the 1960s.

The busy intersection of Broadway, Grant, and Columbus avenues blurs the boundaries of North Beach and Chinatown, and carries the traffic which helped make North Beach into a major nightlife area.

By the late 1950s, North Beach comedy clubs were hosting cutting-edge comics such as Lenny Bruce and Mort Sahl, while jazz clubs in shabby cellars would periodically be taken over by the key players in what became the Beat movement for riotous nights of poetry and bebop.

Another cultural pioneer was Carol Doda, whose silicone-implanted breasts starred in the nation's first topless show, staged at the Condor Club in 1964. The club is now the lackluster Condor Bistro (300 Columbus Avenue); a plaque on an outside wall commemorates its historical contribution.

Testament to the creativity and long-lasting influence of the Beats is provided by City Lights►►► (261 Columbus Avenue). Co-founded by North Beach-born artist and poet

Lawrence Ferlinghetti in 1953, this was the first all-paperback book store in the U.S. and its profits were intended to finance a literary magazine. City Lights gained nationwide notoriety in 1957 when copies of Allen Ginsberg's poem *Howl*, a work destined to become the defining verse of the Beat generation and which City Lights was intending to publish, were seized by U.S. customs and branded obscene. The ensuing controversy alerted the world to North Beach's underground cultural scene and the neighborhood soon filled with goatee-bearded youths and beatnik-seeking tourists.

The Condor's finest moments

As a movement, the Beats may be long gone but City Lights survives and thrives with writings by and about the Beats, and much more, filling its tightly packed shelves.

Facing City Lights across Jack Kerouac Street (named after the author), **Vesuvio's▶** was a popular Beat rendezvous and still draws a faintly bohemian crowd. Another Beat-era favorite was **Caffè Trieste▶** (601 Vallejo Street) which is still a great place for coffee, cakes, and live opera on Saturday afternoons (see page 138).

The 1950s literary associations may have brought North Beach fame, but on its streets the daily concerns of its Italian population are much more in evidence. On the corner of Columbus Avenue and Vallejo Street, the arty window display of **Molinari's Deli▶**—purveyor of fine cheeses, meats and pastas attracts many photographers. Equally mouth watering is the **Victoria Pastry Company▶** (1362 Stockton Street), with its array of Italian cakes and pastries.

Also on Stockton Street, the changing displays at the **North Beach Museum▶▶**, on the mezzanine level of the Eureka Savings Bank (number 1435), make an absorbing social history of the area. Part of that history is the 1912 **Fugazi Hall▶** (678 Green Street), an Italian community hall donated by John Fugazi, a locally born banker and founder of what became the Transamerica Corporation. The ground floor houses the long running revue, *Beach Blanket Babylon* (see page 234). Upstairs are memorabilia and photographs from North Beach's past.

With a statue of Benjamin Franklin in its grassy center and the twin-spired Church of St. Peter and St. Paul on its northern side, **Washington Square▶▶** brings some much-needed open space to North Beach. Each morning, one side is filled with Chinese-Americans going through the slow-motion movements of Tai Chi. On weekends, Bay Area artists and sculptors converge on the square to display and sell their work.

The square's benches cry out to be sat on, but it is hard to resist the allure of the **Church of St. Peter and St. Paul▶▶**. Although construction began in 1922, this engaging Romanesque edifice took 15 years to complete.

137

Tai Chi
A common sight on any morning is scores of Chinese Americans going through the slow, graceful exercises of Tai Chi Ch'uan. This 1,000-year-old form of callisthenics is based on carefully balanced rhythmic movements which use all the body's joints, ligaments, and muscles, and help to regulate blood flow.

North Beach café society

■ **For many residents, copious consumption of high-quality coffee in a public place is what being a San Franciscan is all about. Every neighborhood has its fair share of cafés, and each one differs a little from the next. Some offer newspapers and magazines for perusal by their never-in-a-rush customers, some are bohemian settings with poetry readings and chess matches, others are favored for their post-jog fruit juices or for the fancy cakes which provide an incentive for walking the dog. Every one of them has its devoted group of regulars.....■**

Coffee types

San Francisco's coffee devotees place great stock on the type of coffee bean used by a particular café, but most casual drinkers—and city visitors—are more intrigued by the varieties of coffee offered. Besides espresso (coffee brewed at high pressure) and cappuccino (espresso topped by a creamy milk head), most San Franciscan cafés also dispense *caffè latté* (espresso with steamed milk) and *caffè mocha* (espresso with chocolate). Many also offer house specialities.

The connoisseurs' dream: a North Beach coffee shop (below) and (top) the Caffè Roma

North Beach Italian cafés Probably the first Italian café in the city was **Café Tosca**, opened in 1917 and moved to its current location (242 Columbus Avenue) in 1947. Allegedly serving the first espresso in California, Tosca is still worth a visit but—despite the opera reverberating from its jukebox—it lacks a gregarious atmosphere, not least because its customers are often well-heeled, or would-be well-heeled, socialites.

Much more in keeping with North Beach bohemia, **Caffè Trieste** (601 Vallejo Street) opened in 1956 and quickly became a hang out for the seminal figures of what developed into the Beat generation. Still a great place for entertaining eavesdropping, the Trieste's family owners stage a free operatic performance on Saturday afternoons.

Other North Beach notables are **Caffè Puccini** (411 Columbus Avenue), where the window tables make for North Beach's best people-watching, and **Mario's Bohemian Cigar Store** (566 Columbus Avenue), one of the better spots for snacks and light meals.

Very serious coffee drinkers on the loose in North Beach might prefer to treat their tastebuds—and their noses—to a cup at **Caffé Roma Coffee Roasting Company** (526 Columbus Avenue), which roasts its own beans on the premises.

More cafés
The cafés mentioned here are just a few selected from a very large number and are chosen for being distinguished in some way, by their history, clientele, decor, or mood. Sampling a few of them will give you a good introduction to what San Francisco-style café society is all about. To assist with further investigation, more are described in the Restaurant listings (pages 275–81).

Relaxing at Caffè Trieste: a place for coffee, cakes, and opera

Contemporary bohemia In the heart of the strongly Hispanic Mission District (see page 124), **Café La Bohème** (3318 24th Street) has epitomized the spirit of the bohemian café since its opening in the 1970s. In a less frenetic section of the same neighborhood, **Café Picaro** (3120 16th Street) is also patronized by aging Beats, radical writers, and avant-garde artists. A similarly arty but generally younger clientele gathers at the grunge-influenced cafés of the Lower Haight (east of Haight-Ashbury): favorite rendezvous are **Love 'n Haight** (553 Haight Street), **Café International** (508 Haight Street), and the **Horseshoe Coffee House** (566 Haight Street).

Classy cafés If you prefer sophistication to shabby bohemia, try **Café Tosca** (see page 138); **Café Bastille** (22 Belden Alley), where the staff and many customers like to pretend they are in a stylish Parisian bistro rather than a Financial District alley; or the Marina District's **Just Desserts** (3735 Buchanan Street), where you can sip coffee and listen to classical music.

Window seats are prized commodities: diners at this Italian restaurant have a perfect view of North Beach street scenes

Curious cafés With cafés being a feature of the city, it should be no surprise to find inspired variations on the standard format. In Haight-Ashbury, **Kan Zaman** (1793 Haight Street) is an Arabian-style coffee spot complete with hookahs and pillow-adorned sunken seating. In the Mission District, **Café Istanbul** (525 Valencia Street) recaptures the look of a traditional Turkish coffee house. At **Mad Magda's Russian Tea Room** (579 Hayes Street), the food, drink, and furniture combine to create what has been termed a "bedlam at the Kremlin" style.

Oakland harbor tours
A close inspection of one of the world's largest container docks may not strike everybody as a wildly enthralling prospect, but Port of Oakland Tours (tel. 510/272 1200) offers exactly that on a free boat tour operating daily between May and August.

Oakland Temple
A striking sight in the hills above Oakland, the Oakland Temple (4770 Lincoln Avenue) was erected by the Mormon Church both as a place of worship and as a visitor center to relate the story of Joseph Smith, the religion's founder, and the Mormons' epic cross-country journey to Salt Lake City. The attendants make every effort to interest you in Mormonism but the temple is worth a visit, if only for the great views from it across Oakland and far beyond.

► ►   **Oakland**   45D2
BART: 12th Street or Lake Merritt
Ferry: from Ferry Building
Famously derided by author Gertrude Stein's comment "there is no *there*, there," and still notorious to some as the birthplace of the Black Panthers, Oakland is actually an agreeable mix of old and new, with a strollable waterfront and a lively Chinatown district—plus the wonderful Oakland Museum of California (see pages 142–3).

Ferries from San Francisco berth at what is now **Jack London Waterfront**, an uninspiring conglomeration of souvenir shops and seafood-with-views restaurants loosely themed around the writer. He spent some of his formative years doing odd jobs in the warehouses and canneries built for the goods carried by the ocean-going freighters that once docked here.

London would be unlikely to recognize the area as it is today, though he might remember the turf-roofed log cabin which he occupied during his winter in Alaska's Yukon territory during the Klondike gold rush of 1897. The reassembled cabin sits a stone's throw from **Heinhold's First & Last Chance Saloon►**, where London was known to enjoy a drink or two. The bar's interior is worth a look, as are the photos lining its walls.

More shops occupy the deliberately ramshackle **Jack London Village**, immediately south. Among them, the **Jack London Village Museum and Bookstore** stocks many of the writer's works and displays mementoes of his life, A superior gathering can be seen in the **Oakland Main Library** (125 Fourteenth Street).

Between the waterfront and the elevated I-880 freeway, an energetic **produce market** lines Third Street, but

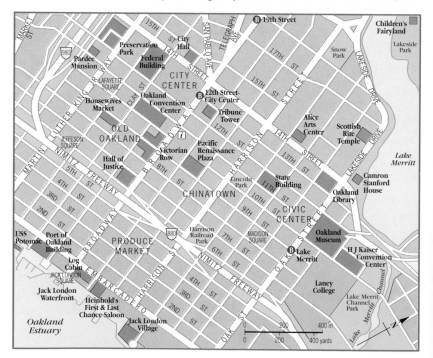

otherwise there is little reason to linger at the waterfront and you should make your way to Chinatown and Old Oakland, which lie on either side of Broadway.

Though it lacks the claustrophobic atmosphere and historical resonance of its San Franciscan equivalent, Oakland's **Chinatown►►**, with its markets and inexpensive Asian restaurants in the streets south of Broadway, justifies exploration. Besides many Chinese-American-run businesses, the district's numerous ethnic groups includeThais, Vietnamese, Koreans, and Burmese.

Cross north of Broadway into Ninth Street and you will discover the restored Victorian buildings of the **Old Oakland Historical District►►**. These handsome structures were at the center of local commercial life a century ago, and most now earn their keep as offices, stores, and food outlets, though one or two house good art galleries.

A block ahead, the mouth watering smells wafting across the junction with Clay Street emanate from the food stands of the **Housewives Market►**.

A symbol of Oakland's booming economy and of the late-1980s regeneration of its downtown area, **City Center►** is an imaginative integration of office space, plazas, and a sculpture garden.

Directly across Fourteenth Street from the modernistic plot, the well-proportioned **City Hall** was considered a breathtakingly high skyscraper when completed in 1914. City Hall's construction came on the heels of another boom: the 1906 earthquake which devastated San Francisco did wonders for Oakland's economy. Superior in design, the adjacent **Tribune Tower►** has been the home of Oakland's daily newspaper since 1923.

Further contrast to City Center is provided two blocks north by the group of vintage Oakland homes that comprise **Preservation Park►**. Most of the houses, the majority dating from the late 1800s, were moved here when the I-980 freeway cut through the neighborhood. The old homes appear to be enjoying their retirement, kept in good order and reached by walking along spotlessly clean pathways. *(Continued on page 144)*

Oakland's Chinatown...

Oakland's twin cities
Fukuoka, Japan
Nakahoda, Russia
Takoradi, Ghana
Dalian, China
Ocho Rios, Jamaica

...has food at every turn

■ **The best museum in the Bay Area, and probably the best anywhere devoted to California, the Oakland Museum explores California's nature, history, and art. On three levels, it will comfortably provide several hours of informative and entertaining insights into the Golden State's past, present, and future.....■**

California ecology Rare is the region which has a more diverse ecology than California, which encompasses high mountains, low deserts, and a 1,200-mile coastline. Spread across a 38,000-square-feet gallery, the **Hall of Ecology** uses dioramas to reveal the broad sweep of plant and animal life which make their homes in vastly different habitats. The **Aquatic California Gallery** does a similar job for underwater life, illustrating the strange goings-on in California's rivers, bays and hot springs, and beneath its ocean waves.

Memorabilia of an earlier California

Californian history Even seasoned California visitors would be hard pushed to find a better or more user-friendly historical record of the state than the **Cowell Hall of History**. Every episode in the region's action-packed past is remembered and the collections are enhanced by interactive computers offering more detailed information on particular exhibits, recorded commentaries from experts and oral folk histories.

The conflicts between indigenous Californians and the Spanish settlers who founded the missions, and the subsequent transformation of California by the discovery of gold, are thoughtfully explored and copiously documented, whether with Native American basketry or a re-created assay office from gold-rich Nevada City.

Equally impressive are the collections illustrating more recent California: the internment of the Japanese during World War II, the rise of Disneyland, and the subcultures of the 1950s and 1960s highlighted with surfboards, a mock-up beatnik coffee house, and assorted hippie-era peace-and-love paraphernalia.

The gallery comes up to date with the invention of the mountain bike and an outline of the state's changing ethnic composition, and poses questions about the economic impact of the end of the Cold War—which has greatly affected the state's defense industries.

Californian art On the museum's top floor, an imaginative gathering of art and artists with Californian connections skillfully demonstrates how the art of the Golden State has developed over the decades.

Admission and guided tours
In 1993, the Oakland Museum broke with a 25-year tradition of free admission and began requesting a $4 donation. Though not compulsory, the sum is well worth paying. Closed on Mondays and Tuesdays, the museum opens Wednesday to Saturday 10–5 and on Sundays noon–7. Free guided tours of the galleries take place most weekday afternoons; information is available from the reception desk.

Landscape artists Throughout the 19th century, landscape painting was the rage in American art and the artists of the day received inspiration by the exploration of the American West, where undeveloped territories teemed with scenes of natural beauty.

Albert Bierstadt was among the main figures to emerge during the mid-1800s, imbuing his canvases with a feeling of nature as a spiritual force: *Yosemite Valley* provides a good example. Working from a studio in the Sierras, another devotee of wild California was Thomas Hill, who is impressively represented here, notably with his own *Yosemite Valley*.

Historical records Besides being quality works of art, Hill's paintings also contributed to the protection of Yosemite as a national park. Several other pieces here carry a significance beyond their aesthetic appeal. Henry Raschen's *California Miner with Packhorse* is an important documentation of the gold rush era, as is George Henry Davis' *San Francisco, July 1849*, a panoramic view of the embryonic city complete with ships abandoned in the bay as their crews headed for the gold mines.

Though painted in the last decades of the 19th century, Davis' painting was acknowledged as accurate and provides an important historical record. Similarly, the same artist's *Fort Ross* captures the Russian settlement on the northern Californian coast prior to its 1840s abandonment.

Twentieth-century art The changing social and artistic mood of California becomes apparent in later periods. Several works by Arthur Mathews, such as *Youth* which puts classical figures into a Californian setting, are examples of the 1910s California Decorative style spearheaded by Mathews and his wife.

More recent works illustrate the growing self-confidence of Californian artists. Among many bold paintings, ceramics, and collages are contemporary works by Richard Diebenkorn, Bruce Conner, and others.

Photography
Among the Gallery of California Art's photographic collection is Dorothea Lange's 1936 *Migrant Mother*, which provided the abiding visual image of the Depression and its effect on ordinary Americans. Lange moved to California in 1918 and established a studio in San Francisco. At one time she was married to Maynard Dixon, who is represented here with some of his emotion-packed studies of the people of New Mexico and Arizona.

Spotlight Tours
Highlighting certain themes and concepts in each of the museum's galleries, so-called "Spotlight Tours" take place on the first and third Saturdays and second and fourth Sundays of each month.

143

California's days of speed and shiny chrome remembered at the Oakland Museum

OAKLAND

Completed in 1931, the Paramount Theater was the crowning glory of Oakland's short-lived art-deco building boom and underwent a successful restoration in 1976

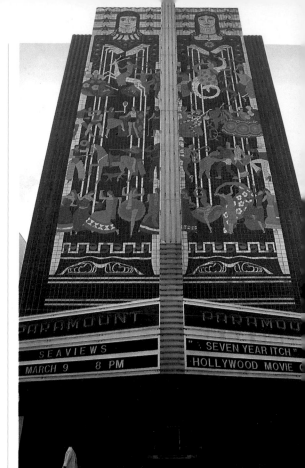

Samuel Merritt
A wealthy land owner and civic leader, Samuel Merritt became mayor of Oakland in 1867 and instigated the damming project which created the lake which now bears his name. In 1888, Merritt loaned his schooner to Robert Louis Stevenson and it was used by the Scottish writer for his voyage to the South Pacific.

Art-deco squirrel

(Continued from page 141) Dotted with yachts and paddleboats, and picturesquely fringed by greenery, **Lake Merritt▶** occupies 150 acres of southwest Oakland and provides a popular weekend recreation spot.

The sole survivor of the extravagant homes which surrounded the tidal saltwater lake at the turn of the century is the **Camron Stanford House▶▶** (1418 Lakeside Drive). Completed in 1876, the house was in private hands until 1910 when it became the site of the Oakland Museum, a role it retained for a remarkable 57 years. Recently saved from the wreckers' ball by community fund-raising efforts, the house has been partly restored to show the lifestyles of some of its former occupants. Guided tours begin with an engrossing slide-show on the history of Oakland.

From here, the present-day **Oakland Museum** (see pages 142–3) is a few minutes' walk away along Oak Street.

▶ **Ocean Beach** *IFCA4*

Stretching for several miles between the Cliff House (see page 80) and Fort Funston (see page 99), Ocean Beach is where San Franciscans might head if, for a few crazed minutes, they ever wanted to pretend that they lived in southern California. Diminishing the appeal of the pebble-strewn strand, however, are the strong winds which frequently blow in off the ocean and a treacherous undertow which makes swimming dangerous.

▶ **Octagon House** *IFCE6*

2645 Gough Street
Bus: 45. Open on the second Wednesday and second and fourth Sundays of the month except during January.
The Octagon House was completed in 1861, one of five eight-sided houses built in San Francisco. The eight sides were considered to bring luck to the occupants. The National Society of Colonial Dames (an organization founded in 1891 to preserve the heritage of the U.S.'s colonial period) acquired the house in 1951, organized its restoration, and now uses it to display decorative arts of the Colonial and Federal periods. (See also page 157.)

▶▶ **Old U.S. Mint** *IFCE5*

Corner of Fifth and Mission streets
Buses: 14, 26, 27
Constructed in neoclassical style in 1874, the granite and sandstone Old Mint survived the earthquake and fire of 1906, and won a place in local hearts by honoring the certificates issued by the city's destroyed banks, allowing cash to reach the stricken population.

Minting operations ceased in 1937, and various government departments used the elegant building until 1968. Restored to U.S. Treasury ownership, the Mint's airy rooms and corridors contain items of numismatic interest—including $1 million in gold bullion—though none of them can detract from the grandeur of the building itself.

A new mint's troubles
In 1937, a new mint opened on a hilltop site in Duboce Street. The mint's fortress-like appearance did little to dampen the eagerness of some of its workers to short-change the U.S. government. During a succession of scandals in the 1960s, tales abounded of mint employees walking out with money taped to their legs and tossing bags of loot out of windows to collect later. In 1966, the mint announced a discrepancy for the year of $15,000—all of it in quarters.

145

The Octagon House

■ **From gold-rush times to the present day, San Francisco has attracted writers by the score, and every neighborhood has at least a few literary landmarks to call its own. The sites mentioned below are merely the most interesting, most accessible, or simply the most curious of a very large number.....■**

The Bohemian Club
Founded in 1872 by city newspapermen, the Bohemian Club included among its members Ambrose Bierce, Jack London, and influential poet George Sterling. As its genuinely bohemian members were replaced by lawyers and financiers, the club steadily became (and remains) a preserve of wealthy—and exclusively male—powerbrokers. A plaque reading "Weaving Spiders Come Not Here," marks the club's present site at 624 Taylor Street.

Top: the plaque marking the birthplace of novelist Jack London Below: Haight-Ashbury's Spreckels Mansion—a lodging for Bierce and London?

North Beach and Telegraph Hill Thanks to what became the Beat generation, North Beach's literary links are plentiful. **City Lights** (261 Columbus Avenue) was the country's first paperback bookstore but more importantly published the earliest of the Beat poets in the 1950s, beginning with Allen Ginsberg's controversial *Howl*.

Ginsberg, City Lights's owner and poet/artist Lawrence Ferlinghetti, and other seminal figures patronized North Beach cafés such as **Trieste** (601 Vallejo Street), while another Beat character, Jack Kerouac, became well known to the bartenders at **Vesuvio's** (255 Columbus Avenue, just across what is now Jack Kerouac Street).

Ginsberg wrote *Howl* while living at **1010 Montgomery Street** on the edge of Telegraph Hill, a neighborhood which appealed to many writers until gentrification took hold. Fans of Armistead Maupin's *Tales of the City* series, however, might pay respects to **60–62 Alta Street**, Maupin's first home in the city and where the first tales were written in the early 1970s.

Pacific Heights and Russian Hill Best-selling romance writer Danielle Steele currently occupies a 42-room mansion in Pacific Heights, but the neighborhood's literary associations stretch way back. Gertrude Atherton, a pre-feminism feminist and one of California's most important 1920s novelists, rented an apartment at **2101 California Street** in 1929 and presided over many literary gatherings there. Also in Russian Hill, Jack Kerouac occupied an attic room at **29 Russel Street** during 1952, revising the drafts of what would become the classic Beat novel, *On the Road*. Three years later, Allen Ginsberg read *Howl* for the first time in public at what was then the Six Galleries (**3119 Filmore Street**).

Nob Hill Dashiell Hammett perfected the hard-boiled private-eye genre in the 1920s, and after several Tenderloin addresses refined *The Maltese Falcon* at **1155 Leavenworth Street** in Nob Hill. Hammett's creation, Sam Spade, left many fictional footprints around the city and often dined at **John's Grill**. The restaurant actually exists (two blocks south of Union Square at 63 Ellis Street) and keeps a replica Maltese Falcon in its second-floor dining room.

SoMa In his writings, Jack Kerouac eulogized the cheap hotels, cargo docks, and rail freight yards of 1950s SoMa. In the same district six decades earlier, Jack London, one of the few internationally known writers to be born in San Francisco, entered the world at a site at **601 Third Street**

now marked by a plaque (see page 169), and is also acknowledged by **Jack London Street, which** runs through SoMa's South Park.

Haight-Ashbury Jack London moved across the bay to Oakland when still a child but returned to the city as an adult, and for a time, occupied (it is claimed) an attic room of Haight-Ashbury's **Spreckels Mansion** (737 Buena Vista Avenue West). The same room (it is also claimed) was once occupied by Ambrose Bierce (see page 37). A leading literary figure in late-1880s California, Bierce was an acclaimed columnist and wrote the darkly witty *Devil's Dictionary*, before he mysteriously disappeared in Mexico.

Minor Beat poet Kenneth Rexroth lived at **250 Scott Street** before Haight-Ashbury's mid-1960s hippie boom, which was underway when maverick journalist Hunter S. Thompson occupied **318 Parnassus Avenue** while conducting the "research" (mostly drunken parties) leading to his name-making *Hell's Angels*.

A literary landmark since the 1950s

Chinatown
Chinatown can also claim literary associations. An impoverished Robert Louis Stevenson first passed the time in Portsmouth Square (he is remembered by a granite plinth, see page 75) in 1879. A riotous atmosphere helped make tiny Sam Wo's (813 Washington Street) a favorite of the Beats in the 1950s. More recently, Amy Tan captured the flavor of the neighborhood in her 1989 novel, *The Joy Luck Club*.

PACIFIC HEIGHTS

Pacific Heights' Union Street is a popular shopping area, with live fashion shows (right) and retail outlets occupying carefully restored 19th-century cottages (below)

► **Pacific Heights** IFCD5

Buses: 3, 22, 41, 45

West of Van Ness Avenue between Nob Hill and the Marina District, Pacific Heights is among the city's most affluent neighborhoods and has two main reasons to prompt a visit. One is the collection of upscale stores and restaurants grouped along a section of Union Street. The other reason is Pacific Heights' impressive diversity of residential architecture, from 19th-century Queen Anne mansions to streamlined 1930s art deco apartment buildings.

On the 1700-2000 blocks of Union Street are the antique shops, boutiques, and chic restaurants where Pacific Heights' well-to-do and fashion-conscious residents like to buy expensive ornaments, select European designer clothes off the rack, and dine on expensive French and Italian food. You do not need an expense account to enjoy the scene, however. For the price of a coffee, a sidewalk table at one of the local cafés can easily provide a happy hour of people-watching.

In the late 1800s, as opulent homes first began appearing on the slopes of Pacific Heights, the valley through which present-day Union Street runs was known as Cow Hollow because of its numerous dairy farms, which supplied the city's fresh milk and cheese. As a result of pressure from the wealthy inhabitants to rid their chosen neighborhood of nasty smells, the farms—and the slaughterhouses which had grown up around them— were closed down in the 1890s, though not all the clapboard farm buildings disappeared.

One of them, at 2040 Union Street, now occupied by stores and a restaurant, was the home of dairy farmer James Cudworth. At number 1980, are the so-called "twin houses," identical bungalows joined by a common wall, which Cudworth built in the 1870s as wedding presents to his two daughters. Many of the other farm buildings remain along Union Street, expensively

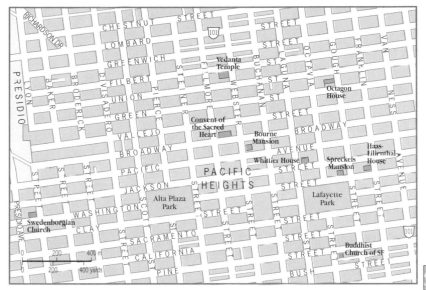

The map shows streets including: RICHARDSON DR, CHESTNUT STREET, LOMBARD STREET, GREENWICH STREET, FILBERT, UNION, GREEN, VALLEJO, BROADWAY, PACIFIC, JACKSON STREET, WASHINGTON, CLAY, SACRAMENTO, CALIFORNIA, PINE, BUSH STREET. Cross streets: PRESIDIO, BAKER, BRODERICK, DIVISADERO, PIERCE, STEINER, WEBSTER, BUCHANAN ST, LAGUNA, OCTAVIA, GOUGH, FRANKLIN, VAN NESS. Landmarks: Vedanta Temple, Octagon House, Convent of the Sacred Heart, Bourne Mansion, Whittier House, Spreckels Mansion, Haas-Lilienthal House, Alta Plaza Park, Lafayette Park, Swedenborgian Church, Buddhist Church of SF. Scale: 200, 400 m / 200, 400 yards

restored, decorated by imitation gas lamps and fronted by neat wrought-iron fences.

A few blocks south of Union Street rise the slopes which give Pacific Heights its name. As you climb, looking back reveals the impressive views across the Golden Gate which encouraged the rich to settle the district in the 1880s. Looking ahead, reveals many of their architecturally adventurous homes. Two of the most intriguing specimens are the **Octagon House** ▶ (2645 Gough Street, see page 145), and the **Haas-Lilienthal**

Union Street's "twin-houses," a wedding gift from the builder to his two daughters

Convent of the Sacred Heart

Architectural criticism
Critic Ernest Peixotto was unimpressed by Pacific Heights' architecture. Commenting on the area in 1893, he described its homes as "nightmares of an architect's brain piled up without rhyme or reason—restless, turreted, loaded with meaningless detail, defaced with fantastic windows and hideous chimneys."

Perry Mason's birthplace
Fans of lawyer-sleuth Perry Mason may care to pay their respects to 1700 Octavia Street, on the corner with Bush Street, the house where prolific writer Erle Stanley Gardener created the character during 1933.

House►► (2007 Franklin Street, see page 105).

Many interesting clusters of Victorian and early 20th-century homes can be found by strolling the neighborhood. Faced with the steep slopes, however, you might prefer to focus your attention on a few properties.
The 1896 **Bourn Mansion**► (2550 Webster Street), was designed by Willis Polk (see panel, page 112) for William B. Bourn II, who ran gas and water companies and inherited a gold-mining fortune. Polk also designed Bourn's country home, Filoli (see panel, page 203).

The **Convent of the Sacred Heart►►** (2222 Broadway) occupies a trim granite mansion erected for bartender-turned-silver-baron James Flood in 1912. An earlier Flood mansion, successfully modified in the mid-1960s, stands close by, housing the very select and academically renowned **Hamlin School for Girls** (2120 Broadway).

Modeled by architects Swain & Tharp on the brownstone town houses of New York, the **Whittier House**► (2090 Jackson Street) was completed in 1896 for paint manufacturer William Whittier. The mansion's red sandstone walls enabled it to survive the 1906 earthquake and fire. This was one of the first homes in the city with electric lights and central heating.

Overlooking Lafayette Park (see page 104), the **Spreckels Mansion►►** (2080 Washington Street), was built for sugar mogul Adolph Spreckels and his wife Alma, largely, or so it seems from the features, in deference to Mrs. Spreckels' French ancestry.

▶ **Pacific Heritage Museum** *IBCD4*

608 Commercial Street
Buses: 1, 15, 69
The Bank of Canton on the edge of Chinatown might be an appropriate setting for several floors holding changing exhibitions which explore the links between the countries of the Pacific Rim. Anyone who regards San Francisco as having more in common with New York than Hong Kong should find plenty of food for thought here.

The Bank of Canton building sits on the site of the city's first U.S. Branch Mint which, in 1875, was replaced by a new U.S. Subtreasury. The story of both is told within the brick-walled vault: exhibits include coins, bullion bags and the sturdy carts, required to move large consignments of gold. The Subtreasury was eventually superseded by what is now the Old U.S. Mint (see page 145).

▶ **Pacific Stock Exchange** *IBCD3*

301 Pine Street
Bus: 12 (weekdays only)
A row of neoclassical columns greets brokers as they climb the steps of the Pacific Stock Exchange, presumably intended to instill a serious mood as they enter what has been a citadel of West Coast finance since 1915. The building, formerly a U.S. Treasury, underwent an architectural overhaul in 1930 (see panel), which explains why the more recent features, and the large and arresting sculptures by Ralph Stackpole on either side of the steps, are in the artdeco *moderne* style. Tightened security in the early 1990s resulted in the closure of the public gallery, but you can see the Stock Exchange's impressive Diego Rivera mural by making an appointment through the Mexican Museum (see page 117; tel. 415/441 0445).

The Stock Exchange's architecture
"One of the major sources of modernism in the Bay Area;" this is how the Foundation for San Francisco's Architectural Heritage describes the city's Stock Exchange which, ironically, acquired its form as a result of the 1920s economic crash. The firm of Miller and Pfleuger had been commissioned to build a new stock exchange on a different site, but financial constraints led instead to their radical conversion—employing an inspired blend of classical and *moderne* styles—of the recently vacated U.S. Treasury.

Hi-tech wheeling and dealing...

...on the floor of the Stock Exchange

PALACE OF FINE ARTS

Weeping maidens...

Bernard Maybeck
Born in New York in 1862, Bernard Maybeck studied architecture at the École des Beaux-Arts in Paris and settled in Berkeley in 1889. He assisted Phoebe Hearst in organizing the competition for the Berkeley university campus, but soon began designing buildings of his own around the Bay Area, distinguished by their inspired fusing of diverse architectural ideas, such as the Swedenborgian Church (see page 172).

...help to decorate the Palace of Fine Arts

▶▶▶ **Palace of Fine Arts**   *IFCD6*
West end of Lyon Street
Buses: 28, 30
In 1915, using the opening of the Panama Canal as an excuse, San Francisco announced its recovery from the devastation of the earthquake and fire of nine years earlier by staging the Panama–Pacific International Exposition (see page 40). On land created with sand dredged up from the bay (the birth of the Marina District), a group of noted architects was commissioned to erect temporary structures to house the Expo.

As their theme, the architects adopted the *beaux-arts* style which had graced similar fairs around the U.S. One of the architects was Bernard Maybeck, and it was his dream-like Palace of Fine Arts which captured the imagination of the Expo's 20 million visitors more than any other building.

Designed as a Roman ruin, Maybeck's inspired work used a classical domed rotunda as its centerpiece and flanked this with a fragmented colonnade, each group of columns topped by weeping maidens and decorated by aimless stairways and funeral urns. The intention was to instill a sense of "moderated sadness" to prepare visitors for the classical art exhibited in the Expo's Great Hall (now housing the Exploratorium, see page 82).

As the other Expo buildings were razed, public admiration and the fact that the army owned the land (rather than private speculators, who quickly developed what became the Marina District), enabled the Palace of Fine Arts to remain. By the late 1950s, however, the structure was becoming a genuine ruin rather than a symbolic one, and a campaign was launched to save it.

At a cost of $7.5 million, the restored Palace—its features replicated in concrete—was unveiled in 1967. Though longer-lasting than Maybeck ever intended, the Palace has lost none of its mysterious enchantment. Take a stroll through the archways and stand beneath the 132ft.-high rotunda, and pause to ponder the structure's haunting reflection among the birdlife of the adjacent lagoon.

► **Performing Arts Library & Museum** *IFCE4*

399 Grove Street
Bus: 21

It may have been regarded as the wild capital of the Wild West, but settlers in gold-rush-era San Francisco were quick to display a taste for the performing arts. No fewer than 5,000 operatic performances took place in the city between 1849 and the 1906 earthquake, and during this time all the celebrated performers of the day—be they populist vaudeville entertainers like Lola Montez, adored actresses such as Sarah Bernhardt, or opera stars of the caliber of Enrico Caruso—included San Francisco on their U.S. tours. It was also here that the U.S. saw its first full-length *Swan Lake* and its first complete *Nutcracker*.

The proof of the city's long-thriving cultural scene is to be found among the million or more individual items—spanning posters, programs, costumes, rare footage of early shows on lithograph and more recent ones on video—stored and carefully cataloged by the Performing Arts Library & Museum.

Not surprisingly, not all of the material can be displayed at any one time. The museum does, however, mount stimulating temporary exhibitions, and the library is a great resource for anyone wishing to delve deeper into the city's performing arts past.

► **Potrero Hill** *IFCF3*

Bus: 15

Between the Mission District and the docks of the eastern waterfront, primarily residential Potrero Hill is off the beaten tourist track. Nonetheless, the **Esprit Quilt Collection** (see page 81) provides one reason to visit the area, and another is the **Anchor Steam Brewery►** (1705 Mariposa Street), home of the beer synonymous with the city and offering hour-long tours followed by tastings (for an appointment, tel. 415/863 8350).

Also in Potrero Hill, **Vermont Street** stakes a claim to be even more crooked than Russian Hill's prettier and more famous—and much more crowded—Lombard Street.

The ins and outs of Lola Montez's provocative Spider Dance, which wowed San Franciscan audiences in the mid-1800s, are among the minutiae of the city's cultural life archived at the Performing Arts Library & Museum

The Potrero Hill Russians
One of San Francisco's more curious ethnic footnotes concerns the Potrero Hill Russians. The first Russians to live in San Francisco colonized this area from the 1850s and, half a century later during the Russo-Japanese War, many more arrived to avoid conscription into the Tsarist army. Many of them were dissenters from the Orthodox church and members of pietistic sects. The chickens and goats kept by these resolutely non-urban Russians were a feature of Potrero Hill until the 1950s.

■ **For the latest intrigue at City Hall or simply to find out which restaurants are worth going to, San Franciscans are avid readers and what they like to read about most is San Francisco. When not reading, they turn to the radio or TV for more Bay Area news and views.....■**

Gay publications
Published bi-monthly, the free *Bay Times* is an excellent source of news and information for gays, lesbians and bisexuals. Also free and worth reading is the politically orientated weekly *Bay Area Reporter*, and the strongly gay-male centerd *Sentinel*.

Daily newspapers The city's major newspapers are the *San Francisco Chronicle* and *San Francisco Examiner*, the former appearing in the morning and the latter in the afternoon. Formerly arch rivals, the two papers are now under the same ownership (and are combined on Sundays) with separate staff. Its morning appearance helps make the *Chronicle* the most popular but the *Examiner* often compensates for its later publication with in-depth features.

Top and below: San Franciscan newspaper vendors await customers

Free newspapers The former rivalry of the *Chronicle* and *Examiner* is echoed by the acrimony between the city's major free weekly newspapers, the *San Francisco Bay Guardian* and *SF Weekly*. Both take a left-of-center stance in their reports on city news and the arts, and carry extensive listings. The *Bay Guardian* was founded in the 1960s; *SF Weekly* started in 1989, and demonstrates its youthfulness with a sharper writing style and better coverage of contemporary culture. It is the *Guardian*, though, which is most likely to expose corruption in high places with well-researched investigative journalism.

Magazines
Several glossy magazines devote themselves to city life each month: *San Francisco* focuses on the comings and goings of the rich and chic; *San Francisco Focus* carries lively features on varied San Franciscan affairs and people.

Radio Aided by several college stations and the diverse interests of the local population, San Francisco and the Bay Area have an abundance of radio stations, offering everything from Top 40 pop music to analysis of international affairs.

Television A number of local and foreign-language cable channels add to the usual network fare. Most hotel room TVs carry a selection of cable and pay-TV channels, and/or in-house movie rental channels. The main San Francisco TV channels are 2 KTVU (FOX), 4 KRON (NBC), 5 KPIX (CBS), 7 KGO (ABC), 9 KQED (PBS); only PBS differs from the rest, with no commercials and predominantly serious programs.

► **The Presidio** *IFCC5*

Main Gate at the junction of Lombard and Lyon streets
Bus: 29

Across the more than 1,500 acres of hills and woodlands that cover the northwest corner of the city, the earliest Spanish settlers founded a presidio (or garrison) in 1776 to guard San Francisco Bay—though its limited armory and poor location made the Presidio a token defense—and protect Mission Dolores, then being established in what is now the Mission District (see page 124).

As Mexico sought and eventually acquired independence from Spain, keeping the settlement supplied became more trouble than it was worth for the Spanish, and the Presidio, along with its adobe buildings, was abandoned.

Following the U.S. acquisition of California in 1846, the Presidio regained a military function and spent many years as the base of the U.S. Sixth Army until it was decommissioned in the early 1990s, its land becoming part of Golden Gate National Recreation Area (see page 99).

The heart of the Presidio is on Lombard Street at the junction with Funston Avenue, where several of the 19th-century buildings remain, as does (on Moraga Avenue) the **Officers' Club►**, which still contains part of an adobe wall from the Spanish era and is marked by a small plaque.

A short walk away, more substantial pieces of Presidio history are exhibited in the charmingly verandahed Old Station Hospital, dating from 1857 and the oldest complete building here, which holds the **Presidio Army Museum►**. With uniforms, maps, weapons, and a thousand-and-one pieces of army insignia, the museum tells the story of the Presidio and charts the role of the building itself, which served as a military hospital from 1899.

There is also an excellent display on the city's 1906 earthquake and the 1915 Panama–Pacific Exposition; outside are two of the "refugee cottages," rented to homeless survivors of the 1906 catastrophe for $2 a month.

Presidio pet cemetery

A Spanish view
In 1776, contemplating the outlook from the hill which would later hold the Presidio, Franciscan missionary and expedition cartographer Pedro Font recorded in his diary: "This mesa affords a most delightful view, for from it one sees a large part of the port and its islands...the mouth of the harbor, and all of the sea that the eye can take in."

Emergency earthquake housing, 1906

The Russians of Russian Hill

Russian Hill is believed to have been named after a group of Russians who were working for a fur-trapping company on the northern Californian coast in the early 1800s, when they perished during an expedition and were buried on the southeast crest of what became Russian Hill. The story is given credence by historical records.

Temple Emanu-El

The bulbous Byzantine-style dome that looms above the northern section of the Richmond District belongs to Temple Emanu-El, a 2,000-seat synagogue serving the oldest Jewish congregation in California, founded in 1850. Completed in 1926 at a cost of $3 million, one of the temple's architects was Arthur Brown, of City Hall fame (see page 78).

In the commercial maelstrom of the Richmond District's Clement Street, are some of the best Asian restaurants in the city

► ▓ **Richmond District**   *IFCB5*

Buses: 1, 2, 5, 28, 31, 38

What might otherwise be a fairly bland residential district filling the space between Golden Gate Park and the Presidio, the Richmond District has been enlivened since the mid-1970s by a major influx of Asian-Americans, including particularly large numbers of Chinese. Thirty-five percent of San Francisco's substantial Chinese population now resides here.

The Chinese influence, with Thai and Vietnamese also well-established, is most apparent along the district's main commercial artery, Clement Street, which is lined by Asian restaurants, bakeries, and supermarkets.

Also found on Clement Street, and along nearby Geary Boulevard, are the longer-established German, Russian, and East European cafés and stores reflecting the ethnic origins of earlier generations of Richmond District settlers. Further indication of the Russian presence is provided by the **Cathedral of the Holy Virgin** (6210 Geary Boulevard), the western U.S.'s seat of the Russian Orthodox religion and dating from 1961.

► ▓ **Rincon Center**   *IBCE3*

Mission Street between Spear and Steuart streets
Buses: 1, 32

Enter the spacious atrium of the Rincon Center at lunchtime and you are liable to find snack-munching office workers being entertained by a dinner-suited pianist, the sound underscored by the splashes of a fountain tumbling 90ft. down a wall.

Opened in 1988, the modern building was cleverly grafted onto the rear of the 1939 **Rincon Annexe Post Office►** building, the delectable artdeco form of which is heightened by Anton Refregiar's **murals►►**. Showing scenes from the Spanish conquering of Native Americans to the violent industrial disputes of the 1930s, the hard-hitting murals—financed by a WPA grant (see page 175)—caused predictable controversy on their unveiling and still make for compulsive viewing.

Above: famously crooked Lombard Street. Left: the Rincon Center, inspired modern architecture

Ina Coolbrith Park
A much-admired poet, Ina Coolbrith was a Russian Hill resident and became California's first poet laureate in 1919. She did much to nurture aspiring writers—Jack London and Ambrose Bierce among them—from the time of her arrival in San Francisco in 1862 until her death in 1928. Ina Coolbrith Park (junction of Vallejo and Taylor streets) is the city's only park named in honor of a writer.

Macondray Lane
Steep slopes notwithstanding, much of Russian Hill makes pleasant strolling territory. The slender Macondray Lane is a charming tree-lined street that stretches for two pedestrian-only blocks between Union and Green streets. It can be reached from a wooden staircase which rises sharply above Taylor Street, a block and a half north of Ina Coolbrith Park.

▶▶ **Russian Hill**   *IBCB5*

Buses: 15, 30, 41, 45

Most visitors stay in Russian Hill only long enough to point their cameras at the section of **Lombard Street**▶▶ famously hailed as "the crookedest street in San Francisco;" its descent between Hyde and Leavenworth streets is landscaped into a series of curves decorated by herbaceous plants and shrubs. The steepness of the grade made the street impassable for vehicles until the gardens were added in the 1920s, enabling traffic to make the downward journey in a corkscrewing fashion.

Take a look at Lombard Street, but while on Russian Hill also take the opportunity to visit the **San Francisco Art Institute**, the oldest art school on the West Coast, described fully on page 159.

Russian Hill also boasts many notable examples of the architectural styles that have shaped San Francisco. Several interesting places on the 1000 block of Green Street include the **Feusier Octagon House**▶ (number 1067), one of the city's two remaining eight-sided dwellings, partially hidden by shrubbery (see also Octagon House, page 145).

St Mary's Cathedral, which seems even bigger on the inside than the imposing exterior suggests

The three cathedrals
Anyone visiting Chinatown after touring St. Mary's Cathedral might like to contrast its striking size and modernity with the compact interior of Old St. Mary's Church (see page 72), which served as the city's Catholic cathedral until 1891. From 1891, the role was taken on by a new St. Mary's built in impressively proportioned redbrick style at the junction of Van Ness Avenue and O'Farrell Street, until it succumbed to fire in 1962.

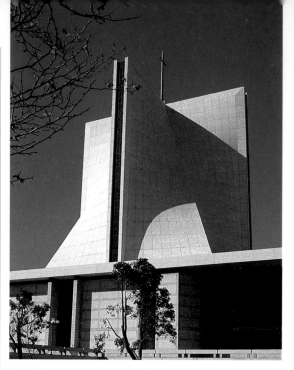

▶▶　　**St. Mary's Cathedral**　　　　　*IFCE5*

Geary Boulevard at Gough Street
Buses: 19, 38
Four hyperbolic paraboloids rising 190 feet into the air and forming the shape of a Greek cross help make St. Mary's Cathedral (formally St. Mary's Catholic Cathedral of the Assumption) the most striking piece of modern religious architecture in San Francisco. Built at a cost of $7 million, the cathedral opened in 1971 and replaced a previous St. Mary's destroyed by fire in 1962 after serving the city's Catholic community for 71 years. Inside, the abiding feeling is one of space. The open-plan cathedral can seat 2,500 people, and its design is intended to eliminate the usual divisions between a cathedral's different areas. Here, the apse, nave, transepts, baptistry, and narthex are undivided beneath the towering ceiling, in the center of which is a skylight in the shape of the Cross. The four stained-glass windows which rise from floor to ceiling in each main wall represent the four elements.

▶　　**St. Paulus Lutheran Church**　　　　　*IFCE5*

Corner of Gough and Eddy streets
Bus: 31
A short walk from the modernist St. Mary's Cathedral is the homely wooden form, in a style dubbed "San Francisco Gothic," of St Paulus Lutheran Church, completed in 1894 at a cost of $65,000. Modeled in part on Chartres in France, the church survived the major earthquakes of 1906 and 1989 more or less intact, but was almost destroyed by fire in 1940. The stained-glass window behind the altar, depicting a descending dove, dates from the original construction. The church is usually only opened for Sunday services; to view at other times, contact the church office (950 Gough Street; tel. 415/673 8088).

▶▶ **San Francisco Art Institute** IFCE6

800 Chestnut Street
Bus: 30
Founded in 1871 (see panel) and moving to its current premises in 1926, the San Francisco Art Institute is the oldest art school on the West Coast, and still one of the region's most respected bases of artistic learning and creativity. Equally as appealing as the student art which hangs in the corridors and galleries, however, is the building itself, styled after a Mediterranean monastery and including a cozy courtyard often enlivened by avant-garde student sculpture.

Acclaimed Mexican muralist Diego Rivera taught at the institute for a brief period in the 1930s and a work of his—an intriguing mural of a mural-in-progress which includes a self-portrait—covers one wall of the **Diego Rivera Gallery**▶ (see also page 151). A 1970 addition, a **café** with inexpensive food, where you might mingle with the students, or just enjoy the views of Fisherman's Wharf. Before leaving, be sure to glance at the bell tower, said to be haunted by the spirits of frustrated artists.

▶ **San Francisco Craft & Folk Art Museum** IFCD6

Building A, Fort Mason
Bus: 28
It may be a tough job to predict what might be on display at the San Francisco Craft & Folk Art Museum, but few of the shows mounted here fail to be informative and entertaining. Recent ones have explored the strange world of the decoy duck, examined the folk art of the former Soviet Union, and focused on improvisation in African-American quilt making.

The mission of the museum is three-fold: to exhibit fine examples of handicrafts; to highlight the folk art of untrained artists which would otherwise be ignored by museums; and to use traditional ethnic art to promote understanding between the diverse cultures which exist among the population of San Francisco and the Bay Area.

A visit here can be a delight: be sure to include it on your Fort Mason itinerary (see page 96).

The Art Institute

159

Art Institute origins
What became San Francisco Art Institute was originally the San Francisco Art Association, set up in 1871 and the first art school west of the Mississippi.

Diego Rivera mural

Matisse's Woman
with the Hat *(1905)*

▶▶▶ **San Francisco Museum of
Modern Art**   *IFCF5*

151 Third Street
Buses: 14, 15, 26, 30, 45
During the 1940s, the decade-old San Francisco Museum
of Modern Art established its forward-thinking credentials
by presenting the first solo exhibitions by the pioneering
artists of abstract expressionism—Ashile Gorky, Jackson
Pollock, Robert Motherwell, and Mark Rothko—but its
continued emergence as a major showplace of modern
art was restricted by lack of space.

With its new custom-built six-storey premises formally
opened in January 1995, however, the San Francisco
Museum of Modern Art finally looks set to become one of
the country's leading art centers, and one with the room
and facilities to mount challenging exhibitions in the new
fields of video, computer, and interactive art.

The core of the permanent collections is shown in the
third-floor galleries, which highlight painting and sculpture
from 1900 to 1970. Here you will find significant contribu-

tions from Europeans, including Pablo Picasso's *Head in Three-quarter View* and *The Coffee Pot*, and what might be the zenith of analytical cubism: Georges Braque's *Violin and Candlestick*.

Be sure not to miss the museum's most prized possession: Matisse's seminal *Woman with the Hat* (1905), a work which made a crucial contribution to what became Fauvism, the century's first radical art movement.

There is also a formidable and engaging stock of German Expressionism and over 100 works by Paul Klee, often arranged into special exhibitions. Surrealism also features, with secondary offerings from primary figures such as Salvador Dali and Max Ernst.

Screaming more loudly for attention, however, are a striking complement of abstract expressionist canvases. Jackson Pollock's *Guardians of the Secret* is foremost among them, but there are notable contributions from fellow gesturist Willem de Kooning, and the last completed work by leading color-field painter, Barnett Newman.

Sharing the third floor are architecture and design exhibitions, ranging from drawings by early San Francisco-shaper Willis Polk (see panel, page 112) to a full set of office furniture by L.A.-based modernist designers, Charles and Ray Eames.

The fourth floor holds some fine 20th-century photography from international greats such as Man Ray and Moholy-Nagy, and equally well-acclaimed local practitioners such as Ansel Adams (see page 56) and Edward Weston. There is a unique collection of 1920s and 1930s experimental photography from eastern and central Europe.

On the fifth floor, the museum keeps its video, audio, and interactive installations.

It is hard to visit the new Museum of Modern Art without forming some impression of the $60-million building which contains it. The museum was the first project in the U.S. by award-winning Mario Botta, a Swiss architect who worked with major figures such as Le Corbusier and Louis Kahn during his formative years. Aiming for a modernist boldness without becoming severe, the museum has a stepped-back brick-and-stone façade with a truncated cylinder rising through its center, decorated in bands of black and white brick. Inside, the cylinder keeps natural light flooding into a full-height atrium, while visitors moving through the galleries enjoy a sense of openness.

Jackson Pollock's Guardians of the Secret *(1943)*

Mexican modernism
While many of the major names of North American and European art are represented in the museum, there are also several welcome examples of modern Mexican painting. Look for Diego Rivera's *Flower Carrier* and *Kneeling Child on Yellow Background*, Frida Kahlo's *Frida and Diego Rivera*, and Joaquin Torres-Garcia's *Constructivist Painting No. 8*.

161

The museum from Yerba Buena Gardens

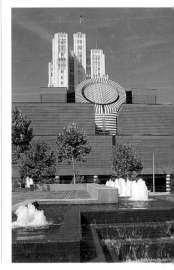

Located several miles from the city center, the San Francisco Zoo requires a special effort to reach. Once there, don't expect the peacocks to show any gratitude

Sutro's library
Adolph Sutro roamed Europe in the 1880s seeking material for what would become the world's largest private library. The treasures he returned with included the world's largest collection of pre-1500 printed books (termed "incunabula"), Lutheran pamphlets including 15 by Martin Luther himself, ancient Hebrew scrolls, and the first four folios of Shakespeare. Sadly, around half of the collection was destroyed in San Francisco's 1906 fire. Much of what remains is devoted to genealogy and U.S. and Mexican history. Although geared to the serious researcher, the library is open to the public and has several cases of objects relating to San Franciscan history.

▶ **San Francisco State University**   *IFCB2*
1600 Holloway Avenue
Buses: 17, 28, 29
Fans of singer Johnny Mathis, once a student here, may enjoy strolling around San Francisco State University, but for anyone else the unprepossessing campus holds little of interest. It does provide a home, however, to the **American Poetry Archives▶**. Works held here are by and about American writers as diverse as Walt Whitman and Amy Tan, and interviews with many recent American authors are available on audiol and video tape.

Books also feature just off campus at 480 Winston Avenue, where the **Sutro Library** (see panel) maintains the vast collection of books bequeathed to the city by wealthy philanthropist Adolph Sutro (see page 171).

▶ **San Francisco Zoological Gardens**   *IFCA2*
Sloat Boulevard and 45th Avenue
Buses: 18, 23
A grizzly bear called Monarch, captured by the *San Francisco Examiner* as a publicity stunt in 1899, is remembered as its first inmate, but the San Francisco Zoo only really began in the 1920s when it acquired a 60-acre plot of land at its present site. While the zoo has greatly improved over recent years, replacing many cages with natural and psychological barriers to keep animals and humans separate, it is not one of the city's top attractions, and its location—several miles southeast of downtown—means a special journey is required to reach it.

The zoo's most successful section is **Gorilla World▶**, costing $2 million in the 1980s and probably one of the most luxurious places for a captive gorilla to find him- or herself. Elsewhere, the zoo has the usual complement of koalas, tigers, lions, and rhinos, insect and reptile houses, and a **Children's Zoo▶** with plenty of furry four-legged creatures waiting to be stroked.

▶▶ **Sausalito**   *44A3*

Buses: Golden Gate Transit
Ferries: from the Ferry Building or Fisherman's Wharf
A 19th-century whaling port and rail terminal, Sausalito also acquired a significant ship-building industry during the 1940s and became a stomping ground of artists, bohemians, and misfits from the 1950s. Few of these things are immediately evident in today's Sausalito, the bayside community having evolved into an affluent—if still non-conformist—San Francisco suburb.

With many of its homes set across a steep-sided hill and linked by winding, tree-lined streets and pathways, the small and picturesque town has also become a major day-trip destination. Try to visit in midweek and arrive on an early ferry, thereby securing at least a few hours of peaceful exploration before the midday crowds arrive.

Besides its scenic appeal and a number of raffish bars located along Bridgeway, the main thoroughfare, Sausalito initially appears to have little other than souvenir shops, ice-cream outlets and a few noted restaurants.

But climb up any near-vertical street (some are accessed by stairs) for a taste of local living and a memorable view of San Francisco across the bay, and then continue for half a mile or so north along Bridgeway—leaving the commercial area behind—to discover two of Sausalito's best-kept secrets.

Built by the Army Corps of Engineers, the **Bay Model**▶▶ is a scale re-creation of San Francisco Bay across a 2-acre indoor site. Enabling the study of water flow and tidal patterns in the bay, the model has gangways lined with informative texts on Bay Area ecology; an introductory film describes the model in detail.

Further along Bridgeway is a community of brightly painted **houseboats**. These floating homes have been decorated with individual flair by their owners, who have resisted attempts to be moved.

William Richardson
Sausalito's name derives from the Spanish word *saucelito*, or willow grove, which was given to the 20,000-acre ranch granted in 1838 by California's Mexican governor to English-born William Richardson. Previously a whaler, Richardson had settled in Yerba Buena (as San Francisco was then known) in 1822 and married the daughter of the Presidio's commander. Responsible for enforcing Mexican trade bans and collecting taxes from vessels using the bay, Richardson allegedly also led a smuggling operation from Sausalito's sheltered coves.

163

Escape from the pressures of freeway driving: live on a Sausalito houseboat and commute to work by yacht

■ **Sports have a hold on the American mind, and few San Franciscans are exceptions to this rule. Where they differ noticeably from the residents of many other U.S. cities, however, is in their embracing of participant sports. The passion for getting out and keeping fit is perhaps induced by an extraordinarily high level of health awareness, and by living among some of the finest surroundings for outdoors pursuits to be found anywhere in the country.....■**

Golf

San Francisco not only has affordable public golf courses but it also has some of the most dramatic landscapes in which to birdie, bogey, or just lose your ball. There is an 18-hole course at Lincoln Park (entrance at 34th and Clement streets; tel. 415/221 9911) and a pitch-and-putt 9-hole course in Golden Gate Park (tel. 415/751 8987). Greens fees are slightly more expensive at Lincoln Park than at Golden Gate Park.

Radio station KNBR supports the Giants!

Bay to Breakers

Held on the third Sunday in May, the Bay to Breakers race draws tens of thousands—athletes, weekend runners and exhibitionists—to compete over a 7.5-mile course from the Ferry Building to the Great Highway.

Baseball During the April to October baseball season, the **San Francisco Giants** draw large crowds to Candlestick Park, 8 miles south of the city. Tickets are available from the stadium box office (tel. 415/467 8000) and through an agency, BASS Ticketmaster (tel. 510/762 2277). On game days, the "Ballpark Express" bus runs between the city and Candlestick Park.

(Note that the Giants have plans to move to a new venue during the mid-1990s.)

Across the bay, the **Oakland Athletics** (or "A's") play in a different league from the Giants and have the ultramodern 50,000-seat Oakland Coliseum Stadium to call home. Tickets (similarly priced to the Giants') are available through the BASS agency mentioned above, and from the Coliseum box office (tel. 510/638 0500). The BART system (see page 252) links San Francisco to Oakland, where the Coliseum has its own stop.

Football The five-times Superbowl winners **San Francisco 49ers** are also based at Candlestick Park ("49ers" relates to the 1849 gold rush in which San Francisco played a major part, see page 32). Their season runs from August to December with most games played on Sundays, kicking off at 1p.m. For ticket details, tel. 415/468 2249. Be warned, however, that all seats are usually sold months (if not years) in advance. Some tickets may be available at marked-up prices (the face value is generally upwards of $25) through agencies such as Ticketron (tel. 415/392 7469).

Avid football fans unable to obtain a ticket for the 49ers might cross the bay to the Berkeley campus, where the professionals of tomorrow play for the University of California's **Golden Bears** at the campus's Memorial Stadium. Tickets (usually under $10) are sold on campus at the Athletic Ticket Office; for details, tel. 1-800/GO BEARS.

Basketball Basketball fans resident in San Francisco must travel to Oakland to see the Bay Area's sole professional basketball team—the **Golden State Warriors**—in Western Conference action at the Coliseum Arena (see above). The basketball season runs from October to April, and most games are played on weekday evenings from 7.30p.m. Tickets are available through the BASS agency and at the Coliseum box office.

Participant sports No visitor to San Francisco who arrives with jogging clothes and energy to burn will find themselves running alone. The city has innumerable popular jogging places: Golden Gate Park, Marina Green, Golden Gate Promenade (between Fisherman's Wharf and Fort Point), and Lake Merced (near Fort Funston, part of Golden Gate National Recreation Area) are just four of the many popular locations. Hills notwithstanding, the simplest and most enjoyable participant sport for visitors is **cycling**. The city has two excellent posted scenic bike routes. One stretches from Golden Gate Park to Lake Merced, the other winds south to north across the city and crosses the Golden Gate Bridge into Marin County. Depending on the model, bike rental costs around $5 an hour (or $20 a day). Rental outlets are plentiful along Stanyan Street, on the east side of Golden Gate Park; many others are listed in the Yellow Pages. More daringly, **Golden Gate Parasailing and Power Boat Rides** (tel. 415/399 1139), provide the chance to parasail above San Francisco Bay or skim across it in a powerboat. Meanwhile, the 200ft.-high cliffs at Fort Funston are a hang-glider's delight.

Baseball fills Candlestick Park to capacity

San Francisco marathon
On a Sunday in mid-July, several thousand runners compete in the San Francisco marathon (regarded by San Franciscans with less affection than the Bay to Breakers race) that includes a crossing of the Golden Gate Bridge en route to the finish line in Golden Gate Park.

Below and opposite, top: San Francisco 49ers

SOMA

South of the Slot
In the days when cable cars ran along Market Street, SoMa was known as "South of the Slot," a reference to the cable-car slot in the middle of the road. A ballad of the day ran:

"Whether you know your
   location or not,
The heart of the city is
   south o' the slot!
That is the spot,
True to the dot,
The heart of the city is
   south o' the slot"!

The media attention focused on SoMa over the last few years has brought about a revival of interest in some of the neighborhood's architecturally distinguished older structures, such as the U.S. Post Office and Court of Appeals Building, shown below, dating from 1902

▶ **SoMa** *IFCF5*

Buses: 15, 30, 45

No part of San Francisco has changed as quickly or as dramatically over the last 10 years as SoMa (its name an abbreviation of its location, South of Market Street), a traditionally industrial, downtrodden, and sometimes dangerous area, which is now a showplace of art and architecture and home to a growing population of creative professionals.

In the late 1800s, while the city's rich were outspending each other building palatial homes on Nob Hill or in Pacific Heights, the flatlands south of Market Street were exclusively the domain of the laboring classes. Unloading cargo ships and toiling in rail freight yards were SoMa's main occupations, and many of the city's militant labor leaders of the 1930s emerged from the neighborhood.

As shifting economic and transportation patterns caused SoMa's warehouses and factories to be abandoned during the 1970s, a small group of artists—eager for light-filled loft apartments—moved into some of them, and avant-garde galleries opened at ground level to display the artists' output.

Simultaneously, a section of Folsom Street suddenly found itself at the center of the city's newest nightlife scene, with a host of clubs and restaurants opening up to take advantage of SoMa's rising profile and its still comparatively low rents.

When the vast Moscone Convention Center opened in 1981, it provided the icing on the cake of SoMa's gentrification. In its wake came high-rise hotels—such as the distinctive Marriott—bringing more money and people into the district.

By far the most ambitious project, however, is the still-evolving **Yerba Buena Gardens**▶▶, a 12-block area enclosed by Market, Harrison, Second, and Fifth streets. Encompassing a landscaped garden complete with

Close up: the U.S. Post Office and Court of Appeals Building

SoMa's streets of sin
Three of SoMa's side streets—Jessie, Clementina, and Minna—are said to be named after a trio of the city's best-known 19th-century prostitutes.

Art-deco plumbing
After the 1906 earthquake and fire devastated the city, the authorities were determined that San Francisco would never again be left without an emergency water supply. An innovative system of pumps was devised, and the San Francisco Fire Department Pumping Station, 698 Second Street, was unveiled in 1920, destined to be better appreciated for its early art-deco style than the usefulness of the apparatus which it housed.

The 1920s Pacific Telephone Building, which houses the Telephone Communications Museum

Yerba Buena Gardens—new territory for SoMa joggers

decorative waterfall, Yerba Buena Gardens also holds the bold and expansive **Yerba Buena Arts Center**, with a theater, galleries, and facilities for mounting the latest hi-tech multimedia exhibitions.

Set to become the city's cultural heart, Yerba Buena Gardens is in the process of acquiring several of the city's institutions: the California Historical Society (see page 66), the Cartoon Art Museum (see page 68), the Mexican Museum (see page 117), and the Jewish Museum (see page 115), are all planning to move here (and some may have done so by the time you read this). One which has already relocated is the San Francisco Museum of Modern Art (see pages 160–1), into stunning new quarters at 151 Third Street.

If you are already familiar with Telegraph Hill's Coit Tower (see pages 174–5), you might like to contemplate the similarities between it—one of the city's favorite landmarks—and **One Park Center**, part of the Yerba Buena Gardens complex under construction on the corner of Mission and Third streets. A 28-story cylindrical office tower, One Park Center allegedly takes its inspiration from Telegraph Hill's best-known feature.

Just along Mission Street, the dark-glass peak of the **Marriott Hotel▶** can be seen across much of San Francisco and generally wins more favor among visitors than locals. Derided as the "jukebox Marriott," the building seems set to endure the fate of the Transamerica Pyramid two decades earlier—loathed at first but eventually welcomed as a distinctive addition to the city skyline.

If the hotel does not appeal, one way to escape from the sight of it is by going inside and taking the elevator to the 39th-floor View Lounge, for a city panorama spared what many San Franciscans consider its latest eyesore.

Quaint and anachronistic it may appear in the Marriott's shadow, but the Gothic-style **St. Patrick's Church▶** (756 Mission Street) is a sturdy survivor. Still bearing the scars of the 1906 earthquake, the church is decorated with the Irish national colors of green, white, and gold, ancient Celtic patterns are embroidered on its vestments, and its stained-glass windows depict scenes from the life of Saint Patrick.

Even so, St. Patrick's original Irish congregation has long since departed, and its regular worshippers are now predominantly Filipino. This is one of the few places in San Francisco where you will hear mass conducted in Tagalog.

Another survivor is the elegant, stepped-back skyscraper completed in 1925 for the Pacific Telephone Company (140 New Montgomery Street). Enter the lobby of this fine building and turn right for the **Telephone Communications Museum►►**, where rope-like cables, vintage switchboards, and many weird and wonderful telephones combine to tell the tale of moving messages around the West Coast, and where a special display reveals the innermost secrets of the telephone pole.

A few blocks south of Yerba Buena Gardens, the elevated I-80 cuts above SoMa carrying traffic to and from the Bay Bridge. Just beyond the freeway between Second and Third streets, **Jack London Street** is named after the writer born in the district in 1876. Although the site is disputed, a plaque on the wall of the Wells Fargo Bank (601 Third Street), near the junction with Brannan Street, claims to mark the precise location of **Jack London's birthplace**.

► Sunset District   *IFCB3*

Buses: 66, 71

In most U.S. cities, a home overlooking the ocean is the stuff dreams are made of. This is rarely the case in San Francisco, where regular fog renders what might be a stunning ocean vista invisible, and cause local temperatures to drop as other parts of the city bask in sunshine.

At the city's western edge and known as the Great Sand Waste before the creation of Golden Gate Park—immediately north—stimulated its settlement, the Sunset District sometimes has the spectacular sunsets which its name suggests, but to enjoy them locals must leave their tidy, suburban-style homes and make their way across the Great Highway to Ocean Beach (see page 145)—and hope for the fog to stay away.

SoMa's Ukrainian Orthodox Church
St. Patrick's is not the only SoMa church to have seen its original congregation move on. The 1906 Ukrainian Orthodox Church of St. Michael (345 Seventh Street), a striking twin-towered affair approached by a double stairway flanked by palm trees, no longer sits at the heart of a sizeable Ukrainian community. It does, however, retain an important cultural significance for the city's Ukrainian *émigrés* and their descendants.

Viewed from Yerba Buena Gardens, the controversial Marriott Hotel towers above St. Patrick's Church

The vast Sutro salt-water baths in their heyday

A Sutro Park lion

▶ **Sutro Heights Park** IFCA5

Buses: 18, 38

Part of the 1,000-acre plot purchased and developed by the remarkable Adolph Sutro (see page 171) in the 1880s, and what is now Sutro Heights Park was formerly the site of Sutro's mansion home. A pair of stone lions and a statue of Venus are the main remnants of the house, occupied by Sutro's daughter, Emma, until her death in 1938.

Take an invigorating stroll across the breezy, tree-studded park and then wind your way across Point Lobos Avenue to the site of the Sutro Baths. Again, only ruins remain from what was Sutro's most cherished contribution to San Francisco: a salt-water bath house spread across a 3-acre indoor site that opened in 1896.

A devout capitalist but one with socialist leanings, Sutro never worried about recouping the $600,000 he spent on the baths and undermined the profit-crazed Southern Pacific Railroad company by laying his own streetcar line to bring people to the baths from the city for a fare of just 5¢.

A 40-piece orchestra playing from a floating platform celebrated the baths' opening, and subsequent entertainment included circus acts—one was a man credited with "eating, drinking and smoking" underwater—and competitions for the public, such as underwater walking races.

The baths used an ingenious engineering system to pipe 1.8 million gallons of salt water from the ocean into seven separate pools, each one maintained at a particular temperature. Meanwhile, three levels of galleries displayed some of the objects—medieval armor, Aztec pottery, stuffed animals, and more—which Sutro had acquired on his world travels and which he hoped would inspire and educate the citizenry.

The baths remained enormously popular into the 1920s, but with his heirs not sharing Sutro's altruistic bent, they fell steadily into decline and were destroyed by fire in 1966.

Adolph Sutro

■ **Rarely in the history of American cities has a mayor been as popular or as altruistic as Adolph Sutro, a millionaire philanthropist elected to San Francisco's highest public office in 1894 but, curiously enough, still best remembered for his salt-water bathhouse.....■**

Born in Prussia in 1830, Adolph Sutro arrived in San Francisco at age 21, eager to claim his share of the gold rush. In fact, he ran a tobacco shop before heading for the mining regions, and it was fortuitous shares in a silver, rather than a gold mine which brought him his first taste of serious money.

Sutro's major venture, however, was a new system of tunneling, using improved methods of drainage and ventilation to allow miners better access to the lucrative seams. Although the silver barons of the time attempted to outwit him, Sutro went ahead with his plans, raising $6.5 million and winning federal approval for a 3-mile tunnel with 2 miles of lateral branches through Nevada's silver-rich Comstock Lode.

Recognizing that the silver bonanza was about to end, Sutro sold the tunnel in 1879 and moved what was by now a substantial personal fortune into San Franciscan property, eventually owning a twelfth of the city and creating the 1,000-acre area still known as Sutro Heights.

Sutro's battles against the Big Four—the merchants turned corrupt railway barons who used their wealth and power to dominate Californian politics (see page 37)— earned him grassroots respect and helped him become the city's mayor in 1894, running as a Populist candidate. Occupying this political hot seat did not suit Sutro, however: the stubbornness which contributed to his success in business did not help him at City Hall, and his inability to delegate wrecked his eagerly awaited anti-corruption program. Sutro described the end of his two-year term as a "perfect blessing."

Before his death in 1898, Sutro financed two Cliff Houses (see page 80), founded what quickly grew into a major collection of rare books (see panel, page 162), donated land to the University of California and, most famously of all, built the Sutro Baths (see page 170), putting the healthy pleasures of indoor saltwater bathing within reach of every San Franciscan.

A man of the people, Adolph Sutro (below) also had friends in high places, such as President Harrison, with whom Sutro is pictured (above)

Sutro and eucalyptus
In the late 1800s Sutro played a part in the import of millions of eucalyptus seedlings into San Francisco for use as windbreaks and ground cover. This, however, has left California with an environmental headache: the fast-spreading eucalyptus has damaged other plant life and, when dead, its wood is a major fire hazard.

SWEDENBORGIAN CHURCH

Swedenborgian
Church

Swedenborgianism
San Francisco's
Swedenborgian Church is
one of 45 such churches
(serving an estimated 3,000
Swedenborgians) in the
U.S., the first of them
founded in the early 1800s
as the works of Swedish
scientist/mystic Emanuel
Swedenborg spread from
Europe. Believing that "the
church is within man, and
not without him",
Swedenborgianism values
personal development and
tolerance, and encourages
involvement in social
issues.

Tattoo art

▶ **Swedenborgian Church**   *IFCD5*
2107 Lyon Street
Buses: 3, 43
Few San Franciscans would be able to pinpoint the
whereabouts of the city's Swedenborgian Church,
though if you are in the area it would be a shame to miss
visiting this relatively minor but extremely intriguing
example of religious architecture.

In keeping with the Swedenborgian philosophy, which
regards nature as the symbol of the human soul, the
church is designed along the lines of a simple log cabin,
complete with fireplace and rough-hewn wood beams,
and its doorway is reached by passing through an effu-
sively planted garden.

Completed in 1895, the church is also a fine specimen
of the turn-of-the-century Arts & Crafts movement, which
the original pastor, Joseph Worcestor, helped to become
established in the Bay Area, partly by means of the brown
shingle homes which he himself designed.

The main architect of the church was Arthur Page
Brown, a seminal figure of the time and also responsible
for the Ferry Building (see page 83). Brown worked from
plans drawn up by, among others, Bernard Maybeck, better remembered for the Palace of Fine Arts (see panel,
page 152), and the mystically inclined Bruce Porter, who
designed the church's stained-glass windows.
Meanwhile Gustav Stickley's furniture, handcrafted from
Californian timber, continues the church's prevailing
themes, as do William Keith's landscape paintings.

▶ **Tattoo Art Museum**   *IBCC5*
837 Columbus Avenue
Bus: 30. Open afternoons and evenings only.
Getting a tattoo may not be top of your list of things to do
in San Francisco, but if you have ever considered
indulging in this form of body decoration, look inside this
working tattoo parlor—lined by photos of extravagantly
tattooed people.

▶ Telegraph Hill

Bus: 39

Telegraph Hill, rising with formidable steepness between North Beach and San Francisco Bay, once housed a strong complement of impoverished writers and artists but is now one of the city's most coveted residential addresses, graced by million-dollar homes offering stunning views. Standing on top of Telegraph Hill is the unmistakable Coit Tower, a memorial to the city's volunteer firemen erected in 1933 (see pages 174–5).

The steep slopes of Filbert and Greenwich streets as they lead from the tower down towards the bayfront Embarcadero have resulted in sections of each being traversed by stairways: the Filbert and Greenwich steps.

A wooden walkway comprises the uppermost portions of the **Filbert Steps▶▶** and is lined with greenery; the lush vegetation is the fruit of a 30-year labor-of-love by local resident Grace Marchant. It was the late Marchant who turned what was—believe it or not—a garbage dump into the welcome array of plants and shrubbery that you see today.

Carefully maintained Victorian cottages, far more expensive than their diminutive size might suggest, and said to have been saved from the 1906 fire by being dowsed in red wine, can be seen from the steps. The oldest among them, number 224, dates from 1863. Along the impossibly slender **Napier Lane▶**, just a few feet wide and accessed only from the steps, are more tiny cottages though, understandably, their residents do not appreciate casual visitors lingering longer than they need to.

The **Greenwich Steps▶** are also wooden for part of their course and cross Montgomery Street close to the landmark Julius Castle, a haphazardly assembled wood-framed restaurant built in 1923 and offering expensive northern Italian food.

From a slightly more recent period, take a look at the nautical motifs adorning the 1936 art deco apartment building at 1360 Montgomery Street. It was here that Humphrey Bogart took a glass-sided elevator to Lauren Bacall's apartment in the 1947 film, *Dark Passage*.

Filbert Steps: walking down is easier than walking up

173

Telegraph Hill's name
What is now Telegraph Hill has had a number of earlier names. During the 1840s, it was known as Windmill Hill but became Signal Hill following the installation of a semaphore on its summit, intended to notify city dwellers of ships entering the bay. The present name stems, simply enough, from the West Coast's first telegraph station, built on the hill in 1853.

■ **Uncharitably said to resemble a fire hose, Coit Tower sits at the top of Telegraph Hill and—strange but true—owes its existence to a young girl's fixation with San Francisco's firefighters. Much more than a city landmark, Coit Tower also holds a remarkable collection of 1930s murals, the political content of which put the tower at the center of a bitter controversy at the time of their completion.....■**

Fires and Lillie Coit
Various explanations have been put forward for Lillie Coit's obsession with fires and the men who put them out. One suggestion is that the young girl's fancy was really taken by the horses which then pulled the fire trucks. Perhaps more likely is the tale that as a child Lillie lost two of her friends when a fire broke out at the empty house in which they were playing and Lillie, after raising the alarm, tried to extinguish the flames herself.

Above and below: Coit Tower's murals. The detail shown below is from the "City Life" mural

Lillie Coit When the seven-year-old Lillie Hitchcock arrived in San Francisco in 1851, she began what would become a lifelong obsession with fires and firefighters—ferocious blazes being a regular feature of life in the fast-growing city.

Although groomed to take her place in high society (she was once presented to Napoleon III in Paris), Lillie became better known for her eccentric behavior. Even in San Francisco, it was considered unusual for women to wear men's clothes, play poker with dock workers, and smoke cigars, but Lillie (who married Howard Coit in 1868) did all three, and also relished her honorary membership of one of the city's fire crews.

When she died in 1929, Lillie left $100,000 for the beautification of the city, and it was decided to use these funds to erect a memorial to the city's volunteer firefighters. Volunteer companies were private firefighting organizations which existed prior to the creation of a municipally run Fire Department.

Arthur Brown, better known for City Hall, was chosen as the project's architect and the tower—actually a 210ft.-high reinforced concrete column—was completed in 1933.

174

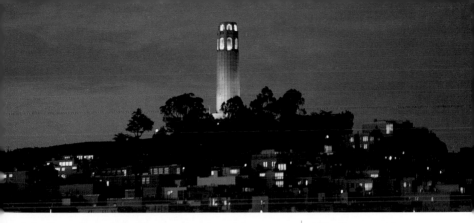

Coit Tower's murals

The long-running debate over whether or not it resembles a fire hose (the architect insisted that this was not part of the design), the tower's form and the views from its observation level play second fiddle to its interior decoration, a superb collection of Depression-era murals which cover the ground-floor walls.

As economic gloom gripped the country, 25 artists were each paid $94 a month by the Works Project Administration (WPA, which created work during the Depression) to cover the tower's interior walls with frescoes depicting life in California (see also page 156).

Controversy ensues

In the tradition of muralists such as Diego Rivera, many of the Coit Tower artists depicted the ordinary working people of California—the steel workers and farm laborers, and reflected the radical political ideas percolating through the financially stricken state.

When the murals were due to be unveiled in 1934, one of the bloodiest episodes in San Francisco's labor history (a dock workers' strike during which battles between strikers and police left two people dead) was in progress.

Against this background, a hammer-and-sickle, a copy of Karl Marx's *Das Kapital,* and a scene showing copies of the *Daily Worker* on sale at newsstands, all present in the murals, proved too much for the city authorities, and the opening was canceled. Following a picket by the Artists' Union, the tower and its murals were eventually opened in October 1934—but not until the offending hammer-and-sickle image had been removed.

Viewing the murals

While the murals vary greatly in style and quality, they collectively comprise one of the state's most important examples of public art and can be viewed for free.

Look in particular for the idealized farm workers in Maxine Albro's *California,* for John Langley Howard's *California Industrial Scenes* and its contrasting of migrants' camps with wealthy capitalists, and for Bernard Zakheim's *Library,* and its controversial image of a worker's hand reaching for *Das Kapital.*

Another mural worth studying is Victor Arnautoff's *City Life,* depicting the junction of Montgomery and Washington streets in San Francisco's Financial District. In the human maelstrom, a man is robbed at gunpoint as the unconcerned crowd flows by.

Whether or not it resembles the end of a fire hose is open to debate, but Coit Tower undoubtedly looks its best in the early dusk, silhouetted against the sunset sky

WPA art in San Francisco
The WPA's arts project was extremely active in San Francisco. In addition to the Coit Tower works, its money financed murals at the San Francisco Zoo and at the Rincon Annexe Post Office (see page 156), and Lucien Labaudt's depictions of recreational pursuits in 1930s San Francisco which adorn the walls of the Beach Chalet, a Willis Polk-designed building (currently closed to the public, though its murals can be glimpsed through the windows) beside the Great Highway on the western edge of Golden Gate Park.

Paper sons and daughters
The loss of official records in the 1906 fire stimulated a boom in "paper" sons and daughters from China claiming kinship with a U.S. resident. Officials at Angel Island devised intimidating questions for would-be immigrants, who could be held for weeks before being granted or denied entry. In the 30 years to 1940, 175,000 passed through successfully; some carved despairing poems on the walls, later published by the Chinese Cultural Foundation.

▶ **The Tenderloin** *IFCE5*
Buses: Any Civic Center bus
Bordered by the Civic Center and Mason Street, the Tenderloin is San Francisco's most depressing quarter, its bedraggled occupants living proof of the failure of the authorities—even in this supposedly liberal and enlightened city—to find a solution to large-scale homelessness. Although the problems of drug use and petty crime affect the area, and some sections are used by male and female prostitutes to solicit business from passing drivers, in the daytime the Tenderloin's streets are generally less dangerous than they may appear. You do, however, need to exercise greater than usual caution.

Currently, much is being made of the Tenderloin's growing band of Vietnamese and Cambodian restaurants, which have taken advantage of low rents, and almost always offer great food at bargain prices. Despite frequent claims to the contrary, however, restaurants alone are unlikely to rejuvenate the whole unhappy area.

Tiburon, an easy ferry ride from the city

Angel Island
The largest island in San Francisco Bay, Angel Island lies close to Tiburon and can be reached by Red & White Fleet ferries from Fisherman's Wharf, and by a summer service from Tiburon. Criss-crossed by cycle and foot trails, the island also contains buildings from its time as a military prison and immigration processing center.

▶ **Tiburon** *44B3*
Ferry: from Ferry Building or Fisherman's Wharf
While Sausalito (see page 163) is the major destination for tourists venturing across San Francisco Bay, discerning travelers opt instead for the quieter and smaller community of Tiburon, a few miles east of Sausalito and occupying a bucolic bayside niche.

Once ashore, you will find that Tiburon proper comprises little beyond Main Street and the shops and galleries which make up **Ark Row▶**, occupying dainty wood-framed buildings and, in some cases, one-time houseboats. To discover more, head for **Lyford House▶**, the home of a 19th-century doctor who tried to lure San Franciscans across the bay with the promise that Tiburon was better for their health and free of "vices and vampires." The house now serves as headquarters for the **Richardson Bay Audubon Center**, which administers a 900-acre wildlife refuge.

▶ **Transamerica Pyramid** *IFCF5*

600 Montgomery Street
Buses: 15, 42, 69

Since its 1972 unveiling, the Transamerica Pyramid has had no rivals as the dominant feature on the San Francisco skyline. Emerging from the Financial District's forest of even-sided high-rises, the 853ft. Pyramid's unique profile—a slowly-tapering spire flanked by windowless wings and with a tower continuing for 212 feet above the 48th floor—has even won over the majority of San Franciscans, despite widespread initial antipathy to the structure.

The building looks its best from a distance. The struts which support the Pyramid from ground level may offer improved earthquake safety but do nothing to enhance Montgomery Street. Similarly, the view from the 27th-floor **Observation Level** is not the dramatic panorama that might be hoped for, but is restricted to the parts of the city directly north of the tower.

Transamerica Redwood Park
On the eastern side of the Transamerica Pyramid, Tom Galli's half-acre Transamerica Redwood Park—a fountain and concrete plaza fringed by genuine redwood trees—offers a chance to escape the Financial District hubbub. On Friday lunchtimes during the summer months, the park hosts free concerts.

Financial District by moonlight

177

▶ **Treasure Island** *IFCG7*

Access by car only from Bay Bridge

A man-made island in San Francisco Bay, Treasure Island was created with the aid of a $3-million grant from WPA (a federal body administering funds to create jobs during the Depression) as the site of the 1939 Golden Gate International Exposition. Deemed unsuitable for its proposed post-Expo role as the city's airport, the island has been a U.S. Navy base since 1941. The **Treasure Island Museum** has exhibits on the Marine Corps and the U.S. Coast Guard, but of greater interest are those on the creation of the 400-acre island, the 1939 Expo and 1930s mementoes from Pan American Airways' China Clipper sea-plane: the last word in luxury trans-Pacific travel during the late 1930s.

Treasure Island resident

Money laundering
The St. Francis (now the Westin St. Francis) Hotel overlooking Union Square is the site of a major money laundering operation. In the 1930s, seeing the white gloves of society ladies soiled by grimy coins, the hotel began to clean all the coins that came into its possession. The practice continues today.

Union Square (below) and (above) its Dewey Monument

Buses: 30, 45

Dotted with climate-defying palm trees and cruised by hungry pigeons, Union Square is a pocket-sized piece of lackluster landscape gardening in the heart of the city which struggles to retain its dignity amid traffic noise and bustling pedestrians.

With big-name department stores, high-fashion retail outlets, and luxury hotels such as the esteemed St. Francis Hotel (see panel) overlooking the square, you might get the impression that Union Square itself is a part of San Franciscan high society. In fact, most people come here only to take a short cut or to retrieve their vehicles from the multi-level parking lot built beneath the square in the 1940s; this was the first parking lot of its kind and one which, in the war years, served the city as a potential bomb shelter.

San Francisco's first mayor, John W. Geary, allocated a plot of what was then rough scrubland for development as a grassy public space in 1850, but not until large-scale pro-Union rallies were staged on it prior to the Civil War did Union Square acquire its lasting name. In 1903, the square also acquired the 97ft. granite column topped by a figure of Victory to mark Admiral George Dewey's triumph over the Spanish fleet at Manila during the Spanish-American War.

Surviving the 1906 earthquake intact, Victory has since looked down upon numerous organized protests—from 1960s anti-Vietnam War marches to the 1990s gay political street theater of the Sisters of Perpetual Indulgence—which have exploited Union Square's central position, and on countless soap-box orators who have sought the ears of passersby.

Normally, the level of activity around the square discourages a leisurely rest on one of its benches, but the weekend art shows are a different story, as are the square's annual events such as April's Rhododendron Festival and August's Cable Car Bell-Ringing Contest (see page 26).

Wells Fargo History Museum   *IBCD4*

420 Montgomery Street
Buses: 15, 42, 69
Having established an express mail service in the eastern U.S. by the 1840s, Henry Wells and William G. Fargo began viewing the opportunities offered by gold-crazed California with relish and opened an office in San Francisco in 1852. Whether buying, selling, or transporting gold, transferring funds, or delivering mail, the company earned a reputation for trustworthiness in an era dominated by rogues.

By 1861, Wells Fargo & Co. provided the main line of communication between California's gold-mining towns and, by the late 1860s, monopolized the movement of mail and people across the entire western U.S.

A few steps from the site of the company's 1852 office, the Wells Fargo Museum records the rise of the company, now one of the country's major financial institutions. Sitting inside an 1860s stagecoach provides the highlight for some visitors, but there is much more to see amid the clutter of a re-created gold-rush-era Wells Fargo office: among the debris are gold-weighing scales, bulky mining tools, and numerous aging letters which miraculously survived their trip across the Wild West.

Western Addition   *IFCD5*

Buses: 5, 31
Squeezed between Haight-Ashbury, Japantown, and the Tenderloin, the Western Addition (its name derived from its being a "western addition" to the 1858 city, whose western edge was defined by Van Ness Avenue) is among San Francisco's less revered areas, home to a largely low-income African-American population with many of its remaining Victorian homes suffering from neglect.

The Western Addition is far from being an inner city ghetto, however. The gentrified Alamo Square (see page 54) is particularly worth discovering, while anyone on a pilgrimage to flower-power San Francisco will enjoy finding the site of the **Fillmore Auditorium** (1805 Geary Boulevard), a legendary 1960s venue for rock concerts and psychedelic happenings, and recently revived as a music venue.

WESTERN ADDITION

With wagons as rickety as the one pictured here, the Wells Fargo Company blazed a trail across the Wild West in the 1860s

Church of John Coltrane
On the edge of the Western Addition, the St. John's African Orthodox Church (351 Divisadero Street) is popularly known as the Church of John Coltrane. Each Sunday, a four-hour service is presided over by the sax-playing bishop who founded the church after undergoing a religious experience when hearing the late jazz musician John Coltrane play live in the 1960s. All are welcome at the services, and those who bring instruments are encouraged to play them.

What made San Francisco...

Excursions

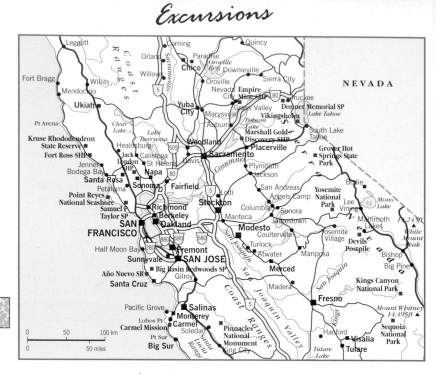

San Francisco may be a captivating city, but it is also a surprisingly small one, and visitors are liable to feel they have exhausted it after a week of energetic sightseeing.

Fortunately, the city is ideally placed for traveling further, be it a simple day trip to the rugged hills and picturesque coastal towns of Marin County, a 2–3-day tour around the old towns of the Gold Country or through the wild vistas of the northern coast, or a few days spent sampling the pastoral surroundings and highly rated produce of the Wine Country.

In fact, so wide-ranging are the possibilities within easy reach of the city that some San Franciscans, who may take several short vacations each year, seldom consider it necessary to venture out of northern California at all.

A landscape for lovers: Lake Tahoe's Emerald Bay

180

Empire Mine State Historic Park, Grass Valley

Gold Country and Lake Tahoe Like San Francisco, Sacramento, 85 miles east, grew rich and powerful following the 19th-century discovery of gold. Sacramento has matured into a likeable, modestly sized state capital and is an excellent place for gaining an understanding of California's unique history. Several defining moments in the state's development occurred here and are well documented in a fine complement of museums.

Scores of gold-rush towns—some immaculately preserved, others a pile of ruins beside the road—are found along the routes east of Sacramento and recall the boom-and-bust days of old. Some of the most engrossing and prosperous of the towns are found in the grassy, tree-studded slopes of the Sierra Nevada foothills and can make atmospheric overnight stops.

The same foothills, their greenery giving way to exposed granite and (even in summer) snow-capped peaks, provide a stunning setting for Lake Tahoe, a massive cobalt-blue body of water which straddles the California–Nevada border. Besieged by skiers in winter, and by gamblers year-round (massive casinos lie immediately across the California–Nevada state line), the idyllic alpine surroundings of Lake Tahoe are also perfect for walking, hiking, or simply relaxing beside the enormous pine-bordered lake—and perhaps taking a sightseeing cruise across it.

Marin County Just a few minutes' drive from the hurly-burly of the city, the untamed hills and canyons of Marin County give a glimpse of how coastal California once looked. Here the wild landscapes and seascapes of the Point Reyes National Seashore will stay in your mind for years, and also offer a close-up look at how earthquakes,

When to go
Geography and geology conspire to give northern California a number of "micro-climates"; the weather is likely to vary considerably over a short distance. Overall, however, you can expect conditions not to vary too much from those described on page 250. Exceptions are the Lake Tahoe area and parts of the Gold Country, which are almost certain to see snow between late October and early April, and the northern coast, which endures considerable rainfall between November and February.

The coastal landscapes at Point Reyes National Seashore are the work of the San Andreas Fault

in particular the rumblings of the infamous San Andreas Fault, have rumpled California's surface over the centuries.

Marin County can be used as a prelude to the longer northern coast excursion. Alternatively, treat it as a day trip and take the inland route back to San Francisco, passing a noted piece of modern architecture on the way.

The Monterey peninsula The Monterey peninsula, 120 miles south of San Francisco, has a rich history, displayed in a wealth of 19th-century buildings. Monterey's modern sights, such as the excellent Monterey Bay Aquarium and the shops of Cannery Row, are also worthwhile and have greatly contributed to the area's recent upsurge in popularity.

Nonetheless, Monterey is still far from over-commercialized and the peninsula's other communities—Carmel with its whimsical architecture and beautiful mission, and Pacific Grove which faces the windy ocean from a granite headland and is usually invaded by colorful butterflies—offer plenty of scope for unhurried exploration and lots of possibilities for spending the night within earshot of crashing surf.

The northern coast The northern coast should be a compulsory excursion for anyone who thinks that the Californian coast means sun, sand, and surfers. Beyond Marin County (see above), the vista quickly becomes one of wave-battered headlands, a restless ocean far too dangerous for swimming in, and far-flung communities set in sheltered coves and populated by a few hundred hardy souls.

The dipping and winding Highway 1 follows a route through the region, revealing some of the state's most spectacular landscapes and passing the restored site of a 19th-century Russian settlement before reaching the

Car rental
All the larger towns described on the excursions can be reached by public transportation but it is far more convenient, and sometimes cheaper, to rent a car from San Francisco. If you are sure of your plans, you may save money by arranging car rental in advance. Otherwise, all the best-known firms have desks at the airport, offices in the city, and are reachable on the toll-free numbers given on pages 254–5.

time-locked village of Mendocino and the comparative metropolis of Fort Bragg, a town built on the timber trade.

The San Francisco peninsula Travel south from the city along the San Francisco peninsula and you will quickly be rewarded with picture-postcard coastal views and major points of interest such as Stanford University, its immense campus the scene of many a scientific breakthrough.

Computer buffs searching for Silicon Valley—a nickname for the Santa Clara Valley—will be relieved to find San Jose, the self-proclaimed capital of the region whose futuristic downtown symbolizes its place at the heart of the state's electronics industries. Sizeable chunks of the valley resemble southern California-style suburbia, but a cluster of offbeat attractions adds spice to a navigation of the area's web of freeways.

The Wine Country Wineries exist all over California, but the most successful lie in the Sonoma and Napa valleys, 50 miles northeast of San Francisco. It was the Napa Valley which brought international recognition to the state's wine industry from the 1970s, although commercial wine production in California actually dates back to the 1850s.

Almost all wineries, be they multi-million-dollar concerns with well-equipped visitor centers or family-run operations where the vintner might personally greet you, offer free tours and tastings which are intended to delight beginners and seasoned oenologists alike.

Only minutes from the city: the hills of Marin County

EXCURSIONS

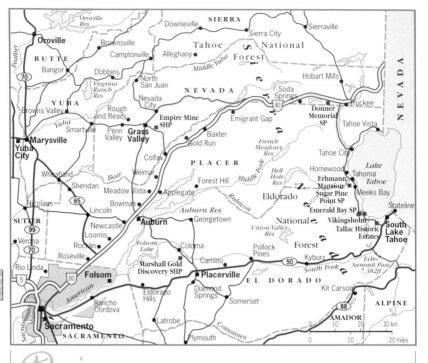

Drive Gold Country and Lake Tahoe

Heading west from the state capital of Sacramento towards the Sierra Nevada mountains, this drive passes through some of the more note-worthy of California's 19th-century gold-mining towns, which do much to evoke the flavor of bygone days. Later, the route swings south and makes a spectacular approach to Lake Tahoe, an immense expanse of water surrounded by snow-capped granite peaks and intensely green swathes of pine forest.

Places of interest in Gold Country and Lake Tahoe are fully described on pages 185–9.

Gold Country bric-à-brac

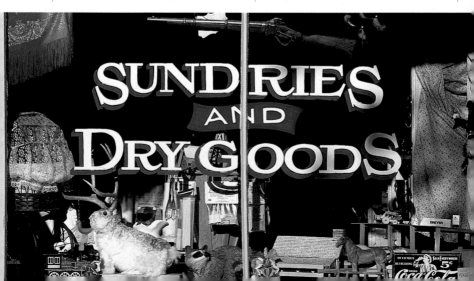

▶▶▶ Gold Country and Lake Tahoe

California's personable state capital, Sacramento, provides the gateway to the Gold Country, where some of the key communities of 19th-century California remain in evocatively preserved form. Within easy reach, too, is Lake Tahoe, the world's second largest alpine lake and a contributor to some of the state's most memorable landscapes.

Sacramento Small, sedate, and filled with trees, Sacramento▶▶▶ might seem an unlikely place to be California's capital, but during the mid-19th century the men and machinery destined for the state's thriving gold mines arrived here on the Sacramento River (deep enough to carry the ocean-going vessels of the time) and helped turn a thinly populated farming settlement into a thriving commercial center

In 1874, 20 years after it became state capital, Sacramento's leaders unveiled the $2.5-million **State Capitol Building▶▶▶**, symbolizing California's enormous independent wealth and sending an unmistakable signal to the federal government, still recovering from the Civil War, that California was not to be pushed around.

Inevitably, the power and grandeur suggested by the sheer size of the State Capitol a century ago has diminished, but it remains as a majestic marker to the state's riches, and is the perfect place to begin seeing Sacramento.

Between 10a.m. and 4p.m., free guided tours depart hourly from the lobby (weekdays only during winter), or you can wander around on your own viewing the restored period rooms, the portraits of former governors (look for the semi-abstract portrayal of Jerry "Governor Moonbeam" Brown), or, when it is in session, watch the state legislature in action.

As big and as imposing as the national Capitol Building in Washington D.C., California's State Capitol (above) was intended to demonstrate to the world at large that the gold-rich state was a force to be reckoned with

The Governor's mansion
Erected in 1877 as one of Sacramento's most luxurious residences, the elegant wooden house at the corner of 16th and H streets was the official residence of 13 California state governors until 1967, when newly elected Ronald Reagan decided to live elsewhere. Stuffed with Victoriana and items reflecting gubernatorial taste, and with a lively anecdote at every turn, the house can be explored on hourly guided tours (daily 10–4).

EXCURSIONS

Old Sacramento: railroad maintenance...

Placerville's hangtown fry
Drop into almost any restaurant in Placerville and you are liable to be offered "hangtown fry". This local specialty comprises eggs, bacon, and fried oysters, and is a dish allegedly consumed by Placerville miners to mark special occasions.

...and auto preservation

Old Sacramento For a clearer impression of the incongruous size of the State Capitol at the time of its completion, make the short walk to **Old Sacramento►►**, where souvenir stores, restaurants and several historical collections fill dozens of two-story wooden buildings dating from the mid-1800s.

The gold rush enabled Sacramento's merchants—many based in what is now Old Sacramento—to amass fortunes without ever going near a mine. Among those to thrive were the so-called Big Four—Charles Crocker, Mark Hopkins, Leland Stanford, and Collis P. Huntington (see page 37)—who not only became millionaires but also wielded considerable political power, largely through their Pacific Railroad Company. This company oversaw the construction of the transcontinental railroad, California's first fixed link with the rest of the U.S.

The story of the Big Four and the transcontinental railroad is told inside Old Sacramento's **California State Railroad Museum►►►**, which also finds space for a tremendous stock of aging but well-maintained locomotives and carriages from the great days of American train travel.

Whatever the advantages of traveling by rail, there are few Americans who would opt for a train when they can be at the wheel of a car. On the periphery of Old Sacramento, the **Towe Ford Museum►** displays an enormous number of (predominantly Ford) vehicles—from Model Ts to Thunderbirds—which will consume several hours of any auto enthusiast's day.

Should art and local history hold more appeal than cars, head instead for the **Crocker Art Museum►►**. This is the oldest art museum in the western U.S., although the exhibits are actually less impressive than the building itself: a voluminous Italianate villa completed in 1873 for Edwin Bryant Crocker, brother of Charles Crocker (of Big Four fame).

Sutter's Fort Sacramento's oldest structure, **Sutter's Fort►►**, stood at the center of the 48,000-acre land holding acquired by German-born John Sutter in 1839. It was on Sutter's land that gold was discovered, although the find was to result in Sutter's bankruptcy and eventually his impoverished death. Within the adobe-walled fort, several workshops have been reconstructed and are regularly staffed by volunteers in period dress.

Already decimated by European diseases carried by the mission-building Spanish, California's Native Americans were caused further harm by the gold rush. Next door to Sutter's Fort, the small but engaging **State Indian Museum►►** chronicles what little is known about the lives and lifestyles of the region's indigenous peoples.

Folsom and Placerville East of Sacramento on Highway 50, **Folsom** makes a pleasant base for state capital commuters and has some briefly entertaining relics from its gold-rush origins displayed in the **Folsom Museum►**. Most Californians, however, know the community for **Folsom Prison**, the oldest section of which dates from 1880 and is concealed behind a surprisingly picturesque granite gatehouse. A **museum►** (closed Tuesday and Wednesday) describes some of the murderers, thieves,

Left: a period-attired guide awaits visitors to Sutter's Fort Below: a monument to the man on whose land California gold was discovered

187

and all-round undesirables who spent time incarcerated here over the years.

Continuing east, **Placerville** provides a more typical example of a Gold Country community. Known as "Hangtown" in the days before law and order replaced vigilantism, Placerville has dozens of wood-framed buildings along its main street, copious examples of the tools of the gold-miner's trade assembled in the **El Dorado County Museum**▶, and the tourable tunnels of the **Gold Bug Mine**▶▶.

North on Highway 49 A few miles north of Placerville on Highway 49, **Marshall Gold Discovery State Historic Park**▶▶▶ preserves the spot where, on January 24, 1848, James Marshall, an employee of land-owner John Sutter, spotted flakes of gold in the American River. The chance discovery, and its profound impact on California, is documented in the park's museum. Follow the park's short foot trails and you will also find a replica of Sutter's sawmill and the cabin where Marshall died broke and dispirited in 1879, never having benefited from his find.

First impressions of **Auburn**▶, 20 miles further north, are uninspiring, but a closer look reveals the cobblestoned streets of the **Old Town**▶▶, where many of Auburn's 19th-century structures are impressively preserved. The **Gold Country Museum**▶▶ traces the affluence which Auburn enjoyed during the days of the gold rush, with mining implements and explanatory displays, plus some informative artifacts from the Chinese community which settled here.

The Leland Stanford mansion

The extremely grand home of Leland Stanford—entrepreneur, railroad tycoon, and one of the Big Four—on the corner of 8th and 9th streets is in the process of being restored to its 1860s appearance, the period during which the Stanford family took up residence. Currently, intriguing tours of the house focus on the painstaking archaeological detective work necessary to uncover clues to the house's history and ensure accurate restoration. For more details, tel. 916/324 0575.

EXCURSIONS

Downieville
On highway 49 north from Nevada City, Downieville retains, along with many 1850s buildings, the gallows that brought the town the dubious distinction of being the one mining community ever to hang a woman.

Rough and Ready
Four miles west of Grass Valley, Rough and Ready, now a few buildings off Highway 20 but once a thriving gold-rush community, is the only town ever to secede from the U.S. Angry over a new federal miners' tax, its citizens elected to leave the union on April 7, 1850. Denied supplies of alcohol, however, they rejoined on July 4.

Grass Valley Two more significant—and more enjoyable—gold-rush communities lie in close proximity north of Auburn. The first, **Grass Valley▶▶**, prospered from the fruits of California's most technologically advanced mine: the Empire Mine produced an annual yield of $5 million in its peak years. The **Empire Mine State Historic Park▶▶▶** offers a chance to explore some of the mine's buildings and penetrate a modest section of its 367 miles of tunnel. The mine's success was partly due to the know-how of Cornish miners; a by-product of their migration from Britain were the Cornish pasties which are a specialty of many local restaurants. One Grass Valley settler who never ventured beneath ground was Lola Montez, a European dancer of great flamboyance and notorious in the U.S. for her sensual "spider dance." A replica of her home in the 1850s now houses the local tourist office and carries a few remnants from her eventful life.

Nevada City Grass Valley may have enjoyed its 19th-century affluence, but 5 miles further on Highway 49, **Nevada City▶▶▶** was at that time California's third-largest city, growing rich as the seat of Nevada County, a region which produced half of the state's total output of gold.

Throughout the easily walked town, markers to the great days of the past are numerous. The 1865 **Nevada Theater▶** is believed to be the oldest continuously operating theater in the western U.S.; author Mark Twain gave his first public lecture here. The **National Hotel▶▶** opened in 1856 claims to be the western U.S.'s oldest hostelry, a boast which becomes easy to believe after viewing its antique-filled lobby and bar area. More organized historical detritus fills the 1861 **Firehouse Museum▶**, and exhibitions of arts and crafts fill the former workshops of the **Miners Foundry and Culture Center▶**.

Nevada City

The Sierra Nevada foothills West from Nevada City, Highway 20 and then I-80 carry you further into the conifer-covered foothills of the Sierra Nevada mountains. For 19th-century pioneers at the mercy of the elements, the Sierra Nevadas were a potentially fatal obstacle on the overland journey to California. In 1846, the **Donner Party**—a wagon train of 89 men, women, and children hoping to reach Sutter's Fort (present-day Sacramento)—became trapped by winter snow at what is now Donner Pass, through which I-80 travels. As food supplies were exhausted, 40 of the travelers died and the survivors resorted to cannibalism to stay alive. At **Donner Memorial State Park▶▶**, a museum tells the travelers' sad tale.

The Lake Tahoe shoreline Traveling south from Truckee, Highway 89 reaches Lake Tahoe at **Tahoe City**. Despite its name, Tahoe City has just 5,000 inhabitants and the **Gatekeepers Museum►**, which keeps the dust off a collection of local historical artifacts. Far more alluring are the lakeside landscapes which proliferate on the southbound route—green hillsides studded by grey granite boulders rising above the glacier-sculptured shoreline of the vibrantly blue lake. Such views were savored by the cream of 1920s San Franciscan society from the **Erhmann Mansion►►**, built two decades earlier for a wealthy banker (guided tours). The stone and wood structure also serves as a visitor center for **Sugar Pine Point State Park►** and its 2,000 acres of view-laden hillside trails.

Continuing south and passing through **Emerald Bay State Park►**, Highway 89 rises above a tree-lined inlet holding Lake Tahoe's sole island, **Fanette Island**. A mile-long trail descends from the highway to the extraordinary **Vikingsholm►►►**, a 38-room mansion built in the 1920s by a Swedish architect in the style of a 9th-century Nordic castle as a retreat for heiress Lora Josephine Knight.

South Lake Tahoe Scenery gives way to commerce as you reach **South Lake Tahoe**, the largest lakeside community and one which offers accommodations but little else. Of chief appeal for many arrivals are the casinos of **Stateline►**, adjoining South Lake Tahoe but actually over the border in Nevada (where, unlike California, gambling is legal).

On the Californian side, the **Lake Tahoe Historical Society Museum►►** focuses on Lake Tahoe's geology and its human history. At **Tallac Historic Estates►►**, a number of structures have been re-assembled around the sites of the Tallac Hotel and Casino, built by the legendary "Lucky" Baldwin in 1898 and scene of much high living.

Vikingsholm, in Emerald Bay Park

Lake Tahoe cruises
The *Tahoe Queen*, a 1920s paddle-steamer, makes an enjoyable voyage between South Lake Tahoe and Emerald Bay daily (in summer), and at night hosts a dinner-dance cruise (tel. 916/541 3364). The MS *Dixie* plies between Zephyr Cove (on the Nevada side of the lake, a few miles north of Stateline) and Emerald Bay, and makes several other lake cruises.

California's gold
No precise records were kept of the value of the gold mined in California during the peak years of the gold rush. Nonetheless, the following statistics are considered reliable:
1848 $ 245,301
1849 $10,151,360
1850 $41,273,106
1851 $75,938,232
1852 $81,294,700
1853 $67,613,487
1855 $55,485,163
1860 $44,095,858
1865 $17,930,858

EXCURSIONS

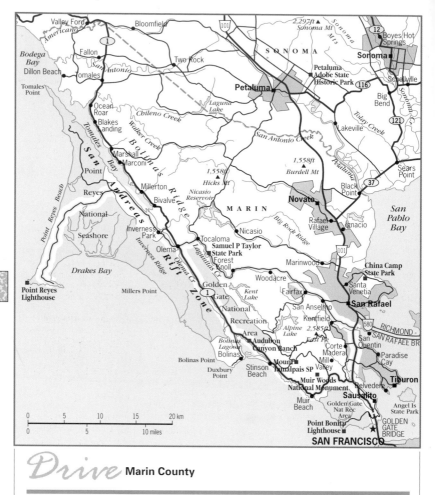

Drive Marin County

A day outing from San Francisco, this drive reveals many impressive natural features of coastal California. Once over the Golden Gate Bridge, the route navigates the undeveloped landscapes of the Marin Headlands, part of the Golden Gate National Recreation Area (see page 99), and continues along the San Andreas Fault to the Point Reyes National Seashore and its isolated lighthouse. Returning, the drive explores forested inland hillsides and passes several attractive towns before returning to the city. Marin County is fully described on pages 190–1.

▶▶ Marin County

Marin County begins as soon as you cross the Golden Gate Bridge and reach the hills of the Marin Headlands.

Along Highway 1 Branch off Highway 101 to join Highway 1 and after a winding 20-minute drive you pass the small town of Muir Beach. Here the **Pelican Inn** does its best to imitate a 16th-century British hostelry.

A few miles north, the 3-mile-long **Stinson Beach▶** is a favorite haunt of sea-and-sand loving San Franciscans, but although the ocean is free of the rip tides which limit swimming elsewhere along the coast, its waters are notoriously cold.

Immediately beyond, Highway 1 skirts the edge of **Bolinas Lagoon►►** and passes a side road leading to the **Audubon Canyon Ranch►**. A nature refuge and research center, the ranch welcomes amateur ornithologists to its canyon trails between mid-March and July.

Anyone interested in observing people rather than wildlife should detour off Highway 1 along Horseshoe Hill Road, which hugs the western side of the lagoon and eventually reaches the tiny town of **Bolinas►**. This close-knit community discourages commercial tourism by sabotaging street signs so that it cannot be found.

Point Reyes Heading north, Highway 1 follows the line of the San Andreas Fault. The fault is responsible for the extraordinary landscapes of the **Point Reyes National Seashore►►►**. Outside Point Reyes' informative **Bear Valley Visitors Center►**, the **Earthquake Trail►►** reveals evidence of the 1906 quake (epicentered locally), and a second path leads to **Kule Loklo►►**, a re-created Native American settlement of the kind used by the Miwok people, the original inhabitants of what became Marin County.

Heading back To return to San Francisco, take Sir Francis Drake Boulevard. This inland route passes the hillside towns of **Fairfax**, birthplace of the mountain bike, and the antique-shop-filled **San Anselmo►►**. Above San Anselmo, two 19th-century stone buildings form part of the **San Francisco Theological Seminary►**, where future ministers of the Presbyterian Church are trained. The public are welcome to share the stupendous views from the seminary's 21 acre grounds.

Your final stop should be the county seat, **San Rafael►**, where the replica of the town's 1817 Spanish **mission** is less significant than the **Marin County Civic Center►►**, the last work of the influential architect, Frank Lloyd Wright, completed beside the highway in 1969.

...a possession of Queen Elizabeth I and named it Nova Albion, or 'New England'.

Muir Woods National Monument
Head inland from Muir Beach along the aptly named Panoramic Highway to Muir Woods National Monument and you will find a modestly sized grove of California redwood trees. The world's tallest living things, redwoods can reach 350ft high, and most of the world's population are found along a narrow stretch of the northern California and Oregon coast. While in the area, you should also visit Mount Tamalpais State Park.

For the Bay Area's best views, choose a fog-free day, pack a picnic lunch, and climb Marin County's Mount Tamalpais

From the historic heart of Monterey, this short but spectacular drive weaves along the peninsula's northern side to reach Pacific Grove and reveal stunning coastal vistas of crashing waves and wind-tormented cypress trees. Turning south, the drive continues through some exclusive residential areas and alongside lushly landscaped golf courses before reaching the pretty community of Carmel and ending at the beautiful Carmel Mission.

Places to visit on the Monterey peninsula are fully described on pages 192–5.

The Old Monterey Jail
Among the more curious of Monterey's many historic structures is the Old Monterey Jail, its entrance behind Colton Hall. Incarcerating its first unfortunate in 1854 and its last a century later, each of the jail's gloomy cells is arranged to re-create an episode from the past—such as the the short, unhappy stay of Anastacio Garcia, described as "the very *beau ideal* of a brigand" and murdered in his cell in 1857.

Monterey Bay Aquarium

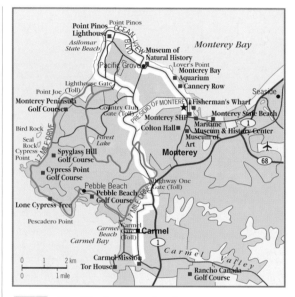

▶▶▶ **The Monterey peninsula**

Between them, the three distinctive communities of the Monterey peninsula offer substantial insights into Californian history, some memorable ocean vistas, and an example of town planning at its most bizarre and insular.

Monterey A fine natural harbor encouraged the Spanish to land and settle at what they named Monterey in 1770. The town became California's administrative base during the mission-building period, retaining this role through the region's Mexican era and during the early years of statehood.

The well-preserved buildings—ranging from Spanish adobes with their elaborate decorative tilework intact to the neoclassical Colton Hall, the seat of California's first state legislature—which make up **Monterey State Historical Park** are among the ordinary offices and stores which comprise the compact core of modern-day Monterey. To locate the old buildings (not all of them are open to the public but each merits at least a quick look), use the widely available *Path of History* map.

Three places of historical worth you should be certain to

see are the **Old Customs House▶**, stuffed with the intriguing mix of essentials and exotica typical of an 1830s ship's cargo; **California's First Theater▶▶**, scene of dramatic productions since 1846; and the **Robert Louis Stevenson House▶▶**, where the Scottish writer spent part of 1879 and which now holds mementoes from his stay, his literary career, and his South Seas travels.

Stevenson was just one of a number of writers drawn to Monterey in its heyday. As the town's fortunes waned—it ceased to be the seat of California's legislature in 1849 and, by the 1920s, had acquired a less glamorous position as the world's largest sardine-canning center—another writer, John Steinbeck, penned the novels *Tortilla Flat* and *Cannery Row* describing life on the Monterey waterfront.

This rough-and-ready area, defined by fish-guts, low-paid workers, and prostitutes as described by Steinbeck, is now the spick-and-span tourist magnet of **Cannery Row▶**, the old warehouses consumed by souvenir shops, seafood restaurants, and the entirely lacklustre **Spirit of Steinbeck Wax Museum**.

Better places to spend an hour are the **Monterey Bay Aquarium▶▶▶**, a state-of-the-art facility exploring and explaining the intricacies of life beneath the Pacific waves, and the $6-million **Maritime Museum and History Center**, charting Monterey's role as a seaport with a multitude of maps, model ships, and nautical knick-knacks.

Pacific Grove Joined to Monterey and extending to the northern tip of the peninsula, **Pacific Grove** acquired its first visitors in 1875 when a band of vacationing Methodists pitched tents on the then-uninhabited headland and founded a summertime religious retreat.

193

Getting lost is hard in Monterey

The Shoreline Bike Path
Many miles of scenic bike paths can be found in California, but few can surpass the Monterey Peninsula's Shoreline Bike Path for easily enjoyed coastal views. The flat, 3-mile route runs between Monterey's Fisherman's Wharf and Lover's Point, beside Ocean View Boulevard in Pacific Grove. Bikes can be rented from Bay Bikes (640 Wave Street; tel. 408/646 9090).

Cyclists admire Pacific Grove

Pacific Grove lodgings

The 17-Mile Drive
Snaking between Pacific Grove and Carmel, the 17-Mile Drive is a marked toll route with views of craggy headlands and the famous Lone Cypress Tree, growing in defiance of ocean winds from an inaccessible outcrop. Maps of the drive are issued at the entry gates on Sunset Drive (in Pacific Grove) and San Antonio Avenue (Carmel).

Point Lobos, near Carmel

Today, Pacific Grove is a very nice place to live. Its main thoroughfare, Lighthouse Avenue, is lined by intriguing stores and cozy cafés and is also where you will find many impressive examples of wood-and-shingle Victorian architecture.

Pine trees are another common sight. Between November and March, many of the trees' branches appear to be hung with yellow and black flags. In fact, these are the wings of **Monarch butterflies**, thousands of which migrate to Pacific Grove from Alaska and Canada. The small **Pacific Grove Museum of Natural History►** has a display on the butterflies, and highlights other aspects of local history and ecology.

Do not leave Pacific Grove without taking a drive along **Ocean View Boulevard►►►**. Beginning just west of the Monterey Bay Aquarium, the road follows a scenic coastal route and eventually swings south to pass the tiny **Point Pinos Lighthouse►►**, which has cast its beam into the distance since 1855. The lighthouse's 19th-century furnishings and historical displays are open to visitors on weekend afternoons.

Carmel Literary notables George Sterling and Mary Austin led a band of artists, writers, and academics to **Carmel►►►** in the early 1900s, dreaming of an idyllic bohemian existence on this then-isolated and thinly populated coastal bluff.

Their presence turned out to be temporary, however, and by the 1920s an ambitious architect was busy creating half-timbered cottages which, combined with the oceanside setting, attracted wealthy San Franciscans. The town's tudor-style look has been rigorously preserved by its residents, the local authorities even banning fast-food outlets, neon lighting, and live entertainment in bars and restaurants, to keep Carmel's charm intact.

The town center, with its boutiques, art galleries and restaurants, justifies an hour's stroll. (See also page 56.) A few minutes' walk away at the foot of Ocean Avenue, **Carmel Beach►►** comprises several miles of white sand framed by cypress groves. Bring your own picnic supplies

Carmel Beach

and you can enjoy a barbecue using one of the beach's fire pits.

One writer who arrived in Carmel on the heels of the would-be bohemians, and not only stayed but built a strange and imposing home for himself and his family, was poet Robinson Jeffers. Completed in 1919, Jeffers' **Tor House▶▶** was constructed from granite stones hauled up by horses from the cove beneath. The building was intended to resemble a Tudor barn which the poet had seen in England, and it provided a home for Jeffers until his death in 1962. There are guided tours on Fridays and Saturdays by reservation (tel. 408/624 1813).

Carmel Mission Perhaps Carmel's greatest day came in 1771 when it acquired the mission founded a year earlier in Monterey, the second link in the California mission chain. The **Carmel Mission▶▶▶** served as the main base of Junipero Serra, the leader of Spain's Sacred Expedition to establish the missions, convert Native Americans to the Catholic faith, and co-opt their labor for the colonial cause. Largely due to a comprehensive rebuilding programme carried out during the 1930s, the Carmel Mission has become one of the best restored and most evocative of all the state's missions. The centerpiece is an eye-catching sandstone **church** with twin Moorish towers; completed in 1879, the church replaced the simple adobe chapel of Serra's time. Behind the church, a **museum** stores remnants from the mission's earliest days, the reconstructed living quarters of Serra, a few of his 600 books, and the sarcophagus which holds his remains: Serra died here in 1784, aged 71.

As you stroll around the fountains and bougainvillea-lined pathways of the mission's extremely well-maintained **gardens**, you might contemplate the controversy surrounding Serra's beatification in 1988. With California's native population dying out through contact with European diseases, and their cultures suppressed and eventually destroyed by the mission system, many believe that the Spanish impact on the native population amounted to genocide, and that the Catholic Church was wrong to put Serra on the road to sainthood.

195

Carmel's Bach Festival
For two weeks beginning each July, Carmel's Bach Festival celebrates not only the German composer but also his 18th-century musical contemporaries. Concerts, opera, and ballet are staged at the town's Sunset Cultural Center, but the climax of the festival is a special candle-lit performance at the Carmel Mission. For details, write to Carmel Bach Festival, PO Box 575, Carmel, CA 93921.

Carmel Mission

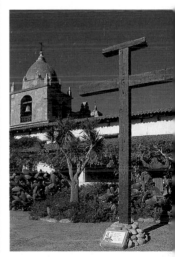

 **The northern coast**

This drive follows Highway 1, a route which winds along the entire Californian coast and in this section holds some of the most dramatic ocean landscapes to be found anywhere in the U.S. From the fishing hamlet of Bodega Bay north to the logging town of Fort Bragg, the two-lane highway makes endless twists and turns, and navigates sharp grades to reach dizzying clifftops revealing fabulous ocean views. The northern coast is fully described on pages 196–9.

Alfred Hitchcock's Bodega Bay

Much of Alfred Hitchcock's 1963 film *The Birds* was shot in Bodega Bay. While some landscapes may be recognizable, the schoolhouse and the boarding house which appear in the film are actually located in the town of Bodega, 5 miles inland (on Bodega Highway, off Highway 1). The Tides restaurant, where locals seek refuge as the birds attack, still exists in Bodega Bay, but in a different location from that of Hitchcock's time.

Bodega Bay birds

▶▶▶ **The northern coast**

To Bodega Bay Beyond Marin County (pages 190–1), Highway 1 spans 200 miles of spectacular coastline and links some of California's most distinctive oceanside communities. The first town reached, **Bodega Bay▶**, sits beside a sheltered lagoon. Though much depleted since its commercial heyday, the fishing fleet is still one of the largest in the area. The main appeal, though, is simply the

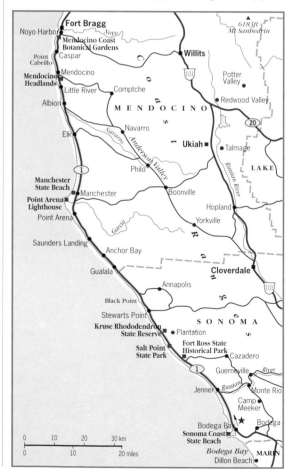

setting, the relaxed ambience, and the discernible community spirit. The latter is apparent during April's **Fishermen's Festival**, which includes a Blessing of the Fleet and the hilarious Bathtub Race.

North from Bodega Bay, Highway 1 passes a succession of coastal towns and 13 miles of which collectively comprise **Sonoma County State Beach▶**. Strong currents render the beaches unsuitable for swimming, but beachcombers, fishermen, and anyone who enjoys peering into tidepools will find much to their liking.

Towards Fort Ross After crossing the Russian River (look for seals basking on its banks), Highway 1 spends the next 11 miles making steep and twisting ascents—bringing tantalizing glimpses of ocean surf pounding against the granite outcrops many feet below—before dropping sharply downwards.

This stretch of coast still looks much as it did in the early 19th century, when Russian fur-trappers purchased a 125-mile strip from Native Americans and founded a colony at Fort Ross, now remembered by **Fort Ross State Historical Park▶▶▶**.

With their crops failing and sea otters (pursued for their pelts) being hunted to near extinction, the colony was abandoned in 1841. Weather and earthquakes subsequently took their toll on the fort's traditional style wooden buildings, but thorough restoration has turned the living quarters, warehouses, and Orthodox chapel into an absorbing reminder of the Russian presence in California.

A few miles north, **Salt Point State Park▶**, spans 6,000 wild coastal acres and has an underwater portion allowing divers to explore the marine life of Gerstle Cove. On dry land, the park's hiking trails reach sites of Native American habitation, and the neighboring **Kruse Rhododendron State Reserve▶▶** is an essential stop in springtime.

Gualala Less spectacular views predominate for the next 30 miles, until the small town of **Gualala** appears. Stretch

Bodega Church

Californian crafts in Russia
The Russians at Fort Ross enjoyed good relations with the local Native American community and frequently traded with them. Often the Russians exchanged otter fur for feathered baskets, important symbols of native cultural identity and the specialty of the Pomo Indians who lived along this part of the California coast. Consequently, one somewhat bizarre legacy of the Russian settlement is that the world's largest collection of Kashaya Pomo basketry is held in St. Petersburg, Russia.

Russian built Fort Ross

EXCURSIONS

Northern coast whale watching
From mid-December to the end of March, the much-loved California gray whales are likely to be spotted on their annual migration between the Arctic Ocean and the warmer waters off Baja California (in Mexico). Marked whale-watching points are a feature of the northern coast, and most have texts and maps describing the whales and their migration. Mendocino and Fort Bragg confirm their admiration for California's state mammal by staging a Whale Celebration Week each March.

your legs with a walk around the town's art galleries—showcases for the work of the area's many painters and sculptors.

North from Gualala Leaving Gualala and approaching **Saunders Landing**, the hills retreat inland, allowing Highway 1 to follow an unusually level section of the coast. This is largely because the San Andreas Fault, a rift of geological instability, moves westwards and continues beneath the ocean. **Manchester State Beach**, a desolate and windswept area of dunes and driftwood, consumes 760 acres here, and on its southern edge stands the 1908 **Point Arena Lighthouse►►**. Reached by Lighthouse Road, off Highway 1, the present lighthouse replaced a wooden original which was destroyed in California's 1906 earthquake. A museum recounts the story of the lighthouse.

Mendocino If mist is swirling across the highway as you reach **Mendocino►►►**, 30 miles from Point Arena, this town of 1,000 souls nestling on a coastal bluff could well be mistaken for a ghostly apparition.

Founded by New England lumbermen a century ago, Mendocino retains much of the ramshackle wooden architecture of their time. The isolated location deterred property developers from razing the town, and strict building codes have recently been enforced to preserve the mid-1800s look.

As the logging industry declined, Mendocino fell upon hard times until a colony of get-away-from-it-all artists and writers began arriving in the 1950s and 1960s. Today, many of Mendocino's old homes are bed-and-breakfast inns, and numerous art galleries are aimed at visitors.

Despite the commercial trappings, Mendocino is enormously appealing and has much to be enjoyed on a half-hour stroll. Drop into the 1854 **Ford House►**, which now serves as a visitor center, for background on the town and local wildlife, and into the **Kelley House Museum►►** for a more personalized insight into local

The bluffs of Mendocino—not for beach lovers

Mendocino flora

Northern coast wineries
Though less celebrated than their counterparts in the Wine Country (see pages 204-9), the wineries dotted along Highway 128, which cuts inland from Highway 1 south of Mendocino and runs through the gloriously wooded Anderson Valley, are well worth investigating. The free Anderson Valley Winegrowers leaflet (from local chambers of commerce) lists them and their creations. This route can also be used to return to San Francisco, by continuing to Boonville and heading south on Highway 101.

history through archive photographs, original Mendocino furnishings, and temporary exhibitions.

When it all seems too much of a metropolis, Mendocino residents put on their windbreakers and take contemplative walks across the **Mendocino Headlands▶▶**, a protected area of striking wildness and beauty adjacent to the town.

Fort Bragg Just 10 miles north, **Fort Bragg** could hardly provide a greater contrast. The gas stations and fastfood franchises which are banned in Mendocino seize the opportunity and proliferate in what is by far the largest town in a 200-mile stretch of coast.

Originating as an army fort in the 1850s and intended to subdue Native American opposition to white settlement, Fort Bragg quickly became dominated by the Union Lumber company, succeeded in recent times by the Georgia-Pacific (or G-P) company.

As Highway 1 enters the town, you will see G-P's sprawling sawmill robbing the town of what might otherwise be a rewarding ocean view. Tours of the sawmill are periodically available, but more valuable background information on the local logging industry lies within the **Guest House Museum▶**, occupying the elegant former home of a 19th-century Fort Bragg swell.

Two places on the town's southern periphery merit a call. The **Mendocino Coast Botanical Gardens▶** offer winding walkways through 47 acres of impressively landscaped headland. **Noyo Harbor**, meanwhile, located off Highway 1, is where locals head when they want fresh seafood. The catch is unloaded from the small fishing vessels which fill the harbor and is then served in no-frills restaurants.

The Skunk Train: linking Fort Bragg and Willits

The Skunk Train
Fort Bragg's Skunk Train, which once transported timber and was nicknamed for the smell of its engine, makes a 40-mile inland run to and from Willits, a scenic trip above rivers and redwood groves. Visitors can enjoy the ride as a half- or full-day trip. For details, tel. 707/964 6371.

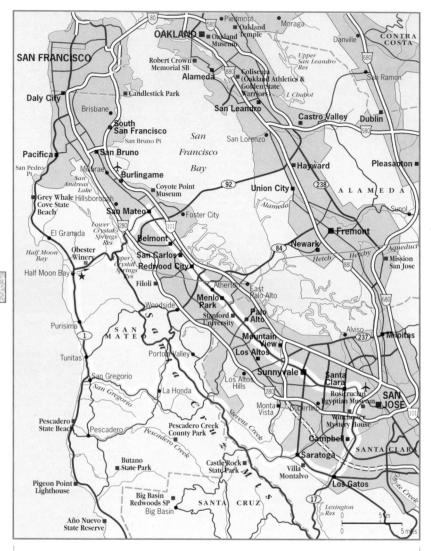

Drive The San Francisco peninsula

On either side of its hilly spine, the San Francisco peninsula splits into distinct sections. On the ocean side, secluded coves and pocket-sized communities are separated by wind-swept farmlands. The bay side, by contrast, is a ribbon of commercial and residential development.

This loop drive explores both sides. Facing the Pacific, picturesque Half Moon Bay is a scenic starting point from which the route moves south, passing unspoiled beaches, before swinging inland to cross the peninsula to Palo Alto and Stanford University. From there, the drive explores San Jose and its environs, a thickly populated area but one with some surprising finds. The peninsula is fully described on pages 201–3.

▶▶   **The San Francisco peninsula**

Along the coast Skimming the coastline as it threads south from San Francisco, Highway 1 passes several beaches—among them Gray Whale Cove, a popular spot for nudists—before reaching **Half Moon Bay**▶▶, its dainty proportions doing little to suggest that this is the peninsula's largest coastal town. Antiques and craft stores, cafés, bakeries, and numerous 19th-century homes converted into bed-and-breakfast inns line Half Moon Bay's handful of streets. Locals who know their pumpkins head for Half Moon Bay just before Halloween: the fields around the town grow the state's plumpest pumpkins and the fact is celebrated by October's Art and Pumpkin Festival.

Highway 1 continues along more sparsely populated coast, passing the handful of homes which constitute **Pescadero**, founded by Spaniards in 1856, the photogenic Pigeon Lighthouse, and the Año Nuevo State Reserve (see panel), a protected breeding ground of thousands of elephant seals (males weigh up to 3 tons).

Heading inland As it cuts inland from Half Moon Bay, Highway 92 takes you past the commendable **Obester Winery**▶ (tel. 415/726 9463), open for tastings of its Sauvignon Blanc, Riesling, and Chardonnay—sip from your glass while overlooking acres of pumpkins.

The highway continues east between the Montara and Santa Cruz mountains, crossing Crystal Springs Reservoir, which was created by the San Andreas Fault.

Highway 92 reaches San Francisco Bay at **San Mateo**, grown large and uninteresting partly through its proximity to San Francisco International Airport. Just north of San Mateo, however, the interactive computers, dioramas, and general exhibits of the **Coyote Point Museum**▶▶ provide cogent insights into the natural life of San Francisco Bay and the problems it is facing.

A young visitor surveys a Half Moon Bay pumpkin farm

Año Nuevo State Elephant Seal Reserve
Thousands of elephant seals come ashore here between December and March to mate. The males spend several months battling for supremacy before the victors copulate noisily with 50 or so females. This memorable spectacle can be seen in the company of a park ranger (reservations essential); tel. 1-800/444 PARK (reservations); 415/879 0227 (information).

Pigeon Point Light

EXCURSIONS

Stanford University

The peninsula railway
Fittingly perhaps, one way to reach Silicon Valley is with the state-of-the-art CalTrains rail link which connects San Francisco with Palo Alto (trip time 58 minutes) and San Jose (93 minutes). Services are most frequent during rush hours. For more information, tel. 1-800/660 4287.

San José de Guadalupe
San Jose takes its name from Mission San José de Guadalupe (long ago discarding the accent), located 15 miles northeast. Founded in 1797, the mission was the fourteenth built in California and was treated to a much-needed $5-million restoration in the 1980s. The mission's chapel and small museum are both worth visiting, not least because the latter includes some of the musical instruments played by the only orchestra of neophytes (Native Americans converted to Christianity) in California.

Stanford University Unrelenting sprawl and heavy rush-hour traffic are the prime features of Highway 101 as you travel south from San Mateo, quickly reaching **Palo Alto** where you should watch for the University Avenue exit. This leads to **Stanford University**, an academic institution which brings 13,000 students to the otherwise bland and lifeless town. Founded by railway magnate Leland Stanford and his wife in 1885 in memory of their son, Stanford University remains a privately run institution and conservative counterpart to the radical University of California at Berkeley (see pages 58–61). Stanford students pay approximately $20,000 tuition per year, and the university reputedly earns $5 million annually in royalties derived from patents of its research departments' inventions. The older part of the campus was designed by Frederick Law Olmstead, fresh from laying out New York's Central Park, and its center-piece is the Main Quad, framed by sandstone buildings in Romanesque and Byzantine style.

The mural-decorated **Memorial Church►** is particularly eye-catching, but the Main Quad is dominated by **Hoover Tower►**. With a good view across the campus and far beyond from its 285ft. peak, the tower is named after Herbert Hoover, a member of Stanford's first class of 1891, and elected U.S. president in 1929. Elsewhere on the campus, the **Stanford Museum of Art►** holds interesting items collected by the Stanford family, such as the shovel that was used to begin the building of the transcontinental railway, and a diverse collection of art which is generally less impressive than the works by Rodin which fill the neighboring **Cantor Sculpture Garden►►**.

Easily the most memorable part of a Stanford University tour is the **Stanford Linear Accelerator Center►►►**, stretching for 2 miles into the hills immediately northwest of the campus. Explaining the basics of particle physics to scientific beginners, the two-hour guided tours are highly recommended. For reservations, tel. 415/926 2204.

Silicon Valley The breakthroughs achieved at Stanford helped the peninsula area gain a reputation as a center of innovative electronics from the 1940s. Four decades later, the development of the (locally invented) silicon chip and the personal computer revolution earned the region—the Santa Clara Valley—the nickname "Silicon Valley."

South of Palo Alto, **San Jose** became the self-acclaimed capital of Silicon Valley, expanding at lightning pace as highly-paid computer company employees flooded in, stimulating an economic boom but creating some of the worst smog in California as they commuted to and from work in the city's new industrial centers. The **Tech Museum of Innovation►►** highlights the region's scientific achievements with impressive interactive exhibits.

Egyptian artifacts Of several areas of interest on the periphery of San Jose, none provides a greater contrast to the town's high-tech ambience than the stunning assemblage of amulets, mummies, textiles, scrolls, and other antiquities from the cultures of Assyria, Babylon, and Egypt, which are displayed inside the **Rosicrucian Egyptian Museum►►**. The entryway to the museum is modeled on the Egyptian town of Thebes, and its gardens

are planted with Egyptian trees and plants, and decorated by sphinxes and obelisks.

A mystery house Just as unlikely, but much more commercially oriented, is the **Winchester Mystery House**▶ (525 S. Winchester Boulevard). Sarah Winchester, heir to the rifle fortunes, believed she was haunted by the spirits of those killed by Winchester weapons and was certain to die if the house was ever completed. At her insistence, construction work continued day and night for 38 years, until her death in 1921. Inside, stairways lead nowhere, corridors narrow to a width of a few inches, some of the 2,000 doors and 10,000 windows open onto blank walls.

Villa Montalvo Hugging the hillsides on the southwestern area of San Jose, **Saratoga** is a snug and affluent community and one which, with **Villa Montalvo**▶, makes a pleasant conclusion to a peninsula excursion. James D. Phelan, U.S. Senator, local mayor, and patron of the arts, built and lived in the 19-room villa. Later it provided a home for the writers, painters, and musicians chosen as recipients of a Phelan endowment.

The 160-room Winchester Mystery House sprawls across nine acres

Filoli
Designed by Willis Polk (see panel, page 112), Filoli is an exquisite 43-room mansion completed in 1919 for William B. Bourn II, inheritor of a gold-rush fortune. The house may be familiar from the opening sequences of the TV serial *Dynasty*. At least as memorable are the gorgeous gardens, certain to have something in bloom at any time of year. Filoli is close to Woodside, off I-280 just inland from Palo Alto.

Drive The Wine Country

These drives explore Sonoma Valley (pages 204–7) and Napa Valley (pages 208–9). Although less famous than the neighboring Napa Valley, Sonoma Valley holds several of the state's best wineries and is less congested than Napa. The route runs from the history-laden town of Sonoma—with the most northern of California's Spanish missions—to the very modern Santa Rosa. The second excursion, from Napa, travels past more wineries, including the oldest in the Napa Valley, and two literary shrines before reaching the spa town of Calistoga. Beyond are geysers, a petrified forest, and an (extinct) volcano. (*See map opposite.*)

Sonoma Plaza

The Wine and Visitors Center
Just off Highway 101 between Santa Rosa and the dairy town of Petaluma, the user-friendly computers of the Sonoma County Wine and Visitors Center hold extensive information on the many wineries of Sonoma County and will even print out an itinerary listing details of those you choose to visit.

►► **The Wine Country**
Sonoma Valley Quieter and less commercialized than the better-known Napa Valley immediately east, the Sonoma Valley nevertheless boasts some of the state's finest—and oldest—wineries, and has historical and literary associations worth savoring as much as the produce of its vines.

At the southern end of the valley, the town of Sonoma►► grew around the site of California's last and most northern Spanish mission. By the time the mission was completed, control of California had passed to Mexico and General Mariano Vallejo was developing Sonoma as a base for his enormous agricultural estate.

Besides the impressive chapel funded by Vallejo, the Sonoma Mission► itself is not particularly interesting, but it does sit neatly among the 19th-century adobe and wood buildings which form the perimeter of the 8-acre plaza at Sonoma's center.

Many of these buildings now have stores, hotels, and

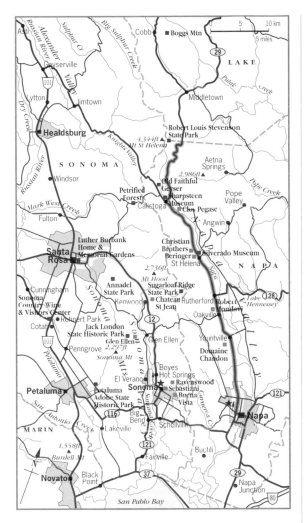

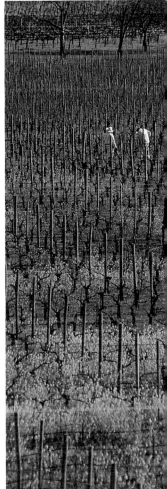

Springtime vineyards

restaurants, although several on the northern side have been restored and contain historical displays and exhibits.

The most substantial collection is inside the **Sonoma Barracks►►** and focuses on the 1846 Bear Flag Revolt, when a group of U.S. fur trappers descended on the town, took Vallejo and Sonoma's small Mexican garrison captive, and declared California an independent republic (a few weeks later came the declaration of full U.S. rule).

Although his enormous *rancho* was broken up, Vallejo accepted the change in government and became a member of the new state's first senate, moving in 1851 into a pretty wooden house named **Lachryma Montis►►**, a few minutes' walk from the plaza. Today, the house holds mementoes of Vallejo's occupancy and a small museum which makes clear his deep influence on the Sonoma region.

First wines It was Vallejo's vineyards which encouraged a visiting Hungarian, Agoston Haraszthy, to import European vine cuttings and start a winery just outside

Zinfandel: mystery grape
While most Californian grapes are clearly of European origin, the roots of Zinfandel are shrouded in mystery. A Black Zinfandel wine appeared on the U.S.'s East Coast in 1838, and Zinfandel grapes were first grown in California 20 years later, but where the grapes actually come from is uncertain: Experts have cited southern Italy, Slovenia, and even California itself, as the true home of Zinfandel.

Sonoma. Haraszthy's wines triggered the growth of the California wine industry during the 1880s, earning him the sobriquet "the father of California wines." Haraszthy died in Nicaragua in the 1860s, and his abandoned winery was severely damaged by the 1906 earthquake, but the **Buena Vista Winery**►► (tel. 707/938 1266) was restored and resumed wine production in the 1940s. It can now claim to be the oldest premium winery in the state.

Lacking such historical resonance but winning plenty of acclaim for its wines, the **Sebastiani Vineyard**►► (tel. 707/938 5532), within walking distance of Sonoma's plaza, is another promising visit; so too is **Ravenswood**► (tel. 707/938 1960), which specializes in Zinfandel (see panel, page 205).

Glen Ellen North from Sonoma, Highway 12 runs the 17-mile length of the valley, but opting instead for the less congested Arnold Drive will carry you 6 miles into the town of **Glen Ellen**, where you should veer off along London Ranch Road and climb steeply into the hills.

Jack London After several rapidly ascending miles, the route takes you to the entrance of **Jack London State Historic Park**►►►. This covers roughly half of the 1,400 acres of meadows and woodlands which the San Francisco-born writer bought in the early 1900s with the intention of building a home—the 26-room Wolf House—and running a farm. He named the area the Beauty Ranch. Tragically, the Wolf House, three years in construction and costing $80,000, was destroyed by an unexplained fire just days after its completion in 1913. London died here in 1916.

Near the park's entrance, the **House of Happy Walls**►►, lived in by London's widow until her death in 1955, now serves as the park's visitor center. It holds two floors of engrossing London-related material, spanning his writings and travels, and also displays some of the custom-built furniture intended for the Wolf House. Outside, a short footpath leads to the still-upright stone

... the Napa Valley Wine Train

walls of the **Wolf House►►**, making clear the building's layout and incredible size.

A side trail leads to London's **grave site**, where his ashes were buried beside the graves of two pioneer-era children. Another trail loops back to the parking lot and continues to the remains of London's farm and the wooden cottage where he and his wife briefly lived.

Kenwood Returning to Glen Ellen and continuing north, **Kenwood** is another friendly town and one with several worthwhile wineries. The best-known among them is **Château St. Jean►►** (tel. 707/833 4134), as appealing for its beautifully landscaped grounds and stone buildings as for its award-winning white wines.

North from Kenwood, **Sugarloaf Ridge►** and **Annandel►** state parks protect wide areas of hillside; both offer a chance to shake off wine-induced lethargy and strike out across many miles of hiking trails.

Santa Rosa Impossible to miss from a high vantage point in either park is the urban sprawl which consumes the northern end of the valley, where Highway 12 swings westwards to reach **Santa Rosa**. This is the route you should take to return to San Francisco (joining Highway 101 from Santa Rosa). If you have time to spare, drop into Santa Rosa's **Luther Burbank Home and Memorial Gardens►►** (415 Steele Lane), the home and experimental garden of a now-legendary horticulturalist.

Santa Rosa was also the birthplace in 1908 of Robert L. Ripley, whose *Believe It or Not!* cartoons, illustrating odd phenomena from around the world, began in the 1920s and mushroomed into the Believe It or Not! museums dotted around the U.S. today. The **Ripley Memorial Museum►** (492 Sonoma Avenue), which commemorates his achievements, is housed in the subject of one of his first cartoons: the Church of One Tree, a gothic-style chapel built from a single redwood.

Wineries in all directions

Valley of the Moon
Jack London's 1913 novel, *Valley of the Moon*, was set in and bestowed a lasting nickname on the Sonoma Valley. In fact, the term originated from a mistaken translation of the Native American word for the valley.

Sonoma City Hall

EXCURSIONS

Sonoma Cheese factory

Napa Valley by train
The 1915 Pullman cars of the Napa Valley Wine Train—locally dubbed the "swine train" for its noise, diesel fumes, and gung-ho tourists—runs between Napa and St. Helena, serving expensive gourmet-standard food and a selection of Napa Valley wines for lunch or dinner (or weekend brunch). The return-trip costs between approximately $25 and $70, to include food. Early reservations are strongly advised (tel. 1-800/427 4124).

Napa Valley by bike
The Napa Valley's Silverado Trail, a route running parallel to the busy Highway 29, makes for trouble-free bicycle touring, provided you do not overdo the wine tasting on the way. Bikes can be rented for around $15–$25 a day from a number of outlets including St. Helena Cyclery, 1156 Main Street, St. Helena (tel. 707/963 7736), and Jule's BikeRents, 1227 Lincoln Boulevard, Calistoga (tel. 707/942 0421).

Napa Valley by balloon
Soaring above it in a helium-filled balloon is one way to tour the Napa Valley, and several companies offer a few hours aloft for around $150. A light meal and a few glasses of champagne are usually included in the price. Reserve early and keep your fingers crossed for a wind-free day (strong gusts may cause the ride to be canceled). Among the many operators are Adventures Aloft (tel. 707/255 8688), and Once In A Lifetime (tel. 707/942 6541).

The Napa Valley An hour's drive from San Francisco and marking the southern end of the Napa Valley, the town of **Napa** grew rich as a transit center for the produce of the Napa Valley's wineries in the mid-19th century and has many Victorian buildings in its historic riverside area.

The town has few wineries, however, and a better first stop in the valley is **Yountville▶**, a few miles north on Highway 29 (which runs the length of the valley), where champagne devotees will be in seventh heaven sampling the fare of **Domain Chandon▶** (tel. 707/944 2280), owned by the first-rate French company, Moët.

Oakville and Rutherford Many of the valley's best wineries are scattered along Highway 29 near the neighboring towns of **Oakville** and **Rutherford**. Here, the one-hour complimentary tours and tastings offered by the **Robert Mondavi Winery▶▶** (tel. 707/259 9463) are recommended for learning something about the intricacies of Californian wines and the wine-making process.

St. Helena A favorite weekend getaway for San Franciscans, St. Helena has numerous gourmet restaurants and bed-and-breakfast inns. Wood-framed buildings of the late 1800s line the pretty Main Street. Inheritor of a goldrush fortune, William B. Bourn built the distinctive stone building which houses the town's **Greystone Cellars▶▶** (tel. 707/967 1100) where, in addition to tastings, tours take in a collection of historic wine-making equipment.

Historically, the Californian wine industry has endured two major setbacks. A plant louse destroyed almost all the valley's vines in the 1870s, while during Prohibition the only wineries able to continue production were those manufacturing sacramental wine for the Catholic Church. St. Helena's **Beringer Vineyards▶** (tel. 707/963 7115) was one which did so, and is the valley's oldest continuously operating winery.

Scottish writer Robert Louis Stevenson passed through St. Helena in 1880 and based his novel, *The Silverado Squatters*, on the area's silver-miners. He is remembered with a collection of memorabilia at the **Silverado Museum►►**. A lesser-known writer's shrine is the **Ambrose Bierce House►**, a compact bed-and-breakfast inn dating from 1872, now named after and containing an intriguing collection devoted to Bierce, a Californian journalist and novelist of the late 1800s (see page 37).

Seven miles north of St. Helena, what **Clos Pegase►►** lacks in historical pedigree—the winery opened in 1986—is more than compensated for by its design. The complex has an imposing Greco-Roman look.

Calistoga Strange as it may seem, water and mud do more to bring visitors to **Calistoga►►** than does wine, the mineral-rich springs, and volcanic mud of the valley's northernmost town having done wonders for people's health since prehistoric times. Calistoga was developed as a spa resort in the 1860s by Sam Brannan, a flamboyant California pioneer and millionaire (see page 37). The dioramas of the **Sharpsteen Museum►►** illustrate the town's growth, and the museum keeps one of Brannan's original resort cottages furnished in 1860s style.

Geysers and volcanoes Any doubts about the area's geothermal activity will quickly be dispelled by the **Old Faithful Geyser►**, a mile north of Calistoga, which propels a jet of boiling water 60 feet skywards once or twice an hour. A less dramatic but more impressive manifestation of the area's seismic rumblings is the **Petrified Forest►►**, 5 miles west of Calistoga off Petrified Forest Road. A grove of redwood trees which stood on this site 6 million years ago was uprooted by an eruption of nearby (and now extinct) Mount St. Helena. Chemicals in the volcanic ash reacted with the wood and the trees were turned to stone.

Mount St. Helena 3,000 acres of the desolate slopes of Mount St. Helena form **Robert Louis Stevenson State Park►►**, where the writer enjoyed a two-month honeymoon, sharing the bunkhouse of an abandoned silvermine with his Oakland bride, Fanny Osbourne.

In Sonoma County, Petaluma Adobe State Park holds the 19th-century buildings and implements of the ranch of General Mariano Vallejo, a major Californian figure prior to U.S. rule

Calistoga—a spa town

Accommodations

From fax-equipped suites in marble towers to four-poster beds in wood-framed Victorian mansions, places to stay in San Francisco are as abundant as the hills and as varied as the views. The choices appeal to all tastes and budgets, and even better is the fact that San Franciscan accommodation is a fiercely contested business, with an overabundance of hotels, motels, and inns all vying for your dollar.

Price ranges A few hotels are able to offer very inexpensive accommodation, as low as $45 per night, by providing small rooms without private bathroom, TV, and phone (though frequently such establishments do offer rooms with these items for $10–$15 extra). Spend anything upwards of $65, however, and you can expect a pleasantly decorated private bathroom, color TV (usually with cable channels), and a direct-dial phone as standard features.

Not surprisingly, room prices rise with room size and also reflect the quality. As the price rises above about $140 a night, your expectations should include a well-stocked mini-bar, a video library from which movies can be rented and, in the bathroom, a hair-dryer and a fine array of soaps, shampoos, and lotions.

Spend $240 or more and you really start tasting the good life, with private jacuzzi, stunning view, perhaps a CD player, round-the-clock room service, and complimentary morning newspapers.

Special levels Many top hotels have a particular floor where the rooms may be no different to those on other floors but are priced (upwards of $280) to include use of meeting areas and a communal room, where complimentary newspapers, magazines, snacks, and drinks are replenished throughout the day, and where staff are on hand to attend to your every whim. More often than not, guests reach this exclusive level with a special elevator key.

City areas San Francisco is small and easy to get around with few unpleasant areas, therefore choosing where you stay is a much less critical consideration than it is in some U.S. cities. The densest concentrations of hotels are in

Haight Street inn

210

Budget lodgings

and around tourist dominated Fisherman's Wharf and the geographically convenient Union Square.

Increasingly, however, adventurous visitors are discovering the smaller and less impersonal hotels and bed-and-breakfast inns which are scattered throughout characterful residential neighborhoods such as Pacific Heights and Haight-Ashbury. By contrast, the area around the junction of Van Ness Avenue and Lombard Street has been dubbed "motel row" with dozens of motels offering clean if uninspired rooms ($50–$70).

Obviously, there is no need to spend all your San Francisco nights in one location, and a night or two outside the city (see panel) is also worth considering.

Hotel types San Francisco hotels come in all shapes and sizes. Many of the major chains such as Holiday Inn and Sheraton have recently built properties in the Fisherman's Wharf area. There are few bargains to be found in this neighborhood (prices are generally $90–$160), but these hotels provide dependable bases and are where many package tourists find themselves staying.

Around Union Square, the heart of the city as far as most visitors are concerned, many mid-priced ($70–$120), medium-sized hotels benefit from proximity to the city's transportation centers, as well as having much of interest (Chinatown, North Beach, Nob Hill, and more), within walking distance.

Expensive lodgings: the Westin St. Francis and Tower, over-looking Union Square

Outside the city
Spending a night across the bay provides an enjoyable change of pace and scenery. Sausalito has several hotels perched on its hillsides; none are cheap and all are fully reserved on weekends, but they offer a chance to stroll in the quaint village after the day-trippers have departed. A stopover in Berkeley encourages a long and leisurely gourmet meal in one of the town's award-winning restaurants without the prospect of indigestion induced by a dash back to the city.

ACCOMMODATIONS

Accommodations agencies
San Francisco accommo-
dation can be reserved
through most travel agents
or by contacting a particular property directly. In
addition, San Francisco
Reservations, 4th Floor, 22
Second Street (tel. 415/227
1500), provides a free
reservation service for its
200 member hotels, and
B&B accommodations can
be arranged through Bed &
Breakfast International,
P.O. Box 282910, San
Francisco, CA 94128-2910
(tel. 1-800/696 1690, reservations 1-800/872 4500, fax:
415/692 1699), and Bed &
Breakfast San Francisco,
PO Box 420009, San
Francisco, CA 94142 (tel.
415/479 1913).

*Chinatown's Holiday
Inn*

Japantown's Miyako

Also close to Union Square, the Financial District and its
environs are dotted with high-rise hotels (from $180) tar-
geted at expense-account guests. While the facilities—
such as in-room fax machines and a complimentary *Wall
Street Journal* each day—may be the stuff of business
travelers' dreams, the vacationer may be tempted instead
by attractive weekend discounts liable to bring prices
down to $120, or less.

Boutique hotels Mostly scattered between Union
Square and Nob Hill, a growing number of "boutique
hotels" (typically $80–$140) have turned what might once
have been an affluent family home into a small, elegantly
furnished hotel with as few as 20 rooms. Boutique hotels
pride themselves on fostering a close, informal
relationship with their guests. Breakfast is normally
included, and complimentary wine or sherry will often be
served in the early evening.

Bed and breakfast Many rambling Victorian homes
throughout the city have been refurbished and converted
into bed-and-breakfast inns. Widely fluctuating prices
($60–$190) reflect the fact that both the individual
properties and the rooms within them can vary greatly.
Some rooms may be small with a shared bathroom,
others might be fully-equipped suites with jacuzzi and
ultramodern CD sound systems.
B&Bs commonly serve complimentary wine and sherry
in the afternoon or evening, sometimes with nuts, fruit,
and an array of homebaked cakes. Breakfast is included
and, in most cases, is far more delicious and nutritious
than a trip to the local diner. Some B&B rooms do not

have TVs or phones as standard features (and some B&Bs celebrate the fact that they offer an escape from such things), but these can be provided if required.

The popularity of B&Bs means that you should make a reservation early, especially if arriving during the summer or staying over a weekend. Besides contacting the B&B directly, reservations can be made through the specialist agencies listed in the panel on page 212.

Gay accommodation Wherever they stay in this tolerant and liberal city, gay and lesbian travelers are unlikely to encounter unpleasantness or hostility from hotel staff although, obviously, not every homophobic visitor to San Francisco leaves their potentially offensive attitudes at home. A number of hotels and bed-and-breakfast inns, particularly in the Castro district, are staffed by, and cater specifically to, gays and lesbians.

Budget accommodation While hotel rooms may average $100 a night, San Francisco is still good news for travelers on tight budgets, with a number of official AYH and privately run hostels, plus a YMCA, offering beds in small dormitories for around $14 a night, and single and double rooms for $25–$40. The hostels include the 170-room San Francisco International Hostel at Fort Mason, the largest youth hostel in the U.S. Others are found all across the city, giving a wide range of location options. Many hostels impose a three-night maximum stay during the busy summer season, and some operate an evening curfew.

Seasonal considerations Most visitors to San Francisco arrive from June to August, when it is wise to reserve accommodations well in advance of arrival. Prices are $10–$30 higher throughout this period than during the rest of the year (when advance reservations are advisable, though not absolutely essential). Keep in mind, however, that San Francisco enjoys its best weather from late September to early November, when sunshine is common and unhindered by the fogs which cool many summer days.

Except for hotels especially geared for business travelers, weekend prices are always higher than weekday prices. Be warned that accommodations can sometimes be at a premium when the city hosts a major convention, though this chiefly applies to Financial District hotels and those in SoMa near the Moscone Convention Center.

Hidden extras The prices quoted are average rates for double rooms but—like most advertized rates—do not include a total tax surcharge of 12 percent which, once added to bills, can provide a shock for unsuspecting guests when they check out. If your room has a mini-bar, be sure to scrutinize the price list before helping yourself: prices can be three or four times higher than normal.

Ecclesiastical bed-and-breakfast: Alamo Square's Archbishop's Mansion

213

Food and drink

San Franciscans are enthusiastic eaters

Eating and drinking are major preoccupations in San Francisco, a city which boasts as many restaurants as New York (around 4,000 at the last count), offering everything from downhome American diner fare to cuisines culled from every corner of the globe. For Californians with cultured palates—or just big appetites—San Francisco is much less about bay views, cable cars, and the Golden Gate Bridge, than it is about putting the latest restaurant to the test and keeping up with the comings and goings of the city's top chefs.

Prices Fierce competition helps keep prices to levels which Europeans in particular will find impressively low. All but the most exclusive restaurants are well within the range of the majority of travelers, and it is fairly easy to eat well wherever you are in the city.

As a general rule, budget for $6–$8 per person for breakfast, around $10 for lunch, and $15–$20 for dinner. Expect all of these figures to rise sharply as the quality of the setting improves, and for a special evening meal with liberal amounts of wine, expect to spend $50–$75 per person. Wherever you dine, a tip of at least 15 percent is expected; reward extremely good service with a tip closer to 20 percent.

Breakfast fare Breakfast is the only dish of the San Franciscan day which differs little from what is found all across the U.S. A three-egg omelette with a choice of fillings likely to include various cheeses, vegetables, ham, and even fruit, accompanied by hash browns (a version of fried potatoes) and toast (or a muffin) are staple offerings in most coffee shops, where the breakfast menu will also include waffles and generous helpings of pancakes.

Classier places, and the on-site restaurants of many upscale hotels, can provide a more varied breakfast, offering any combination of the above plus cereals, fresh-baked breads and muffins, fruit, and fresh juices.

Eating with children
All but the most exclusive San Franciscan restaurants welcome children. Young diners will often be handed toys and coloring sets as soon as they sit down and those who are old enough to read will find they have their own section of the menu, where child-sized portions and perennial kids' favorites such as burgers, chips (called 'fries'), onion rings, and ice cream feature prominently.

Culinary neighborhoods Like the local climate, food in San Francisco can change considerably within the space of a few blocks, some neighborhoods being synonymous with a particular ethnic fare. North Beach (Italian food) and Chinatown (Chinese) are the obvious examples and both are worth exploring. Elsewhere, be it the new influx of Asian restaurants taking root in the Tenderloin, the Salvadorean bakeries of the Mission District, the high-class French restaurants of Nob Hill, or the nouveau hippie hangouts of Haight-Ashbury, lies much more to stimulate the touring gastronome.

Eating Italian The streets of North Beach are jammed with Italian restaurants offering first-rate regional cuisine from every inch of the Mediterranean country. Almost all of them provide excellent value: a simple fresh pasta dish is unlikely to be more than $7, and a six-course dinner for less than $20 is not unknown.

North Beach dining is no secret, however, and for evening meals you should plan to dine early (before 7p.m.) to avoid the worst of the crowds, especially on Fridays and Saturdays. The more upscale North Beach restaurants will accept reservations, but many of the more intimate and enjoyable places do not.

Earlier in the day, you should have no difficulty finding a cosy niche inside one of the neighborhood's many atmospheric cafés, where you can linger over a cappuccino and a wide choice of light Italian lunches and dessert delicacies to your heart's (and your stomach's) content.

North Beach may be the spiritual home of Italian cuisine in San Francisco (and Italian food is available across the city) but not every restaurant located there is guaranteed to delight. Over the last two decades, the increasing commercialism of the area has caused many locals to stick to the tried and tested haunts (some restaurants are almost old as the city) and give a wide

> **A special crab**
> During its mid-November to June season, look out for Dungeness crab, which many Italian restaurants serve as the center-piece of an Italian-San Franciscan seafood dish called *cioppino*, a throw-everything-in type of fish stew which, the story goes, was first concocted by the wives of the city's late-1800s Sicilian settlers. Dungeness crab also claws its way onto menus elsewhere—in Chinatown, look for it deliciously prepared in ginger and garlic.

215

ITALIAN FRENCH
BAKING CO.
of
SAN FRANCISCO
French Bread & Rolls
Rich Pinocci
(415) 421-3796
1501 Grant Avenue
San Francisco

Italian delis offer plenty of picnic choice

NEECHA
THAI CUISINE

00 SUTTER STREET
ear Steiner)
AN FRANCISCO, CA 94115

LUNCH Mon.-Fri. 11 - 3 p.m.
DINNER Daily 5 - 10 p.m.
TEL: (415) 922-9419

berth to some of North Beach's newer and brasher dining places.

Chinatown fare Chinese food has long been a feature of San Francisco, and Chinatown its culinary hot spot, despite the fact that many of the top Chinese chefs have departed for other areas, notably the Richmond District where Clement Street has many Asian restaurants of merit.

Within Chinatown, prices are exceptionally low ($5 buys a good lunch, $8 a filling dinner), and cooking styles, which reflect every region of China, have been expanded by the diverse ethnic backgrounds of recent immigrants. Besides Cantonese, Mandarin, Hunan, Hakka, and Szechuan fare, unusual Vietnamese-Chinese and even Peruvian-Chinese dishes can also be found enlivening menus.

Only in Hong Kong are you likely to encounter a greater variety of dim sum—pastries and dumplings filled with seafood, meat, or vegetables—than in Chinatown. The most popular dim sum restaurants (locally called "tea houses") are large and lively, and predominantly cater to a neighborhood Chinese clientele. Dim sum is usually served from 10a.m. to 3p.m., though the best dishes have often been consumed by 1p.m. Many dim sum restaurants serve regular Chinese dinners during the evening.

Dim sum is not ordered from a menu but is served from carts which are wheeled around the tables, pausing at each one long enough for diners to make their selections before returning to the kitchen to be restocked. Westerners unfamiliar with this system will do well to look interested but puzzled, and hope that the waiter or waitress will offer a description of what is offered in English. If they do not, just point to what looks good—but remember that one of the carts will be carrying dessert dishes.

When you have eaten your fill (which may take some

216

Dim sum delights
Popular dim sum dishes include _Cha Sil Bow_ – steamed pork bun; _Gai Bow_ – steamed chicken bun; _Chern Goon_ – spring rolls; _Sil Mi_ – steamed pork and shrimp dumpling. Less popular ones among Westerners include _Gai Guerk_ – braised chicken feet, and _Op Guerk_ – braised duck's feet.

A North Beach garlic specialist

time, dim sum is intended to be a leisurely experience), the cost is determined by the number of empty dishes or baskets on your table.

American classics— around the clock

Thai and Indian Many Thai, and a lesser number of Indian restaurants, are well established all over San Francisco, and are much like their counterparts in any other Western country. Anyone with a liking for hot, spicy food should remember that few Americans share this trait and most Indian and Thai dishes will be served in mild forms. Hotter dishes are usually indicated on the menu. Few are budget-priced but most offer good value: expect to pay around $10 for lunch and around $15 for dinner.

More Asian More appealing to the gastronomically adventurous—and the budget-minded—are the batch of Vietnamese, Laotian, and Cambodian restaurants which have appeared on the city's culinary scene in recent years. Many of them are located in the seedy Tenderloin area, which deters some would-be diners, while their bare tables and spartan furnishings come as a shock to San Franciscans weaned on luxurious decor and fancy tablecloths. Within these no-frills surroundings, however, you can feast on barbecued shrimp and sugarcane or spicy chicken in coconut milk and still emerge with ample change from $10.

Seafood at its freshest

Japanese food
In San Francisco, aim for Japantown's Japan Center and you will discover several dozen restaurants and sushi bars providing a treat for the tastebuds for under $7 (lunch) and $12 (dinner).

Mexican Its relative lack of variety and sophistication tends to deter San Francisco's spoiled diners from raving about Mexican food, although a number of reliable restaurants throughout the city present the usual U.S. version of south-of-the-border fare.

Most of these offer a meat-free alternative, such as fish tacos and the cheese-filled *quesadilla*, to the staple beef, pork, and chicken main dishes (served with a variety of corn or flour tortillas), together with margaritas delivered by the glass or pitcher in a variety of frozen and fruit flavors.

FOOD AND DRINK

Asian tastes are easily found

Sourdough bread
Slightly bitter and chewy, sourdough bread has been around for thousands of years in many countries but first appeared in San Francisco during the gold rush, when yeast and baking powder were in short supply and settlers made bread using a sour starter, a fermented mixture of flour and water which enabled the dough to rise (see also panel, page 93).

Vegetarian dining
Most vegetarians need never go hungry in San Francisco, where every restaurant—except possibly the most red-blooded steak house—will offer at least one, usually several, vegetarian dishes. There is also a generous sprinkling of exclusively vegetarian eating places, from the gourmet-standard Greens at Fort Mason Center, to innumerable small, inexpensive ethnic hole-in-the-wall diners.

The "festive" atmosphere of such places is at odds with the simple Mexican restaurants of the strongly Hispanic Mission District, which concentrate much less on atmosphere—bare tables and peeling paint on the walls are the order of the day—than on presenting a large, wholesome meal at a price rarely reaching $5.

Latin American Mexican may be the Mission District's dominant cuisine, but the area also holds dozens of restaurants and bakeries representing many of the countries of Latin America. Here you can sample a Puerto Rican seafood stew, try goat curry, or wrestle with an authentic Cuban sandwich—all for just a few dollars. Even if you find the rough and ready atmosphere of the restaurants—and the staff's lack of English—intimidating, stick around long enough to try a few gluttonous snacks from the bakeries lining Mission and 24th streets.

Bohemian eats For a meal in the company of the city's cutting-edge artists, writers, lesser media celebrities, and full-time nightclubbers, try any of the restaurants and cafés that drift in and out of style along Haight-Ashbury's Haight Street or SoMa's Folsom Street. Many of these serve no more than basic, filling American food—such as enormous omelettes, huge sandwiches, and all types of burgers—but do so surrounded by bizarre decor and a carefully cultivated bohemian atmosphere. Prices are rarely much higher than run-of-the-mill coffee shops, though some turn out food of a standard high enough for food snobs in suits to be found dining next to embryonic poets in thrift-store rags.

Tourist grub Few San Franciscans would dream of eating in tourist-packed Fisherman's Wharf. Despite claims to the contrary, comparatively little of the seafood offered actually comes from local waters, and most dishes can be found in better and less expensive forms elsewhere. Visitors with hunger pangs are well advised to limit their eating to snacks from seafood stalls on the street. Clam chowder in a bowl of sourdough bread (a chewy, slightly bitter bread otherwise best eaten toasted—see panel) is one tasty if expensive—over $3—option. But try to preserve your appetite for more inspiring surroundings. If this proves impossible, forego the seafood for the costly but usually excellent ethnic restaurants found at Ghirardelli Square.

California cuisine In the late 1970s, the upscale restaurants on Berkeley's Shattuck Avenue pioneered what became known as California cuisine. A handful of inventive chefs took the abundant supplies of fresh meat, vegetables, and fruit raised or grown on the state's farms, and the produce of its fish-stocked rivers and the ocean, and began criss-crossing the borders of international cuisine, juxtaposing traditional methods of preparation, flavoring, and styling.

The masterminds of California cuisine selected ingredients for their nutritional balance, appealing to the digestive tract as much as the tastebuds. In some cases, animals were reared and vegetables grown to the exact specifications of a restaurant, and some chefs bought seafood only from known and trusted fishermen. To satisfy the true gourmet's aesthetic sense, color co-ordination was also important, aiding the artful presentation of food on the plate.

The individuality of each chef prevented any single dish, which might be anything from grilled pigeon breasts to red snapper in peanut sauce, from becoming uniquely associated with California cuisine, although the techniques from the period have since been widely adopted—and almost taken for granted—among San Francisco's latest influx of first-rate chefs. The best of a number of San Franciscan restaurants describing their fare as "Californian" continue the themes of California cuisine. On any particular day, the menu will feature whatever ingredients are in season, and preparation will span a diverse assortment of cooking styles. Often a Californian wine will be recommended to enhance the flavor. Do not expect platefuls of red meat but do expect a small portion of food to cost upwards of $25.

Sunday brunch
A mix of late breakfast and early lunch, brunch is a Sunday fixture for many San Franciscans. With the cost depending on the trendiness of the restaurant, and the combination of food and alcohol included in the price, it usually lasts from 10a.m. to 2p.m. The restaurant sections of local newspapers and magazines have plenty of suggestions as to the best brunch spots—but be sure to make a reservation before heading out.

San Francisco has cuisines from all corners

FOOD AND DRINK

Luxury Chinese dining

A more egalitarian offshoot of California cuisine has been the exotically topped pizzas—goat's cheese, duck and lobster are among the favorites—baked in traditional wood-fired brick ovens and delivered to the masses (or anyone who does not mind spending $10–$15) by a number of establishments, including the ever-expanding California Pizza Kitchen chain.

U.S. regional As their tastebuds steadily exhaust the cuisines of the world, many San Franciscans—like their counterparts in other major American cities—are rediscovering the regional cuisines of the U.S. Anyone weaned on blackened cajun catfish in Louisiana or on the fiery fare of the southwest, would be unlikely to find their childhood favorites among the painstakingly prepared dishes which are featured on the menus of the city's "contemporary American" restaurants.

Many of these nestle among the ritzy boutiques of the city's more expensive residential areas, particularly Pacific Heights. Here, top-rated chefs present gourmet variations on regional fare which bear the nutritional and aesthetic imprint of California cuisine and often use regional inspiration in the preparation, spices, and sauces, rather than in the dish itself. Be it jambalaya with duck, or grilled quail pie, regional American fare can be full of surprises, though many restaurants distanced from the frontiers of gastronomy simply include mesquite-grilled seafood (swordfish is a favorite) and steaks as their token regional dishes.

French Legend has it that the French chefs who traveled west from New York with their wealthy, financier bosses in the late 19th century and opted to open restaurants there rather than return, were the root of San Franciscans' obsession with good eating.

The more affordable of the city's present-day French restaurants are the cozy imitation Parisian bistros which usually offer well-priced (around $15) lunchtime fare. In the evening, candlelight and lingering romantic dinners (typically $25 per person plus wine) are the rule. When they feel like dressing for dinner, however, San Franciscans head for one of the city's expensive French restaurants where the tablecloth creases are razor sharp, the staff are as smartly attired as the customers, and full-length gold-framed mirrors reflect the city's great and good wining, dining, and not batting an eyelid at spending over $100 each.

Drinks San Franciscans take drinking almost as seriously as they take eating. Knowing which café has the most flavorful coffee and which Californian winery has produced this year's best Chardonnay are vital concerns, regarded as essential to a person's well being.

Coffee-drinkers' paradise The aroma of freshly roasted beans may waft across North Beach's streets less frequently than in the past, but San Francisco is still a coffee-drinkers' town. Like their counterparts all over the U.S., every city diner will rush steaming mugs of fresh-brewed coffee (75¢–$1) to patrons with the usual choice between regular and decaffeinated, and bring free refills as often as desired.

For its many coffee aficionados, however, the city has hundreds of cafés which earn customer loyalty through the brand of bean they use, and the taste and appearance of the cappuccino or espresso which they serve. Italian cafés are part of North Beach culture but many more—be they refined or bohemian in ambience—are found in every neighborhood (see pages 138–9). In a café, expect to pay $1–$2 per cup.

Tea-drinkers' alternatives The freshness and quality of San Francisco's coffee may encourage devoted tea drinkers to change their habits, at least for the duration of their visit. Tea in San Francisco can mean selecting between high-grade leaves such as oolong or Earl Grey,

Buying alcohol in shops
Antisocial drinkers, or anyone who wants to make their hotel room a more convivial place, will find plenty of choice (provided they are 21 or over) in supermarkets and in most grocery stores between 6a.m. and 2a.m. Californian wines can be exceptionally good value, often costing as little as $4 a bottle. Imported beers and lagers are generally $6–$7 per six-pack, domestic beers around $4 per six-pack. Hard liquor is predictably pricier and cannot be sold between 2a.m. and 6a.m.

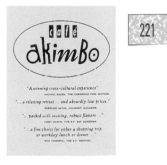

café
aKimBo

"A winning cross-cultural experience"
MICHAEL BAUER, THE CHRONICLE PINK SECTION
"... a relaxing retreat ... and absurdly low prices."
CAROLINE WATER, GOURMET MAGAZINE
"... packed with inviting, robust flavors ..."
JANET HAZEN, THE S.F. BAY GUARDIAN
"... a fine choice for either a shopping trip
or workday lunch or dinner ..."
RON CONSBERG, THE S.F. SENTINEL

Eating al fresco is easy

Above: early evening wine and snacks are a bonus at many hotels
Below: for Italian fare try North Beach

222

which are liable to be offered in the more upwardly mobile cafés and in upscale hotel lounges. Top-rate tea can also be sipped in the company of cucumber sandwiches and scones as part of afternoon tea, an increasingly popular activity among the city's more affluent residents (see pages 132–3).

Irish coffee If a North Beach espresso fails to get the blood flowing, you might try Irish coffee which, allegedly, made its first U.S. appearance when served at the Buena Vista Café (2765 Hyde Street) in 1952. Whatever the truth in this tale, Irish coffee—a mix of coffee, Irish whiskey, sugar, and whipped cream—turns up in many bars, cafés and restaurants, and a glassful will undoubtedly help you face the city's sea breezes.

Alcohol in moderation Although there are exceptions, few San Franciscans drink alcohol with the aim of getting drunk, and they are much more likely to order a glass of wine to stimulate their tastebuds in preparation for dinner, or drop into a bar for a few sociable beers with friends on their way home from work.

Most restaurants are fully licensed, and many cafés also serve a limited range of beer, wine, and spirits. The city's many bars are seldom intimidating affairs, and an unaccompanied woman is by no means a rare sight. Most bars are also refreshingly free (or almost free) from cigarette smoke.

American beers such as Budweiser and Miller are sold on draft and in bottles in virtually every bar, and many establishments also carry a small selection of bottled European lagers (occasionally found on tap) and Mexican beers—imported brews are more expensive but far higher in quality, and strength, than their U.S. counterparts.

Most bars also stock Anchor Steam Beer, which is brewed in San Francisco (and has been since the gold rush) and has many local admirers. If the bar stocks them, the adventurous beer drinker should also investigate the

Opening hours
Legally, bars can be open at any time between 6a.m. and 2a.m., though most choose to open their doors around 11a.m. and close them around midnight (later on Fridays and Saturdays). Provided they are licensed, restaurants can serve alcohol throughout their hours of business except between 2a.m. and 6a.m.

output of California's microbreweries, increasingly prevalent across the state and often making excellent beers. At least two San Francisco bars brew their beer on the premises (see pages 84–5).

California wine Many wine drinkers are drawn to San Francisco by its proximity to the Wine Country (see pages 204–9), the country's major wine-producing region. While the wineries of the Napa and Sonoma valleys (the heart of the Wine Country) undoubtedly lead the field, skilled vintners are found all across the state and often produce wines of impressive quality. The classier a restaurant is, the lengthier its wine list will be (and it may also carry selected European vintages). Asking the waiter for advice is regarded not as a sign of oenological ignorance, but as an indication of genuine interest.

Wines ordered in a restaurant will usually cost $3-$4 a glass, or proportionately less if ordered by the bottle or half bottle. Most bars stock a reasonable selection of wines.

Hard liquor and cocktails Many restaurants and almost every bar will carry a range of hard liquor, including a selection of malt whiskies, Russian vodkas, and various types of bourbon. European visitors should note that these are served in more generous measures than they are at home, and should insist on their drink being served "straight," if they do not want a pile of ice ("on the rocks") in their glass. Some bars have their own specialty cocktails.

Juice power Caffeine- and sugar-laden soft drinks, such as the ubiquitous Coke and Pepsi, have long since fallen from favor among health-conscious San Franciscans, for whom fresh fruit juices are a preferred soft drink. Special protein-packed juice blends—varieties of orange, grapefruit, and carrot juice, combined with parsley, ginger, spinach, and other root vegetables—which are sold in juice bars and at some gyms, are enjoying a surge in popularity. You should expect to spend $2–$4 for an energizing glassful.

Hot-dog lovers will find health-conscious San Francisco has relatively few street food stands, but liquid refreshment is always available

Shopping

From the smooth and sophisticated department stores of Union Square to the wacky and radical shops of Haight-Ashbury, San Francisco has plenty for the discerning and adventurous shopper. Partly because San Franciscans like to cultivate a close relationship with their favorite retailer and partly because the tight-packed peninsula has no spare room, the vast impersonal shopping malls common in other U.S. cities are rarely found here.

Union Square shopping While one-of-a-kind shops may be very much in keeping with its character, San Francisco also has its share of those mid-20th century shrines to consumerism, department stores. Four of the leading names have outlets within a well-filled wallet's throw of Union Square.

The enormous **Macy's** occupies two sites, one on each side of Stockton Street (at the junction with O'Farrell Street). The original store, **Macy's West**, has seven floors of women's fashions, perfumes, and cosmetics, together with home furnishings and kitchen items. Across O'Farrell Street, **Macy's East** carries menswear and children's clothes, and also shows off the latest electronic appliances, gadgets, and gizmos, plus an extensive choice of luggage for those who prefer to travel heavy.

Macy's built a formidable reputation by putting dependable, good-quality merchandise within the budget of middle-income Americans. By contrast, it is expensive evening wear for those with important special functions to attend that fills the racks of **Neiman Marcus** (150 Stockton Street), where several other sections are devoted to fine china and dazzling (and dazzlingly expensive) jewelry.

Department store aficionados will need no encouragement to continue to **Saks Fifth Avenue** (384 Post Street). Compared to its neighborhood rivals, the casual browser might find Sak's short of flair and imagination. Conversely, however, it is the very lack of anything approaching trendiness which endears it to its regulars.

Near Union Square Any money left over after scouring the Union Square department stores will quickly be gobbled up along nearby Maiden Lane. This cobbled street is lined by stylish boutiques, such as **Chanel** (number 155), where three floors are filled with the French company's finest products, and **Candelier** (number 60), with a remarkable stock of candles and candelabras in weird and wonderful forms. Seekers after art should venture inside the architecturally striking (see page 116) **Circle Gallery** (number 140). Close by, **Gump's** (250 Post Street) has forged an unassailable reputation as a home of fine china, crystal, and world-class pearls—all sold at world-class prices—and, by San Francisco standards, has been in business forever (since 1891). A more recent arrival, but one equally well thought of by those who are financially secure and have traditional taste, is **Polo-Ralph Lauren** (90 Post Street).

Saks...Union Square

224

Computer software
With Silicon Valley less than an hour's drive away, it should be no surprise that San Francisco is a good place to buy computer equipment.

If the shops in and around the Union Square area only whet your appetite, gather up your credit cards and head for **Nordstrom** (occupying the top five floors of the San Francisco Shopping Center, 865 Market Street). After riding the spiraling escalators, you will find yourself amidst a colossal assortment of men's and women's fashions. If you fail to find shoes to your liking here, you probably never will—Nordstrom stocks over 100,000 pairs.

Fisherman's Wharf San Francisco's tackiest array of tourist trinkets—garish T-shirts, souvenir mugs, toy cable cars, and worse—fills the shops lining Jefferson Street in Fisherman's Wharf. In the same area, however, are four shopping complexes which may not promise bargains, but do offer a varied selection of merchandise a cut above the usual neighborhood junk: Pier 39, The Cannery, Ghirardelli Square (described below), and The Anchorage (see panel, page 226)

Lining **Pier 39**'s wooden walkways is a large complex of intriguing specialty stores. Southpaws feeling oppressed in a largely right-handed society will find plenty to please at **Left Hand World**, where the corkscrews, can-openers, and watches are all designed with them in mind. A thousand-and-one objects in **Wound About** have one

Crocker Galleria

225

SHOPPING

A piece of Japan

Less than a mile from boisterous Haight Street are
the far quieter environs of
Japantown. As you would
expect, the local shops are
well stocked with
everything from kimonos to
rice cookers. There are
also a number of outlets for
quality Japanese arts and
crafts: to find them, cruise
the shops of Japan Center
(on Post Street) and continue to Nihonmachi Mall,
across Post Street.

*San Francisco T-shirts
come in many forms,
from the typical
tourist versions of
Fisherman's Wharf to
the neo-psychedelic
specialties of Haight
Street*

The Anchorage

With a bright, nautical
theme and 50 shops, The
Anchorage is Fisherman's
Wharf's newest shopping
complex, located directly
across Leavenworth Street
from The Cannery. The fire-
eaters, jugglers, and
clowns who regularly per-
form in its courtyard are
likely to have at least as
much appeal as the stores,
but if you want to get your
Christmas gifts early, the
Incredible Christmas Store
has just what you might
need and is open all year
round.

thing in common—they all need winding. Strange wire
and kinetic sculptures fill **Designs in Motion**.

The Cannery (2801 Leavenworth Street) offers everything from competitively priced local scenes, and other artworks, for sale in the **Print Store** to the classic 1960s
psychedelic posters and prints filling the walls and racks of
Best Comic and Rock Art Gallery. Meanwhile, the
Gourmet Market offers plenty of fine items for a picnic.

Once a chocolate factory, **Ghirardelli Square** (9800
Northpoint) provides more outlets for artistic creations
from near and far. The combined **Folk Art International**
and **Xanadu** are worth browsing for their items (usually)
created by the unsung artisans of the Third World. The
wares of the **California Crafts Museum** are the produce
of some of the state's many painters and sculptors.

Financial District deals The brokers of the Financial
District put their skills of acquisition to the test in the
expensive stores found around the elegant **Crocker
Galleria** (between Sutter and Post, and Kearny and
Montgomery streets). The Galleria's three tiers of walkways, lined by tempting food stands and benches which
make prime vantage points for peoplewatching, wind up
to a pleasant rooftop garden. On the way, **The Polo Store**
is the city's second outlet for Ralph Lauren's elegant
clothing; quality menswear also fills **The Hound**.

Women interested in exploring Scandinavian dress
trends can do so amid the Finnish designer clothing
stocked by **Marimekko**. Also for women, **Versus Gianni
Versace** offers first-class Italian fashions. Anyone seeking
to improve their looks more cheaply might pick up a pair of
snappy shades at **Rigorno Sunglasses**. The Galleria also

offers unusual stationery and greeting cards at **Cardo-Mania** and **Paper-Mania**, and local artists' paintings and ornaments at the **House of Hospitality**.

Purchasing opportunities are more varied and less expense-account oriented at **The Embarcadero Center**, on the Financial District's eastern edge (see page 81). Look for **Bare Escentuals**, with divinely decadent bath oils and lotions, and **La Donia**, glinting with imaginative jewelry.

Discount shopping If serious shopping threatens to burn a hole through your budget, remember that numerous factory-outlet stores can be found in SoMa. Many leading design companies discount their damaged or discontinued lines here, and retail operations pass on some of the savings from the area's low rents. Prices are usually 20–50 percent less than in regular stores. In a hangar-like room, **Esprit** (499 Illinois Street) fills cartons with its brightly colored Californian casualwear; **Spaccio** (645 Howard Street) might appeal to dapper males with its reduced-price Italian menswear; **ACA Joe** (149 Townsend Street) carries quality, natural-fiber sportswear. The jackets, coats, and rainwear on sale at **Coat Factory Outlet** (1350 Folsom Street) may prove attractive for reasons other than their low prices. If you run short of shopping ideas, a cruise around the multi-store outlet complexes might provide inspiration. The two floors of the **Six Sixty Center** (660 Third Street), include **Outerwear**, stocking Icelandic sweaters among other items, and **Kidswear Center**, packed with children's clothing and toys. Another group of discount outlets fills **Yerba Buena Square** (899 Howard Street).

Maiden Lane carries the scent of fine things

Thrift store shopping
Dedicated rummagers will pass many happy hours sorting through detritus—from clothes, books, and ornaments, to 1950s boomerang coffee-tables and valve-driven TVs—which can be found gathering dust in the city's many thrift stores. Every neighborhood has at least a few, their profits usually benefiting charities or the local church. To find the nearest thrift store, consult the Yellow Pages.

Discount shopping: a factory outlet store

SHOPPING

228

Union Street clothing
Seldom will you see a poorly dressed person browsing the stores of Union Street, probably because they are surrounded by some of the city's best French and Italian designer-wear outlets. Among the neighborhood favorites are, for women, American Girl in Italy (number 2163), and Coco's Italian Dreams (number 2254). Men with a hankering for the cultured European look might investigate Sy Aal (number 1864), which boasts a resident wardrobe adviser.

More shops than you can shake a credit card at are gathered under one roof at the San Francisco Shopping Center

Haight Street With its eccentric used-clothing shops, book and record outlets, funky cafés and restaurants, and skateboarding neo-hippies, Haight-Ashbury's Haight Street is rapidly becoming one of the city's most entertaining and innovative shopping strips.

Bellbottom pants, felt hats, lacy dresses, and full-length evening dresses last worn in earnest during the 1920s are all liable to appear among the racks of vintage, bizarre, or just unusual and cheap apparel, in Haight Street's never-boring secondhand clothes stores.

These open and close with great frequency, but the most firmly established include **Aardvark's** (number 1501), which has a very large stock; **Held Over Too** (number 1537), strong on 1950s sartorial favorites; **Dharma** (number 1600), specializing in Third World clothing; **Spellbound** (number 1670), with gladrags from the 1890s to the 1920s; and **Wasteland** (number 1660), which has plenty to tease and please the lover of 1960s togs and strange clothing in general.

Also on or close to Haight Street, **Revival of the Fittest** (1701 Haight Street) recycles and re-creates crazy American household knickknacks of the 1940s and 1950s; **Curious and Candles** (289 Divisadero Street) promises tarot cards, crystals, and "magical" oils; **Positively Haight Street** (1157 Masonic Avenue) carries the boldest tie-dye Tee shirts; and the giant-sized rolling papers and waterpipes of **Pipe Dreams** (1376 Haight Street) recall local concerns during Haight-Ashbury's hippie times.

Music fans in pursuit of vinyl and CDs are also well served by Haight Street. Hours of fun can be had rummaging through the secondhand stocks of **Reckless Records** (number 1401) and **Recycled Records** (number 1377). For new sounds and much more, head for **Rough Trade** (1529 Haight Street).

Union Street In contrast to the wild wares of Haight Street, the 1700–2000 blocks of Pacific Heights' Union Street provide a happy hunting ground for fine—and often very expensive—antiques and curios, and for chic clothing (see panel, page 228).

For pedigree items to hang on the wall or clutter your coffee table, investigate **Paris 1925** (number 1954), stocking art deco ornaments and accessories—rings, clocks, watches, and more, or **Artiques** (number 2167), with paintings by early Californian artists and a good selection of art-nouveau prints.

For more whimsical offerings, call at **Music Box Co.** (number 2201), where hundreds of intricate music boxes range from the genuinely antique to the hideously kitsch.

Eye-catching decorative glasswork is the stock-in-trade of **The Enchanted Crystal** (number 1771), and that long search for a Sino-Tibetan gilt-wood Buddha figure might be ended by a peek inside **Sankum** (number 1810), or **A Touch of Asia** (number 1784). Meanwhile, Chinese silk paintings and Japanese *netsuke* (wooden, bone, or ivory carved toggles) are among the exquisite merchandise of **Fumuki Fine Asian Arts** (number 2001).

More antiques In the unlikely event of antique-seekers' thirst not being quenched on Union Street, a trip to the historic brick buildings of the Jackson Square district is in order. In close proximity to the junction of Montgomery and Jackson streets, a score of upscale antiques galleries are packed to the rafters with 18th- and 19th century European dressing tables, armchairs, chests-of-drawers, Turkish rugs, and fine Asian tapestries and decorative pieces. Little of this will fit comfortably into a traveler's suitcase, but most items can be shipped around the world.

Chinatown enterprise Be it bird's nest soup or colorful kites, Chinatown thrives on buying and selling, and more shops than you can shake a chopstick at fill the neighborhood's frenetic blocks.

Local Chinese buy their essential supplies along Stockton Street and in the district's many alleyways. Visitor attention focuses on Grant Avenue and bustling emporia that stock anything and everything Asian—from sofa-sized hunks of pottery to intricate wood-carved ornaments. Silks, jade, and porcelain are for sale at competitive prices all along Grant Avenue; *netsuke* (if far from great quality) are another bargain buy.

Chinatown is one of the few places in San Francisco where tea is more highly revered than coffee. Many of the fine teas imported by **Ten Ren Tea Company** (949 Grant Avenue), can be sampled at the counter before your selection is stylishly wrapped—you could even buy a complete Chinese tea service.

Should something stranger and stronger be required,

Jackson Square antiques

Chinatown side-streets
The reward for venturing along Chinatown's side-streets and alleys is a plethora of unusual shops all much less tourist-oriented than those of Grant Avenue. For example, at Clarion Music (entrance on Waverly Place, off Sacramento Street) is a wondrous gathering of Asian musical instruments ranging from Burmese temple bells to Chinese egg rattles.

Chinatown shops

Bookshops across the bay
Insatiable bibliophiles will find plenty of stimulation along Berkeley's Telegraph Avenue, where wide-ranging new titles are found at Cody's Books (number 2454), and vast numbers of used volumes fill the shelves of Moe's (number 2476), and Shakespeare & Co. (number 2499). A ferry to Oakland's Jack London waterfront leaves you just steps from a huge link in the Barnes & Noble chain. Crossing to Larkspur, meanwhile, finds a branch of A Clean Well-lighted Place for Books awaiting disembarking ferry passengers.

drop into one of the area's many herbalists, such as **Yau Hing Co.** (831 Grant Avenue) or **Che Sung Tong** (729 Washington Street), where the cure for what ails you is certain to be in stock.

For shoppers looking for nothing more exotic than post-cards, Chinatown is still the place to be; many street stalls offer ten cards for $1.

Bookstores San Francisco is a city of bookworms and has plenty of welcoming bookstores in which to browse, buy, and even hear acclaimed authors reading their work. Widely found chain stores such as **Crown** and **Doubleday** are well-stocked with the latest titles, often at reduced prices, but it is with specialty book stores that the city excels. Many of these also carry a wide range of overseas newspapers and magazines.

Almost every neighborhood has at least one excellent bookstore. Those worth going out of your way to visit include **The Booksmith** (1644 Haight Street) and **A Clean Well-lighted Place for Books** (601 Van Ness Avenue), both with a broad range of recently published fiction and non-fiction; **City Lights** (261 Columbus Avenue), which features writings by and about the Beat generation, as well as a wide range of general titles; **Tillman Place Bookshop** (8 Tillman Place), packed with classy hard-backs, including many on travel; and **A Different Light** (489 Castro Street), the premier spot for books of gay and lesbian interest.

Anyone using San Francisco as a stop on the way to California's great outdoors will find plenty to inform and inspire them at the **Sierra Club Shop** (730 Polk Street), where the publications of the state's long-serving environmental protection organization describe the western U.S.'s wildest areas with informative texts and stunning photographs.

Should you be stumped for what to read about next, weave through the many miles of shelving inside **McDonald's Bookshop** (48 Turk Street), cluttered with everything from vintage *TV Guides* to esoteric occult tomes. Another tremendous stock of used volumes awaits your gaze at **Forever After** (1475 Haight Street), while some of the best used-book bargains turn up at the **Friends of San Francisco Library** outlet at Fort Mason Center (see page 96).

Barnes & Noble
Booksellers Since 1873

Jack London Square
98 Broadway
Oakland, CA 94607
Phone (510) 272-0120
Fax (510) 272-0343

Browsing on Clement Street

Be it ballet or the blues, San Francisco's nightlife has something to satisfy all tastes and all budgets. Even more impressively, the city's diverse range of evening entertainment is on a surprisingly small and friendly scale. Unlike the situation in many major U.S. cities, visitors looking for after-hours enjoyment are more likely to be welcome than treated like gatecrashers at someone else's party.

Everything from comedy clubs to avant-garde dance is included in the nightlife listings carried by the free weekly papers, the *San Francisco Bay Guardian* and *SF Weekly*. The pink "Datebook" section of Sunday's *San Francisco Chronicle & Examiner* also has comprehensive nightlife information for the upcoming week.

Boasting the earliest municipally run opera company in the U.S. and the world's first (and possibly only) lesbian and gay chorus, a vibrant and varied cultural diet is an integral part of San Franciscan nightlife. The major events—socially, none are more spectacular than the opening night of the opera season in September—take place in the buildings of Civic Center's Performing Arts Complex. More esoteric presentations—such as avant-garde music and dance shows—can be found in small and medium venues dotted about the city.

Classical music The San Francisco Symphony perform at the Louise M. Davies Symphony Hall (201 Van Ness Avenue; tel. 415/431 5400), frequently joined in their main September to May season by internationally acclaimed guest conductors and soloists. The summertime program includes a Beethoven Festival, a Pops series, and a special performance in tandem with the highly regarded Los Angeles/New York-based Joffrey Ballet. Tickets are usually around $20, and quickly sell out for top-name appearances.

The Civic Center's **Herbst Theater** (the auditorium of the War Veterans' Building, 401 Van Ness Avenue; box office, tel. 415/392 4400) sees an annual season of chamber music, recitals, dance, and jazz, organized by

Dizzy North Beach neon

Tickets
The major ticket agency, BASS, has numerous outlets including the TIX booth on Union Square (see below); Supermail, Four Embarcadero Center; Headlines, 838 Market Street; and The Wherehouse, 165 Kearny Street. For a credit-card booking or recorded information, tel. 510/762 2277. TIX offers half-price day-of-performance tickets (cash only) for Bay Area arts events from a marked booth on the Stockton Street side of Union Square (tel. 415/433 7827).

Conducting the symphony

San Francisco Symphony Orchestra

San Francisco Performances (tel. 415/398 6449), and often starring internationally recognized performers.

From September to April, the Herbst Theater also hosts the **Philharmonia Baroque Orchestra** (tel. 415/391 5252), performing works by the great composers of the 17th and 18th centuries. The **Chamber Symphony of San Francisco** (tel. 415/495 2919) appears at the same location in a season lasting from January to May.

Away from the mainstream Ears craving more avant-garde musical fare might be in luck at the Green Room of the War Veterans' Building (401 Van Ness Avenue; see page 231), where the **San Francisco Contemporary Players** (tel. 415/252 6235) present modern experimental pieces, or at the same building's Herbst Theater, where the San Francisco Symphony's succinctly titled New and Unusual series takes place each spring.

The under-representation of women in the musical world is addressed by the **Bay Area Women's Philharmonic** (tel. 415/543 2297), performing works by female composers; most concerts take place at the First Congregational Church (corner of Post and Mason streets). Meanwhile, the **Lesbian/Gay Chorus of San Francisco** (tel. 415/861 7067) can be found at the Metropolitan Community Church (150 Eureka Street), and during special events at other venues.

Opera The highly regarded **San Francisco Opera** has a star-studded September to December season at the War Memorial Opera House (301 Van Ness Avenue; tel. 415/864 3330). Guest artists include celebrated opera names, Pavarotti being one. Tickets ($15–$100) for the 3,000-seater auditorium are snapped up by mail order months in advance, although a limited number of low price standing tickets are put on sale at the box office two hours before a performance. Even for these, there is

San Francisco Opera

Home of the hits: Geary Street theater district

strong demand; arrive early to be sure of a place in line.

Any opera buffs visiting out of season might well be content with the enjoyable **Pocket Opera** (tel. 415/989 1853), a small professional company which, from March to July, stages informal interpretations of comic operas in one of the city's smaller theaters (the actual venue varies from year to year).

Dance The **San Francisco Ballet** (tel. 415/703 9400) enjoys a reputation as one of the U.S.'s most accomplished and exciting companies, regularly adding striking new works to the repertoire of favorites which fills its February to May season. Performances take place at the War Memorial Opera House (see page 231), and tickets are priced from around $12. The company returns for Christmas performances of the *Nutcracker*, each presentation promising to be more spectacular than the previous year's.

Unfairly in the shadow of the better-known company across the bay, the **Oakland Ballet** (tel. 510/452 9288) regularly presents innovative modern works—as well as established classics—at the Paramount Theater (2025 Broadway).

Many small, modern dance companies are based in the city and they, and other touring dance companies, can frequently be found at one of the following venues:

A dress rehearsal of the San Francisco Ballet's Sleeping Beauty

Will it never end?
Beach Blanket
Babylon

Beach Blanket Babylon
Now the longest-running theatrical show in U.S. history, *Beach Blanket Babylon* began in 1971 and, in various forms, this witty and raucous high-camp revue—tracing the unlikely adventures of Snow White—has been packing them in ever since. Plays nightly except Monday and Tuesdays at Club Fugazi, 678 Green Street (tel. 415/421 4222); reservations essential.

Cowell Theater (Fort Mason Center; tel. 415/441 5706); Theater Artaud (450 Florida Street; tel. 415/621 7797); Footwork (3221 Second Street; tel. 415/824 5044); and the New Performance Gallery (3153 17th Street; tel. 415/863 9834).

Finally, the students of the San Francisco State University Department of Dance periodically demonstrate their skills at the SFSU Gym, on the university campus (1600 Holloway Avenue; tel. 415/338 2062).

Theater Many visitors are quite happy to explore no more of San Francisco's nightlife than the commercial theaters grouped in close proximity just west of Union Square. Several of these were erected during the 1920s as homes for vaudeville and the best of them have retained—and maintained—their lavish fixtures and fittings. The best seats at a blockbusting show can be $50 but most seats are $12–$25. For smaller theaters, expect to spend less.

A trio of 1920s stalwarts, able to seat up to 2,000, are also the first West Coast stops for the hottest plays and musicals arriving from New York's Broadway. On any particular night (or the Wednesday and weekend matinees), the Curran Theater (445 Geary Street; tel. 415/474 3800); the Golden Gate Theater (1 Taylor Street; tel. 415/441 0919); and The Orpheum (1192 Market Street; tel. 415/474 3800), are all likely to be staging hit plays and musicals.

For theater-goers for whom the *oeuvre* of Andrew Lloyd Webber holds less appeal than that of Molière or George Bernard Shaw, the respected American Conservatory Theater (or ACT; tel. 415/749 2228) can be relied upon to please. ACT's main base is the Geary Theater (415 Geary Street; tel. 415/749 2200), due to reopen in 1995 after repairs for earthquake damage. Meanwhile, ACT productions take place at the Theater on the Square (see page 235) and the Stage Door Theater (420 Mason Street). Across the bay, the Berkeley Repertory Theater (2025 Addison Street; tel. 415/845 4700) has forged a reputation for classy drama, be it modern plays or old chestnuts.

A mix of mainstream and experimental drama is the staple fare of the medium-sized **Marine's Memorial Theater** (609 Sutter Street; tel. 415/771 6900), **Theater on the Square** (450 Post Street; tel. 415/433 9500), and the **New Conservatory Theater Center** (25 Van Ness Avenue; tel. 415/861 8972). Premières—ranging from children's plays to political satire—are the forte of the intimate **Magic Theater** (Building D, Fort Mason Center; tel. 415/441 8822).

Venues for innovative and challenging—and sometimes just pretentious—drama include **Actors Theater** (533 Sutter Street; tel. 415/296 9179), **Climate Theater** (252 Ninth Street; tel. 415/626 9196), and **EXITheater** (156 Eddy Street; tel. 415/673 3847). Blurring the boundaries of drama and performance art, **George Coates Performance Works** (110 McAllister Street; tel. 415/863 4130), explores the combining of pre-recorded film and music with live performance.

The city is also the base of the US's first gay and lesbian company, **Theater Rhinoceros** (2926 16th Street; tel. 415/861 5079), who present a diverse programme, often exploring social attitudes and behaviour.

Comedy In the early 1960s, Mort Sahl and Lenny Bruce were among the stand-up comics who appeared at San Franciscan comedy clubs and, encouraged by the city's liberal and appreciative audiences, began to change the face of American comedy. Even today, the San Franciscan audience is one which appeals to new talents and established names alike, both being fairly easy to find in several dozen comedy clubs.

Most clubs have a cover charge of around $10 (sometimes with a minimum two drinks charge) depending on the night of the week and on the stature of the evening's star performer.

Always good for a laugh: San Francisco comedy clubs

235

Stand up comedy

NIGHTLIFE

Film festivals
The biggest of dozens of film festivals which take place in the city each year, the San Francisco International Film Festival brings new and innovative works from international directors to selected city cinemas each spring. Another major movie event is the International Lesbian and Gay Film Festival, featuring new films of gay and lesbian interest from around the world each June; main screenings take place at the Castro Theater.

The major venue is the plush and comfortable **Cobb's** (The Cannery, 2801 Leavenworth Street; tel. 415/928 4320), which regularly features major names though its strongly tourist crowd can render it short on atmosphere. A better bet might be the long-running **Holy City Zoo** (408 Clement Street; tel. 415/386 4242), or the **Punch Line** (444 Battery Street; tel. 415/397 75730).

A predominantly lesbian and gay audience gathers at **Josie's Cabaret and Juice Joint** (3583 16th Street; tel. 415/861 7933) to hear predominantly gay and lesbian comedians.

Cinema On any given day, San Franciscan cinemas sport a tempting mix of first-run, cult, and even a few foreign-language films in venues ranging from multiscreen complexes to tiny arthouse theaters. The pick of the complexes is the eight-screen **Kabuki Center** (corner of Post and Geary streets; tel. 415/931 9800), where the latest Hollywood offerings make their first local appearance.

When quality of setting matters, however, the discerning film buff watches first-run fare at one of the following: the **Clay** (2261 Fillmore Street; tel. 415/346 1123), built in 1910; **The Balboa** (3630 Balboa Street; tel. 415/221 8184), the city's only surviving 1920s art-deco cinema; the **Coronet** (3575 Geary Boulevard; tel. 415/752 4400), or the **Northpoint** (2290 Powell Street; tel. 415/989 6060), both with massive screens dating from the daring days of Cinemascope.

Cult classics, foreign-language, and arthouse films—often featured as mini-seasons—are the viewing pleasure at the **Castro Theater** (429 Castro Street; tel. 415/621 6120); the **Roxie** (3117 16th Street; tel. 415/863 1087);

236

Specialist seasons and cult movies prevail at the Castro Theater

the **Red Vic** (1727 Haight Street; tel. 415/668 3994); and the **Strand** (1127 Market Street; tel. 415/621 2227).

Nightclubs Unlike their ultra-glamorous counterparts in New York or Los Angeles, San Francisco's nightclubs are rarely places where you will find major celebrities dodging *paparazzi* as they sprint between limo and club entrance. The city does have a few chic and sophisticated discos where the rich and the beautiful glide across the dance-floor with consummate ease, but much more in keeping with its character are the dozens of clubs pulsating to contemporary sounds, often found in the converted ware-houses of SoMa.

As in cities the world over, the nightclub scene is constantly changing. The suggestions below are simply the most interesting of those most likely to be still in operation at the time of your visit.

To sample the nightlife high life—literally as well as figuratively—dress to the nines and take the elevator to the 32nd floor of the St Francis Hotel (Union Square), where **Oz** (tel. 415/774 0116) finds a cool and stylish crowd dancing to international hits and reclining into deep sofas amid decor resembling a wooded glade.

Should you be more intent on simply dancing your legs off, try the highly energetic live and recorded Brazilian beats of **Bahia Tropical** (1600 Market Street; tel. 415/861 8657), or the red hot salsa rhythms at **Cesar's Latin Palace** (3140 Mission Street; tel. 415/648 6611).

A long-serving fixture on the fast-changing alternative club circuit, **Club DV8** (540 Howard Street; tel. 415/957 1730) offers the latest and grooviest dance sounds. Another firmly established favorite is the **DNA Lounge** (375 Eleventh Street; tel. 415/626 1409), where dressed-in-black twentysomethings show up for early evening live bands and dance till dawn to goth, indie and industrial sounds, with occasional House and reggae nights.

Newer clubs in a similar vein include **Nightbreak** (1821 Haight Street; tel. 415/221 9008); **City Nights** (715 Harrison Street; tel. 415/979 8686); and **Club Oasis** (278

North Beach beckons

Guided nightclubbing
If deciding where to strut your stuff in the San Francisco night proves impossible, you might relish the assistance of Three Babes and a Bus (tel. 415/552 CLUB), a company which will carry you—and a bus-load of similarly indecisive individuals—on a four-hour tour of some of the city's hottest nightspots (Fridays and Saturdays only). For around $30 you get admission and special ID allowing you to walk right in, even when there is a line outside.

NIGHTLIFE

Brainwash

If only for the novelty, show up at one of the early evening rock music shows at Brainwash (1122 Folsom Street; tel. 415/861 FOOD). This combined bar and laundromat offers the chance to drink, eat, and tap your foot to live sounds as your dirtiest duds are regaining their whiteness. Bringing a sackful of dirty washing is not compulsory, however.

One of the casinos at Stateline: gambling is not legal in California but San Franciscans who cannot resist the lure need only pop over the border into Nevada

Eleventh Street; tel. 415/621 3200), where the dancing is done on a 30 x 48ft. dance floor.

More daring fare is provided by the **Paradise Lounge** (1501 Folsom Street; tel. 415/861 6906), usually featuring live bands early on and following them with a hit-or-miss conglomeration of multimedia happenings—poetry readings, body painting and tattooing, throbbing disco—liable to be found as you make your way through its three floors.

Should ten-pin bowling and pinball be essential extras for your night on the tiles, you should sample **Park Bowl** (1855 Haight Street), where rock videos are shown on a giant screen above multi-lane bowling, or **Holy Cow** (1535 Folsom Street; tel. 415/621 6087), which offers pinball machines for those who tire of the club's disco beats.

With many gay and lesbian residents enjoying open and assertive lifestyles, visitors might expect San Francisco's gay and lesbian nightclubs to be wild, no-holds barred affairs. In fact, perhaps because the need to get together and let off steam is less great than in more oppressive urban centers, the city's gay and lesbian nightlife is often surprisingly restrained—which is not to say there is not a lot to please hedonistic gay and lesbian travellers.

Of the predominantly gay male bars and clubs, **The Stud** (399 Ninth Street; tel. 415/863 6623) has long been a favored watering hole, both to mellow out with a drink on a quiet week night, and to start an evening of urgent clubbing on the much busier Fridays and Saturdays.

Another popular drinking spot is the **Twin Peaks Tavern** (401 Castro Street; tel. 415/864 9470), a fine place to pose in the heart of the world's premier gay neighborhood. Country & Western fans, however, might be more at home amid the plaid shirts and cowboy boots of **Rawhide** (280 Seventh Street; tel. 415/621 1197), which not only spins C&W discs but provides free country-dancing lessons.

For two to three weeks beginning in late October, the annual San Francisco Jazz Festival finds the top local names and many overseas guests appearing at venues the length and breadth of the city. Tickets for the biggest shows are snapped up early, but many are available for other nights during the festival through the usual agencies and from the San Francisco Jazz Festival Store Box Office (141 Tenth Street; tel. 1-800/627 5277 or 415/864 5449).

239

The historic Italian-American Club Fugazi makes an unlikely home for the wacky Beach Blanket Babylon

Many of the city's nightclubs have a gay or lesbian night once a week, including **Cesar's Latin Palace** (see page 237), which has a lesbian/gay salsa night, but the number one gay and lesbian nightclub is **End-Up** (401 Sixth Street; tel. 415/543 7700), an often riotous disco hosting differently themed nights through the week.

A quieter place for lesbians to socialize is **Café San Marcos** (2367 Market Street; tel. 415/861 3846), with a large bar area, pool tables and a patio.

Jazz In the 1940s and 1950s, San Francisco was one of the hottest spots for live jazz in the U.S. and the sweaty North Beach cellar clubs became particularly revered by bebop enthusiasts. These days, a jazz venue can be anything from a hotel lounge where guests are serenaded with a pianist tinkling the ivories in a vaguely jazz-like manner, to tiny bars where knowledgeable jazz buffs and scruffily dressed art students flip out to the latest uneasily defined jazz genres such as jazz-rap, acid-jazz, and hip-bop.

The majority of jazz venues, however, are the well-equipped backrooms of restaurants, where a bite to eat often (but not necessarily) precedes an evening listening to accomplished mainstream jazz. At any of the following, expect a cover charge of $5–$10 depending on the night of the week and the ranking of the

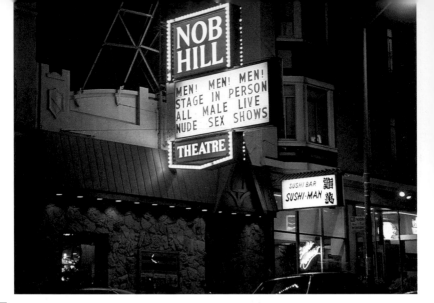

Baring all...

San Francisco Blues Festival
Over a weekend each September, the San Francisco Blues Festival brings some of the genre's leading exponents to day-long open-air concerts at Great Meadow, near Fort Mason Center (see page 96), with a Friday afternoon curtain-raising concert taking place at Justin Herman Plaza, next to the Embarcadero Center (see page 81). For ticket details; tel. 415/826 6837.

performer; on occasions there may also be a minimum drinks charge.

The more enjoyable and dependable of the medium-sized jazz venues are **Pier 23 Café** (Pier 23, Embarcadero; tel. 415/362 5125), an upbeat waterside eaterie which also features mambo and reggae bands several times a week; **Slim's** (333 Eleventh Street; tel. 415/621 3330), a small and pricey club which mixes jazz acts with rock and R&B; **Up & Down Club** (1151 Folsom Street; tel. 415/626 2388), a great spot for catching the cream of the up-and-coming acts; **Rasselas** (2801 California Street; tel. 415/567 5010), a jazz and supper club serving Ethiopian food and presenting some of the better local combos; **Jazz at Pearl's** (256 Columbus Avenue; tel. 415/291 8255), showcasing many of the city's top-rated performers; and **Café Du Nord** (2170 Market Street; tel. 415/861 5016), probably the likeliest venue to catch the hottest fresh talents.

Among the smaller venues which give an airing to less mainstream jazz sounds are **Club 181** (181 Eddy Street; tel. 415/673 8181), **Ace Café** (1539 Folsom Street; tel. 415/621 4752), and **Elbo Room** (647 Valencia Street; tel. 415/552 7788).

Rock music San Francisco gets its share of national and international rock acts, with many of the big names playing south of the city at the **Cow Palace** or across the bay at the **Oakland Coliseum** with tickets available through the major agencies. The largest rock venue in the city, staging concerts three or four nights a week, is **The Warfield** (982 Market Street; tel. 415/775 7722).

More intimate than the major venues, and better places for putting your finger on the pulse of the local rock scene, are the many neighborhood clubs where exotically named unknown, semi-known, and a few almost well-known bands go through their paces, sometimes to packed houses, sometimes to an audience of friends. Admission typically ranges from free to $10.

The likeliest venues are the **I-Beam** (1748 Haight Street;

tel. 415/668 6006); **The Crash Palace** (628 Divisadero Street; tel. 415/931 1914); **DNA Lounge** (375 Eleventh Street; tel. 415/626 1409), **Paradise Lounge** (1501 Folsom Street; tel. 415/861 6906), the last three all doubling as lively nightclubs (see page 237–8) after the bands conclude.

You are more likely to discover no-frills R&B and garage bands at spit-and-sawdust venues such as **The Saloon** (1232 Grant Street; tel. 415/989 7666), **Morty's** (1024 Kearny Street; tel. 415/986 MORT), and **Grant and Green** (1371 Grant Street; tel. 415/693 9565).

By contrast, some of the area's best blues players can be found in the relatively swanky confines of **Lou's Pier 47** (300 Jefferson Street; tel. 415/771 0377), one of the few reasons San Franciscans brave the Fisherman's Wharf tourist crowds.

Poetry It might be the legacy of the Beats or the inspirational qualities of the landscape, but sometimes it seems that everyone in San Francisco is a poet—a feeling compounded by the poetry readings taking place around the city every night.

Each Thursday, the café of the **San Francisco Art Institute** (800 Chestnut Street; tel. 415/749 4567) holds an "open mike" night, when poets and anyone with something to say can seize the moment; **Above Paradise** (1501 Folsom Street; tel. 415/861 1912) is a poets' reading room operating weekly above the Paradise Lounge nightclub (see page 238).

Elsewhere, numerous bookstores, particularly **City Lights** (261 Columbus Avenue; tel. 415/362 8193) and **A Clean Well-lighted Place For Books** (601 Van Ness Avenue; tel. 415/441 6670), frequently have published poets reading from their latest works.

Berkeley poetry
Poetry addicts not satisfied by what is on offer in the city might cross the bay to Berkeley, where regular poetry reading venues include Black Oak Books (1491 Shattuck Avenue; tel. 510 486 0698) and the Tea Spot Café (2072 San Pablo Avenue; tel. 510 848 7376). A likely location to find established poets and prose authors giving readings is Cody's Books (2454 Shattuck Avenue; tel. 510 845 7852).

Streamlined sculptures match the contours of the Louise M. Davies Symphony Hall to the rear, a recent and stylish addition to the Civic Center complex

Children's San Francisco

Not an average place

The Exploratorium

A generous helping of child-friendly museums, wide open spaces and exotic neighborhoods makes San Francisco an enjoyable and rewarding place to explore with children.

With the **Exploratorium** (see page 82), the city has one of the finest places for discovering and learning about science anywhere in the world. Boredom is unheard of amid the hundreds of hands-on exhibits.

Interactive computers, which the Exploratorium has by the dozen, are also a feature of the **California Academy of Sciences** (see pages 64–5). Here, though, it is likely to be the huge aquarium, the dolphins, and the prehistory exhibits which steal the show for younger children; older ones are more likely to be enthralled by the re-creation of San Franciscan earthquakes and the planetarium shows.

Across the bay on the Berkeley university campus, the **Lawrence Hall of Science** (see page 61) is smaller and less well-equipped than the Exploratorium but nonetheless has much to inform and entertain among its science-based exhibits and computer quizzes.

Other museums not specifically targeted at children but likely to be much appreciated by them, include the **Cable Car Museum** (page 63), the **Fire Department Museum** (see panel, page 114), the **Wells Fargo History Museum** (page 179), and the restored sea vessels of Fisherman's Wharf: the **Hyde Street Pier Historic Ships** (page 112), the **National Liberty Ship Memorial** and the **USS Pampanito** (see panel, page 128).

Fisherman's Wharf's more commercial attractions, particularly **Ripley's Believe It or Not!** (see panel, page 93) and the **Guinness Museum of World Records** (page 93) are proven child pleasers, as are the buskers who perform along Jefferson Street and the daytime open-air shows at **Ghirardelli Square** (page 93) and **The Cannery** (page 93). While in Fisherman's Wharf, remember to take a look at the colony of sea lions which have taken up residence close to **Pier 39** (see panel, page 92). More sea lions can be seen frolicking around Seal Rocks, at the

city's western extremity, just beyond the **Cliff House** (see page 80).

Another promising stop is **Fort Point** (page 96), with its Civil War-uniformed guides and proximity to the **Golden Gate Bridge** (page 98), which older children will be itching to walk across. Infants may find the ferry ride to **Alcatraz** more enjoyable than exploring the former prison—but young teens developing a taste for the macabre will relish it.

The city may not have the greatest zoo in the world, but young charges are unlikely to be underwhelmed by the inhabitants of the **San Francisco Zoo** (page 162).

The city's biggest and best open space, **Golden Gate Park** (pages 100–3) has plenty to thrill kids. After a few hours at the **California Academy of Sciences** (pages 64–5), younger ones can be introduced to the residents of the buffalo paddock, watch remote-controlled model boats zipping over Spreckels Lake, or sit on a purple dragon and ride a restored 1912 carousel. Older children might prefer a bike ride through the park, or a paddle-boat cruise around Stow Lake.

The **Golden Gate National Recreation Area** (page 99) is ideal territory for a breezy nature ramble, which might conclude with a picnic at China or Baker beaches. **Fort Funston** has hang-gliders launching off from its tall cliffs every weekend.

San Francisco's ethnic diversity can be an eye-opener for kids (and adults) unused to such a disparate urban mix. A stroll through **Chinatown** (pages 72–5), a walk around **Japantown** (pages 113–14), a tour of the Italian cafés and shops of **North Beach** (pages 134–7), or a trip to the strongly Hispanic **Mission District** (pages 124–5) can all offer new and stimulating experiences.

Pier 39's Carousel

243

Babysitting
The majority of hotels can arrange babysitting or can recommend a company providing this service. Among those with established reputations are American Childcare Service (tel. 415/285 2300), who can entertain your offspring in a hotel room or escort those over 7 on museum visits, and Nannycare USA (tel. 1-800/448 2915), offering everything from babysitting to parties.

San Francisco for free

Always free museums

Cable Car Museum (page 63)

Chinese Cultural Center (page 75)

Chinese Historical Society (page 74)

Fire Department Museum (see panel, page 114)

Fort Point National Historic Site (page 96)

Museum of Money of the American West (page 127)

National Maritime Museum (page 128)

North Beach Museum (page 137)

Old U.S. Mint (page 145)

Presidio Army Museum (page 155)

Society of California Pioneers (page 79)

Wells Fargo History Museum (page 179)

Whether you are a hard-up culture vulture or just a person who likes to get something for nothing, San Francisco offers plenty of enjoyable ways to fill your day without spending a cent. Museum enthusiasts strapped for cash will do well to be in the city on the first Wednesday of the month, when a number of museums waive their usual admission charges. The **M H de Young Memorial Museum** (pages 118–21) and the **Asian Art Museum** (pages 122–3) are both free on the first Wednesday (10am–8:30 or 9pm) and Saturday (10am–noon) of the month. A visit to one or both can easily be combined with an exploration of **Golden Gate Park** (pages 100–3) where the parkland, and the Strybing Arboretum, are free.

Budget-minded parents should note that the city's two most popular child-friendly attractions—the **California Academy of Sciences** (pages 64–5) and the **Exploratorium** (page 82)—waive their admission fees on the first Wednesday of the month, as does the **San Francisco Zoo** (page 162).

The **Mexican Museum** (page 117) is also free on the first Wednesday of the month, although the **San Francisco Museum of Modern Art** (pages 160–1) goes against the grain by allowing free entry on the first Tuesday of the month.

Impecunious art lovers who miss the free museum days have plenty more to content themselves with. Besides a large collection of galleries, such as the **Circle Gallery** (140 Maiden Lane), Frank Lloyd's Wright's model for the Guggenheim Museum in New York (see page 116), several hotels seek to cement their top-class status by lining their public rooms with top-class art. A stroll through the corridors of the **Ritz-Carlton** (600 Stockton Street) reveals 18th- and 19th-century landscapes, seascapes and portraits from English and American painters. At the **Stanford Court** (905 California Street) the

Jugglers in Golden Gate Park

Pier 39, where there is always something to look at

treasures include a diverting collection of Far Eastern pieces, among them 240 theme paintings by Kan Wing Lin and 18th-century hand-painted screens.

The **Sheraton Palace** (2 New Montgomery Street) not only boasts the Garden Court, one of the city's most elegant interiors, but also several stunning murals, including one by Maxfield Parrish valued at $2.5 million.

Lining the **Redwood Room** of the Four Seasons Clift Hotel (495 Geary Street) are works by the turn-of-the-century Viennese artist Gustav Klimt, and the **Compass Rose** room at the St Francis (Union Square) holds several signed photographs by San Francisco-born Ansel Adams. For contemporary fare, head for Hotel Diva (440 Geary Street), where the **Stanza-Diva Gallery** exhibits work by emergent Bay Area artists and photographers.

Some of the finest 1930s public artworks in California can be seen for free in San Francisco, at **Coit Tower** (pages 174–5) and the **Beach Chalet** (see panel, page 175).

Musicians, magicians, clowns and comedians regularly give their services for free (though a donation is appreciated) and are particularly easy to stumble upon at **Fisherman's Wharf**.

Free events often enliven lunchtimes on **Justin Herman Plaza**, at the Embarcadero Center (see page 81), and the slightly seedy **Hallidie Plaza** also features free amusements on some weekday afternoons.

Walking around this pedestrian-friendly city's many distinctive neighborhoods obviously costs nothing—though you might spend more energy than you would like to scaling some of the hills. For Victorian mansions, head for Pacific Heights or Haight-Ashbury. For modern architecture, pace the Financial District and cross Market Street into SoMa for the Rincon Annexe and the Yerba Buena Gardens complex.

Wherever you go, remember that neighborhood churches—with free entry—may be among the city's most intriguing landmarks, be it the soaring post-modern **St Mary's Cathedral** (page 158), or the log cabin-like **Swedenborgian Church** (page 172).

Free walks
Almost every day, the City Guides (tel. 415/557 4266) offer free guided walking tours of many of the city's neighborhoods, and historical and architectural points of interest. From May to October, the Friends of Recreation and Parks (tel. 415/750 5105) conduct free walks around various sections of Golden Gate Park.

Scenic elevators
Two city hotels have glass-sided elevators which offer dizzying views of San Francisco as they whizz between floors. The Tower elevators of the St. Francis Hotel (Union Square) may be the fastest in town (moving at 1,000 feet per minute), but for a truly vertiginous experience ride the Crown Room elevator of the Fairmont Hotel (950 Mason Street).

The perils of partying
Guests booking into the St. Francis to celebrate a business success will be eager to avoid the fate which befell silent-screen comedian Fatty Arbuckle in 1921. Arriving for a weekend party to mark the signing of a new $800,000 contract, Arbuckle booked a suite overlooking Union Square. The subsequent death of actress Virginia Rappe ended Arbuckle's career, despite the fact that he was found not guilty of any wrongdoing in three separate trials.

San Francisco may not be the rich persons' playground that New York or Los Angeles can claim to be, and money certainly is not a prerequisite for enjoying the city. Nonetheless, having much more money than you know what to do with always eases the stresses and strains of travel, and San Francisco has at least a few locations which should be known to the affluent jet-setter.

Heads of state, royalty and the simply mind-bogglingly rich have been regulars at the **St. Francis Hotel** (Union Square) since it opened in 1904. The addition of a modern wing in the 1970s may have upset architectural purists but delighted the guests, who expect top-notch facilities in their $1,000-a-night suites. Afternoon tea in the **Compass Rose** room (see page 133) is a fixture on the social circuit, and the night can be smooched away with the mellow, well-heeled revellers gathered in the 32nd-floor **Oz** nightclub. At the **Big Four** restaurant (1075 California Street), you do not need to be as wealthy as the 19th-century railroad barons for whom it is named, though it helps. This may not offer the city's finest food, but the rich and powerful love to luxuriate within the wood-panelled walls and feast on offerings which include tea-smoked Peking duckling. The curious but financially embarrassed might sneak in for breakfast and escape with change from $20.

The St Francis and the Big Four might well be considered overbearingly traditional by design-conscious, money-laden individuals under 40. For such folk, **Hotel Triton** (342 Grant Avenue), with its artistic fixtures and in-room VCRs and CD players—and its roller blades for hire—is tailor-made. Come dinner time, **Aqua** (252 California Street), serving gourmet seafood to a chic crowd in subdued surroundings, is the place to be if you are photogenic with $100 to spend.

Classy: the Garden Court, Palace Hotel

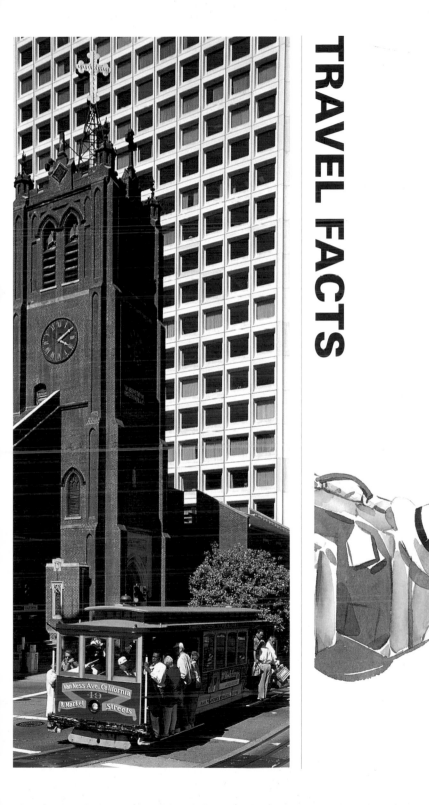

By air

San Francisco International Airport (tel. 415/761 0800) is approximately 14 miles south of the city. American carriers serving San Francisco are **Alaska Air** (tel. 800/426 0333), **American** (tel. 800/433 7300), **Continental** (tel. 800/525 0280), **Delta** (tel. 800/221 1212), **Southwest** (tel. 800/531 5601), **TWA** (tel. 800/221 2000), **United** (tel. 800/241 6522), and **USAir** (tel. 800/438 4322). International carriers include **Air New Zealand** (tel. 800/261 1234), **British Airways** (tel. 800/247 9297), **Canadian Airlines** (tel. 800/426 7000), **China Airlines** (tel. 800/227 5118), **Japan Air Lines** (tel. 800/525 3663), **Lufthansa** (tel. 800/645 3880), **Mexicana** (tel. 800/531 7921), and **Qantas** (tel. 800/227 4500). Several domestic airlines serve the Oakland Airport (tel. 510/577 4000), which is across the bay from downtown San Francisco (via I-880 and I-80), although traffic on the Bay Bridge may at times make travel time longer.

Traveling to and from San Francisco International Airport is easy. The best options for first-time arrivals, and any-one encumbered with luggage, are the numerous privately run minibus-es, such as Super Shuttle (tel. 415/558 8500), which collect passengers from the traffic island directly outside the terminal; simply wait for one to show up. The one-way fare into the city is around $10.

A cheaper alternative is the SFO Airporter (tel. 415/495 8404), a bus that runs every 20 minutes between 5a.m. and 11p.m. from the airport to the hotels near Union Square; the fare is around $8.

Less expensive are routes 7F and 7B of the local SamTrans bus service (tel. 800/660 4BUS). Service 7F is an express service making a 35-minute journey from the airport into San Francisco's Transbay Terminal (First and Mission streets), for a flat-fare just under $2. Service 7B follows a longer (55 minutes, with numerous stops) route to the same destination and charges less. Exact change is required on both buses, and luggage on the 7F is restricted to one moder-ately sized item. The SamTrans buses stop at marked stops outside the air-port's United and Delta terminals.

Depending on traffic condi-tions, a taxi into the city will cost approximately $30–$40.

By bus

Greyhound buses (tel. 1-800/231 2222) into San Francisco finish their journeys at the Transbay Terminal (First and Mission streets). This is also the destina-tion of local long-distance buses, such as the Golden Gate Transit (tel. 415/332 6600), that serve Marin and Sonoma counties.

By train

Taking a train (tel. 1-800/872 7245) to San Francisco means disembarking at the gleaming new train station at Emeryville, between Berkeley and Oakland, and continuing into the city aboard one of the free shuttle buses that meet arriving trains.

Buses are inexpensive and reliable

248

29 SUNSET
To 3rd St/Paul
Daily Approx 7AM-6:30PM

INFORMATION:
DIAL 673-MUNI

The buses carry passengers to the Transbay Terminal (First and Mission streets), a trip of around 40 minutes.

Insurance

Before leaving home, itemize your bags' contents and their worth in case they get lost. To minimize that risk, label them inside and out with your name, address, and phone number. (If you use your home address, cover it so potential thieves can't see it.) Put a copy of your itinerary inside each bag, so that you can be easily located. At check-in, make sure that the label attached by baggage handlers bears the correct three-letter code for your destination. If your bags do not arrive with you, or if you detect damage, file a written report with the airline before you leave the airport.

In the event of loss, damage, or theft on domestic flights, airlines' liability is $1,250 per passenger, excluding the valuable items such as jewelry or cameras that are listed in the fine print on your ticket. Excess-valuation insurance can be bought directly from the airline at check-in. Your homeowner's policy may fill the gap; or firms such as The Travelers Companies (1 Tower Sq., Hartford, CT 06183, tel. 203/277 0111 or 800/243 3174) and Wallach and Company (107 W. Federal St., Box

Shuttle vans are an easy option between the airport and city

480, Middleburg, VA 22117, tel. 703/687 3166 or 800/237 6615) sell baggage insurance.

When to go

San Francisco is enjoyable to visit at any time. The weather is rarely extreme, and numerous festivals and events take place throughout the year. The peak tourist months are July and August, when accommodation reservations should be made as early as possible and when prices may be slightly higher than usual.

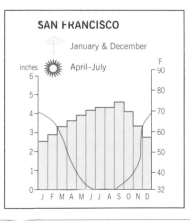

SAN FRANCISCO

January & December

inches   April–July   °F

Climate

Any time of the year is the right time to go to San Francisco, which is one of the most beautiful cities in the world. The fog rolls in during the summer, but it seems less of an inconvenience than part of the atmosphere of this never-mundane place. As long as you remember to bring along sweaters and jackets, even in August, you can't miss.

San Francisco is on the tip of a peninsula, surrounded on three sides by the Pacific Ocean and San Francisco Bay. Its climate is quintessentially marine and moderate: It never gets very hot—anything above 80° is reported as a heat wave—or very cold (as far as the thermometer is concerned, anyway).

For all its moderation, however, San Francisco can be tricky. In the summertime, fog often rolls in from the ocean, blocking the sun and filling the air with dampness. At times like this you'll want a coat, jacket, or warm sweater instead of the shorts or lightweight summer clothes that seem so comfortable in most North American cities during July and August. Mark Twain is credited with observing that the coldest winter he ever spent was one

Fog: a frequent visitor, but seldom staying long

summer in San Francisco. He may have been exaggerating, but it's best not to expect a hot summer in this city.

If you travel to the north, east, or south of the city, you will find warmer summer temperatures. Shirtsleeves and thin cottons are usually just fine for the wine country.

Be prepared for rain in winter, especially December and January. Winds from the ocean can add to the chill factor, so pack some warm clothing to be on the safe side.

For current weather conditions and forecasts for cities in the United States and abroad, plus the local time and helpful travel tips, call the **Weather Channel Connection** (tel. 900/932 8437; 95¢ per minute) from a touch-tone phone.

Money matters

Many automated-teller machines (ATMs) are tied to international networks such as **Cirrus** and **Plus**. You can use your bank card at ATMs to withdraw money from an account and get cash advances on a credit card account if your card has been programmed with a personal identification number, or PIN. Check in advance on limits on withdrawals and cash advances within specified periods. On cash advances you are charged interest from the day you receive the money from ATMs or tellers. Transaction fees for ATM withdrawals outside your home turf may be higher than for withdrawals at home.

For specific Cirrus locations in the United States and Canada, call 800/ 424 7787. For U.S. Plus locations, call 800/843 7587 and press the area code and first three digits of the number you're calling from (or of the calling area where you want an ATM).

You don't have to be a cardholder to send or receive a **MoneyGram from American Express** for up to $20,000. Go to a MoneyGram agent in retail and convenience stores and American Express travel offices, pay up to $1,000 with a credit card and anything over that in cash. You are allowed a free long-distance call to give the transaction code to your intended recipient, who needs only to present identification and the reference number to the nearest MoneyGram agent to pick up the cash. MoneyGram agents are in more than 70 countries (call 800/926 9400 for locations). Fees range from 3% to 10%, depending on the amount and how you pay.

You can also use **Western Union**. To wire money, take either cash or a cashier's check to the nearest office or call and use MasterCard or Visa. Money sent from the United States or Canada will be available for pickup at agent locations in 78 countries within minutes. Once the money is in the system it can be picked up at *any* one of 22,000 locations (call 800/325 6000 for the one nearest you).

National holidays
Banks and all public offices will be closed on all the following holidays, stores may be open on some of these days: New Year's Day (January 1st), Martin Luther King's Birthday (third Monday in January), Lincoln's Birthday (February 12th), Washington's Birthday (third Monday in February), Memorial Day (last Monday in May), Independence Day (July 4th), Labor Day (first Monday in September), Columbus Day (second Monday in October), Veteran's Day (November 11th), Thanksgiving Day (fourth Thursday in November), Christmas Day (December 25th).

Time differences
San Francisco and the rest of California use Pacific Standard Time.

Cash is easily available—but use the right card

Public transportation

San Francisco is a fine city to explore on foot but even the most dedicated walker will want to make use of the excellent public transportation system during some part of their stay, either to experience the delight of a cable-car ride or simply to avoid having to climb another hill.

Traveling across the bay to Berkeley or Oakland will likely involve a trip on the highly efficient BART system, while a visit to Sausalito, Alcatraz or Tiburon can require a ferry across San Francisco Bay. You will only need to use a taxi if you are in a rush, or for late-night journeys when public transportation services are somewhat skeletal.

The BART The Bay Area Rapid Transit (or BART; for information, tel. 510/464 6000) system is chiefly of use for crossing the bay to Berkeley and Oakland, though it also runs through the city and forms a speedy link between the Financial District, the Civic Center, and the Mission District. Fares are according to distance traveled. Tickets can be bought from machines at BART stations, where there are also easy-to-understand maps. The BART system runs from 6a.m. to midnight (from 8a.m. to midnight on Sundays).

The BART system moves people below ground...

...cable cars do the same above ground

Buses The buses and, to some extent, the streetcars (a type of underground train) run by MUNI (tel. 415/673 MUNI) are much more useful for getting around San Francisco than the cable cars.

All MUNI routes are shown in the phone book and at most bus stops. The most useful routes are also illustrated inside the back cover of this book.

On buses, the fare is $1. Exact change is necessary and should be fed into the machine next to the driver when boarding; free transfers (onto other routes) are issued on request. Regular MUNI buses run from 5a.m. to 1a.m. Through the early hours of the morning, MUNI's "Owl Service" buses provide a reduced frequency service on the main routes.

Cable cars A first-time visitor might well expect to find San Franciscans cruising around the city aboard the famous cable cars. In truth, the cable cars, much loved and restored to service in the early 1980s, are much closer to being a tourist attraction than a practical means of getting around. Cable cars operate on just three routes: two between Market Street and Fisherman's Wharf, and the Financial District and Nob Hill. Buy your ticket, which costs $3, from self-service machines before you board the car. During the summer, expect a lengthy line at the Market Street and Fisherman's Wharf stops.

Ferries Few people visit San Francisco and manage to resist the temptation to take a bay cruise or a ride on one of the ferries that sail across the bay to Sausalito, Tiburon or Oakland. Such

Cable cars cover a limited route— but everybody wants to hop aboard

trips provide great views of the city and its two major bridges. Complete ferry details are given on page 89.

MUNI Passports If you are using public transportation a lot, a MUNI Passport (available from outlets around the city) is likely to save a considerable amount of money. The passports are valid on all MUNI services (including cable cars) for 1, 3 or 7 days, and currently cost $6, $10, and $15, respectively.

Taxis It is unlikely that you will need to use taxis in San Francisco, except perhaps during the early morning hours when buses may be scarce.

If you have to move in a hurry, you will usually be able to hail a taxi on a major street within a few minutes (expect a longer wait during rush hours). Taxis can also be ordered over the phone; many cab companies are listed in the Yellow Pages.

Average taxi fares are around $2 for the first mile and $1.50 for each additional mile.

Driving
While public transportation more than adequately serves San Francisco and

A city driving hazard: complex parking laws

much of the immediate Bay Area, a car is a near-essential accessory for distant explorations.

Car rental The nearest locations of major car rental companies can be found by calling the following toll-free numbers: **Avis** (tel. 800/331 1212); **Budget** (tel. 800/527 0700); **Dollar** (tel. 800/800 4000); **Hertz** (tel. 800/ 654 3131); **Thrifty** (tel. 800/367 2277). Unlimited-mileage rates range from $32 per day for an economy car to $47 for a large car; weekly unlimited-mileage rates range from $143 to $180. This does not include tax, which in San Francisco is approximately 8% on car rentals.

San Francisco has many good budget rental car companies: **American International** (tel. 415/692 4100), **Enterprise** (tel. 800/325 8007), and **Reliable** (tel. 415/928 4414) are a

few. At the other end of the price spectrum, **Sunbelt** (tel. 415/771 9191) specializes in BMWs, and Corvette and Miyata convertibles.

You should be careful to read the small print if renting from a small company, and you should also bear in mind that in the event of a breakdown, their back-up service may not be as thorough as that of a nationally known company.

Picking up the car in one city and leaving it in another may entail substantial drop-off charges or one-way service fees. The cost of a collision or loss-damage waiver can be high, also. Some rental agencies will charge you extra if you return the car *before* the time specified on your contract. Ask before making unscheduled drop-offs. Fill the tank when you turn in the vehicle to avoid being charged for refueling at what you'll swear is the most expensive pump in town.

Major international companies have programs that discount their standard rates by 15%–30% if you make the reservation before departure (anywhere from 24 hours to 14 days), rent for a minimum number of days (typically three or four), and prepay the rental. More economical rentals may come as part of fly/drive or other packages, or even barebones deals that only combine the rental and an airline ticket.

Before you rent a car, find out exactly what coverage, if any, is provided by your personal auto insurer and by the rental company. Don't assume that

you are covered. If you do want insurance from the rental company, secondary coverage may be the only type offered. You may already have secondary coverage if you charge the rental to a credit card. Only Diners Club (tel. 800/234 6377) provides primary coverage in the United States and worldwide.

Car breakdown In the unlikely event that your rental car breaks down, phone the emergency number that should be prominently displayed on or near the dashboard (if it is not, simply phone the regular number for the car rental agency). With luck, a rental company representative will shortly arrive with another car in which you can continue your trip. Should you be unfortunate enough to break down far from a phone, stay with your vehicle and wait for a Highway Patrol vehicle to come by. If any other passing motorist stops to offer help, there is every chance that they are genuine, but you should treat their interest with caution. Usually, the best help such a person can provide is to drive to a public phone and make a call on your behalf.

Driving tips In San Francisco, your major driving problem is likely to be parking. Most hotels have designated parking spaces for guests but general parking in the city's busier areas is notoriously difficult. Many parking lots charge by the hour or by the day. On certain streets, parking is forbidden during rush hours. Look for the warning signs; illegally parked cars are towed.

When parking on the city's steep streets, you are required by law to curb your tires. point them away from the curb when facing uphill and

255

City buses are more useful, if less attractive to visitors, than street-cars

towards the curb when facing downhill.

Long-distance public transportation

There is a major move afoot in environmentally concerned northern California to wean devoted drivers away from their cars and develop less polluting forms of mass transportation.

By bus Greyhound serves San Francisco from the Transbay Terminal at First and Mission streets (tel. 415/558 6789 or 800/231 2222).

By plane The Sunday travel section of most newspapers is a good source for bargains on airfares. When making a reservation, particularly through an

unfamiliar company, call the Better Business Bureau and your local or state Consumer Protection Bureau to find out whether any complaints have been registered against the company, pay with a credit card if you can, and consider trip-cancellation and default insurance.

Less expensive fares, called promotional or discount fares, are round-trip and involve restrictions, which vary according to the route and season. You must usually buy the ticket in advance (seven, 14, or 21 days are standard), although some of the major airlines have added no-frills, cheap flights to compete with new bargain airlines on certain routes. These new low-cost carriers include **Private Jet** (tel. 800/949 9400), based in Atlanta and serving Miami, Dallas, St. Thomas, St. Croix, Las Vegas, New York's Kennedy, Los Angeles, Chicago, and

San Francisco. With the major airlines the cheaper fares generally require minimum and maximum stays (for instance, over a Saturday night or at least seven and no more than 30 days). Airlines generally allow some return date changes for a $25 to $50 fee, but most low-fare tickets are nonrefundable. Only a death in the family would prompt the airline to return any of your money if you cancel a nonrefundable ticket. However, you can apply an unused nonrefundable ticket toward a new ticket, again with a small fee. The lowest fare is subject to availability, and only a small percentage of the plane's total seats will be sold at that price. Contact the U.S. Department of Transportation's Office of Consumer Affairs (I-25, Washington, D.C. 20590, tel. 202/366 2220) for a copy of "Fly-Rights: A Guide to Air Travel in the U.S." *The Official Frequent Flyer Guidebook* by Randy Petersen (4715-C Town Center Dr., Colorado Springs, CO 80916, tel. 719/597 8899, 800/487 8893, or 800/485 8893; £14.99, plus $3 shipping and handling) yields valuable hints on getting the most for your air travel dollars.

Consolidators or bulk-fare operators buy blocks of seats on scheduled flights that airlines anticipate won't be sold. They pay wholesale prices, add a markup, and resell the seats to travel agents or directly to the public at prices that still undercut the airline's promotional or discount fares (higher than a charter ticket but lower than an APEX ticket, and usually without the advance-purchase restriction). Moreover, some consolidators sometimes give you your money back. Carefully read the fine print detailing penalties for changes and cancellations. If you doubt the reliability of a company, call the airline once you've made your reservation and confirm that you do, indeed, have a reservation on the flight.

Travel clubs offer members unsold space on airplanes, cruise ships, and package tours at as much as 50% below regular prices. Membership may include a regular bulletin or access to a toll-free hot line giving details of available trips departing from three or four days to several months in the future. Most also offer 50% discounts off hotel rack rates, but double check with the hotel to make sure it isn't offering a better promotional rate independent of the club. Clubs include **Discount Travel International** (114 Forrest Ave., Suite 203, Narberth, PA 19072, tel. 215/668 7184; $45 annually, single or family), **Entertainment Travel Editions** (Box 1014 Trumbull, CT 06611, tel. 800/445 4137; price ranges $28–$48), **Great American Traveler** (Box 27965, Salt Lake City, UT 84127, tel. 800/548 2812; $29.95 annually), **Moment's Notice Discount Travel Club** (425 Madison Ave., New York, NY 10017, tel. 212/486 0503; $45 annually, single or family), **Privilege Card** (3391 Peachtree Rd. NE, Suite 110, Atlanta, GA 30326, tel. 404/262 0222 or 800/236 9732; domestic annual membership $49.95, international, $74.95), **Travelers Advantage** (CUC Travel Service, 49 Music Sq. W, Nashville, TN 37203, tel. 800/548 1116; $49 annually, single or family), and **Worldwide Discount Travel Club** (1674 Meridian Ave., Miami Beach, FL 33139, tel. 305/534 2082; $50 annually for family, $40 single)

By rail
Amtrak (tel. 800/ 872 7245) trains (the *Zephyr*, from Chicago via Denver, and the *Coast Starlight*, traveling between Los Angeles and Seattle) stop in Oakland; from there buses will take you across the Bay Bridge to the Ferry Building on the Embarcadero at the foot of Market Street in San Francisco.

Student and youth travel
Students carrying International Student Identity Cards (ISICs) are entitled to reduced admission to many museums and other attractions.

While not exclusively for young and student travelers, San Francisco's hostels (see under Accommodations, pages 268–74) offer budget-priced accommodations, and several have kitchens, where guests can prepare their own meals, and common rooms for guests to socialize.

Travelers under age 25, especially those without credit cards, may have difficulty renting a car.

Media

San Francisco has two daily newspapers, the morning *San Francisco Chronicle* and the afternoon *San Francisco Examiner* (combined on Sundays), and two major free weekly newspapers, the *SF Weekly* and *San Francisco Bay Guardian*. Several other free publications provide news, views and information to the city's large gay and lesbian population: *Bay Times*, *Bay Area Reporter* and *The Sentinel*. All of the above are easy to find in vending machines on the street.

Standard tourist information can be found in free magazines found in most hotel lobbies, such as *San Francisco Key* and the *Bay City Guide*, and the broadsheet *San Francisco Tourist Guide*. These are usually financed by advertising revenue and their editorial opinions reflect this. They are worth picking up, however, for their many discount coupons, which may save you money when you are shopping or visiting major tourist attractions.

In all but the cheapest hotel rooms you will find a TV. Linked to national networks, the main San Francisco TV channels are 2 KTVU (FOX), 4 KRON (NBC), 5 KPIX (CBS), 7 KGO (ABC), and 9 KQED (PBS). Many hotels also offer selected cable TV channels, and some have a further choice of six or so pay-to-view movies.

Most hotel rooms also have a radio, with which you will be able to sample some of the Bay Area's 80-odd radio stations.

For fuller media details, see page 154.

Get your news from a vending machine or newsstand

Post office

San Francisco's main post office is at 1300 Evans Street. There are plenty of other post offices around the city, however, and you can find the nearest one by looking in the phone book or asking at your hotel. Most post offices are open Monday to Friday 8–6 and Saturdays 8–1. For postal service information, tel. 415/ 550 6500.

Telephone and fax

Some budget-range hotels offer free local calls, but hotel room phone charges are generally considerably higher than those of public phones. A particular hotel's phone charges should be displayed on a card in the room.

Throughout this book, the area code for San Francisco (415) has been included for all telephone numbers within the city.

Almost all hotels are equipped with fax machines, and most will allow guests to send and receive faxes. The charges for this service vary considerably. While all hotels charge to send faxes, some will waive charges for faxes received though others bill guests as much as $3 per page in addition to imposing a $3 or $4 "handling" fee.

Cameras, camcorders, and laptops

If your camera is new or if you haven't used it for a while, shoot and develop a few test rolls of film before you leave home. Store film in a cool, dry place—never in the car's glove compartment or on the shelf under the rear window.

Airport security X-rays generally aren't harmful to film with ISO below 400. To protect your film, carry it with you in a clear plastic bag and ask for a hand inspection. Such requests are honored at U.S. airports. Don't depend on a lead-lined bag to protect film in checked luggage—the airline may increase the radiation to see what's inside.

Before your trip, put camcorders through their paces, invest in a sky-light filter to protect the lens, and check all the batteries. Airport security personnel may ask you to turn on the camcorder to prove that it's what it appears to be, so make sure the battery is charged.

Videotape is not damaged by X-rays, but it may be harmed by the magnetic field of a walk-through metal detector, so be sure to ask for a hand-check.

Security X-rays do not harm hard-disk or floppy-disk storage, but you may request a hand-check, at which point you may be asked to turn on the computer to prove that it is what it appears to be. (Check your battery before departure.) Most airlines allow you to use your laptop in flight except during takeoff and landing (so not to interfere with navigation equipment).

Calling home: it is cheaper to use a pay phone than the one in your hotel room

259

Crime and police

San Francisco has its problem areas – the Tenderloin, the Western Addition, and parts of the Mission District are those where greater than usual caution is required (and each is worth avoiding after dark) – but overall San Francisco rates as one of the country's safest major cities.

In its compact neighborhoods, where the main streets are nearly always bustling with pedestrians, you will seldom be alone, and therefore vulnerable or a target for street crime. It goes without saying, though, that shortcuts through dimly lit alleys or across open areas after dark are reckless and potentially dangerous undertakings.

At all times, you should be careful not to carry easily snatched bags and cameras, or to stuff your wallet into your back pocket. In a bar or restaurant, always keep your belongings within sight and within easy reach.

When not in use, cameras and other valuables should be left in the hotel's safe (some hotels provide in-room safes), and you should never carry more money than you need to for a particular outing.

In order to make an insurance claim, you should report any item stolen to the nearest police precinct (the address of which will be in the phone book). It is highly unlikely that your stolen goods will be recovered but the police will be able to fill out the forms which your insurance company will need to expedite your claim on your return home.

San Franciscan police are seldom far away

Emergency telephone numbers

For fire, police or ambulance, dial 911 and ask for the relevant service. Other emergency numbers include **Rape Crisis Hotline** (tel. 415/647 7273 or 206 3222), **24-hour Crisis Line** (tel. 415/696 5900), and **Travelers Aid** (tel. 415/255 2252).

Traveler's checks

Although you will want plenty of cash when visiting small cities or rural areas, traveler's checks are usually preferable. The most widely recognized are **American Express, Barclay's, Thomas Cook**, and those issued by major commercial banks such as **Citibank** and **Bank of America**. American Express also issues *Traveler's Checks for Two*, which can be countersigned and used by you or your traveling companion. Some checks are free; usually the issuing company or the bank at which you make your purchase charges 1% of the checks' face value as a fee. Be sure to buy a few checks in small denominations to cash toward the end of your trip, when you don't want to be left with more foreign currency than you can spend. Unlike cash, once lost or stolen, traveler's checks can be replaced or refunded if you can produce the purchase agreement and a record of the checks' serial numbers (especially of those you've already cashed). Sign all the checks when you buy them; you'll endorse them a second time to exchange them for cash or make purchases. Common sense dictates that you keep the purchase agreement separate from your checks. Caution-happy travelers will even give a copy of the purchase agreement and checks' serial numbers to someone back home. Most issuers of traveler's checks promise to refund or replace lost or stolen checks within 24 hours. In a safe place—or several safe places—record the toll-free or collect telephone number to call in case of emergencies.

Health and pharmacies

If you need to see a doctor or dentist, find one by looking under "Physicians and Surgeons" or "Dentists" in the Yellow Pages. Alternatively, telephone the **San Francisco Medical Society** (tel. 415/567 6230) for doctor referral or the **San Francisco Dental Society** (tel. 415/421 1435) to find a dentist.

City hospitals with well-equipped 24-hour emergency rooms include **San Francisco General**, 1001 Potrero Avenue (tel. 415/206 8000), and **St. Francis Memorial Hospital**, 900 Hyde Street (tel. 415/ 775 4321).

Access Health Care provides drop-in medical care at two San Francisco locations, daily 8–8. No membership is necessary. Davies Medical Center, Castro St. at Duboce Ave, tel. 415/565 6600; 26 California St. at Drumm St., tel. 415/397 2881.

Several **Walgreen Drug Stores** have 24-hour pharmacies, including

Most hospitals accept emergencies

stores at 500 Geary Street near Union Square (tel. 415/673 8413) and 3201 Divisadero Street at Lombard Street (tel. 415/931 6417). Also try the Walgreen pharmacy at 135 Powell Street near Market Street (tel. 415/391 7222), which is open Monday–Saturday 8a.m.–midnight, Sunday 9a.m.–9p.m.

Lost property

Lost at San Francisco International Airport, tel. 415/876 2461.
Lost on MUNI public transportation, tel. 415/923 6168.
For anything lost elsewhere, call the police station; the local precinct's number will be in the phone book.

For an ambulance, dial 911

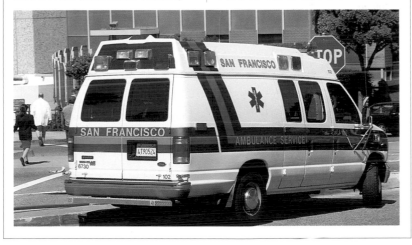

Children

Children are always warmly welcomed. Hotels and motels will usually provide a crib or extra bed in parents' room for children under 12 (sometimes for older children) at no extra charge, and restaurant staff are likely to appear with games, crayons, the children's menu and, if necessary, a high chair as soon as they spot youngsters.

The California Academy of Sciences and the Exploratorium are just two of the city's major attractions that are intended to entertain and educate children. See pages 242–3 for more suggestions.

Travelers with disabilities

In San Francisco facilities for travelers with disabilities are, by world standards, impressive. By law, public buildings must be at least partially wheelchair-accessible and all must provide toilets for the disabled. Most street corners have dropped curbs, and nearly all city buses have lifts for wheelchair-users, designated wheelchair space on board, and can usually "kneel" to make access easier from the curb. All BART stations are equipped with a wheelchair-suitable elevator between street and platform level.

Provided they receive sufficient notice, trains and airlines are legally obliged to provide services for travelers with disabilities, and Amtrak also offers a 15 percent discount to travelers with disabilities. Though less comfortable than the trains, and particularly uncomfortable for wheelchair users, Greyhound buses allow a companion to travel free provided a doctor's certificate can be produced stating that this is necessary.

Some major car rental companies can arrange vehicles with hand controls.

A wealth of material regarding facilities for the traveler with disabilities in San Francisco can be obtained from the Disability Coordinator, Mayor's Office of Community Development, 10 United Nations Plaza, Suite 600, San Francisco, CA 94102 (tel. 415/554 8925).

Maps

The most useful map of San Francisco is the Visitor Map, available from the Visitor Information Center (see Tourist Offices, page 266), and from many hotels. For travel elsewhere around California, use the

Facilities for the disabled are many

free map issued by the California Office of Tourism, which is also available from the Visitor Information Center.

Older travelers

The **American Association of Retired Persons** (AARP, 601 E St. NW, Washington, D.C. 20049, tel. 202/434 2277) provides independent travelers who are members of the AARP (open to those age 50 or older; $8 per person or couple annually) with the Purchase Privilege Program, which offers discounts on lodging, car rentals, and sightseeing, and the AARP Motoring Plan, which furnishes domestic trip-planning information and emergency road-service aid for an annual fee of $39.95 per person or couple ($59.95 for a premium version). AARP also arranges group tours, cruises, and apartment living through AARP Travel Experience from American Express (400 Pinnacle Way, Suite 450, Norcross, GA 30071, tel. 800/927 0111 or 800/745 4567).

Two other organizations offer discounts on lodgings, car rentals, and other travel products, along with such nontravel perks as magazines and newsletters:
The **National Council of Senior Citizens** (1331 F St. NW, Washington, D.C. 20004, tel. 202/347 8800; membership $12 annually), and **Mature Outlook** (6001 N. Clark St., Chicago, IL 60660, tel. 800/336 6330; $9.95 annually).

Note: Mention your senior-citizen identification card when booking hotel reservations for reduced rates, not when checking out. At restaurants, show your card before you're seated; discounts may be limited to certain menus, days, or hours. If you are renting a car, ask about promotional rates that might improve using your senior-citizen discount.

A number of American airlines and hotels offer discounts for older travelers (typically those aged 60 or older), though frequently changing details mean that finding out about the latest offers can be difficult. Your local travel agent may have up-to-date information, but you are more likely to glean the latest facts by contacting the airline directly.

The following tour operators specialize in older travelers: If you want to take your grandchildren, look into Grandtravel (6900 Wisconsin Ave., Suite 706, Chevy Chase, MD 20815, tel. 301/986 0790 or 800/247 7651). Saga International Holidays (222 Berkeley St., Boston, MA 02116, tel. 800/343 0273) caters to those over age 60 who like to travel in groups. SeniorTours (508 Irvington Rd., Drexel Hill, PA 19026, tel. 215/626 1977 or 800/227 1100) arranges bus tours throughout the United States and Nova Scotia, as well as Caribbean cruises.

Money apart, older travelers should be careful not to take on more physical activity than they can manage wherever they go. In San Francisco, a city with many tempting walks, the steepness of the hills should not be underestimated.

Opening hours

The majority of San Francisco's shops open on weekdays and Saturdays from 9a.m. or 10a.m. to 5p.m. or 6p.m. Major department stores, shopping centers, and tourist stores in Fisherman's Wharf and Chinatown, keep longer hours and are also open on Sundays. Smaller or specialized

Banking Hours
Monday-Friday
9am 6pm

24-Hour Customer
Service: 781-2235

No Smoking

CONVERSION CHARTS

FROM	TO	MULTIPLY BY
Inches	Centimeters	2.54
Centimeters	Inches	0.3937
Feet	Meters	0.3048
Meters	Feet	3.2810
Yards	Meters	0.9144
Meters	Yards	1.0940
Miles	Kilometers	1.6090
Kilometers	Miles	0.6214
Acres	Hectares	0.4047
Hectares	Acres	2.4710
U.S. gallons	Liters	3.7854
Liters	U.S. gallons	0.2642

(1 U.S. pint = 16fl oz)
(1 U.S. gallon = 0.8 U.K. gallons)

Ounces	Grams	28.35
Grams	Ounces	0.0353
Pounds	Grams	453.6
Grams	Pounds	0.0022
Pounds	Kilograms	0.4536
Kilograms	Pounds	2.205
U.S. tons	Tons	1.0160
Tons	U.S. Tons	0.9842

MEN'S SUITS

U.S.	36	38	40	42	44	46	48
U.K.	36	38	40	42	44	46	48
Rest of Europe	46	48	50	52	54	56	58

DRESS SIZES

U.S.	6	8	10	12	14	16
U.K.	8	10	12	14	16	18
Rest of Europe	34	36	38	40	42	44

MEN'S SHIRTS

U.S.	14	14.5	15	15.5	16	16.5	17
U.K.	14	14.5	15	15.5	16	16.5	17
Rest of Europe	36	37	38	39/40	41	42	43

MEN'S SHOES

U.S.	8	8.5	9.5	10.5	11.5	12
U.K.	7	7.5	8.5	9.5	10.5	11
Rest of Europe	41	42	43	44	45	46

WOMEN'S SHOES

U.S.	6	6.5	7	7.5	8	8.5
U.K.	4.5	5	5.5	6	6.5	7
Rest of Europe	38	38	39	39	40	41

stores, some of which may be closed on Mondays but open every other day, frequently begin business as late as 11a.m. or noon and close at 9p.m. or 10p.m.

Typical bank hours are Monday to Friday from 9a.m. to 3p.m. or 3:30p.m., with some branches staying open until 6p.m.

Museum opening hours vary according to the size and popularity of the museum. Larger ones generally open daily from 9a.m. or 10a.m. to 5p.m. or 6p.m., though smaller museums keep shorter hours and may be closed on one or more days during the week (and may only open during the afternoon). Where a museum has unusual opening hours, the details are given in the A–Z section of this book.

Places of worship

As you might expect in a city with such an ethnically diverse population, San Francisco's places of worship are many and varied, reflecting many faiths. Some of the most interesting churches are detailed in the A–Z section of this book. Your hotel reception will be able to advise on those in your neighborhood, and the telephone book carries a comprehensive list.

Sales tax

Added to the marked price of everything you might purchase in the city is San Francisco's 8.5 percent sales tax. Elsewhere in California, the sales-tax may be slightly lower.

Tipping

How much you tip is entirely up to you, but the general rule in a restaurant or coffee shop is to leave the server 15 percent of the total bill, or slightly more—generally up to 20 percent, though there is no hard and fast rule—for particularly good service. It is customary to tip drivers around 15–20 percent of the fare. The amount need not be exact, however, and most people (if the amount works out within reason) simply tell the driver to keep the change as they hand over the fare.

Tip hotel porters, especially if they are red in the face and short of breath after carrying your bulging suitcases up several flights of stairs. Again, the amount you tip is entirely discretionary, but you should probably plan on an average of 75¢–$1 per bag.

Toilets
Every public building in San Francisco is obliged to provide public toilets. Such toilets are almost always maintained in immaculate condition.

Wine and beer
Many visitors to San Francisco put aside time to sample the produce of the neighbouring Wine Country (see the excursions described on pages 204–209 to Sonoma Valley and Napa Valley), but California's native beers are also worth seeking out.

San Francisco's Anchor Steam Beer is nowadays enjoyed in bars across the world, and there are numerous micro-breweries in the area making exceptionaly good brews that are a totally different experience from the weak and taste-less mass-market American beers.

Women travelers
In San Francisco as in any city in the world, women on their own—whether residents or visitors—may attract unwelcome attention. However, this is more likely to be annoying than threatening and can usually be dealt with simply by ignoring it or delivering a sharp verbal rebuff. Common sense dictates that women on their own should avoid isolated, poorly lit areas at night and cheap hotels in seedy districts.

A women's bookstore on Valencia Street

Organized tours

San Francisco lends itself to being discovered at your own pace, perhaps with the aid of the guided walking tours detailed on pages 94–5. If you are pressed for time, however, you might consider a whistle-stop guided tour of the city and surrounding area.

Among numerous companies offering such trips, **Tower Tours** (tel. 415/434 TOUR) has a half-day city tour and a tour crossing the Golden Gate to Sausalito and Muir Woods, either of which can be combined with a cruise on the bay. **Gray Line Tours** (tel. 415/558 9400) offers much the same as Tower Tours for a slightly higher price, but the company also has an evening tour that includes a walk around Chinatown and optional dinner.

If you want to stay in San Francisco but see some more of California, Tower Tours offer a wine country trip and a tour around the Monterey peninsula.

InterAmerica Tours (tel. 415/381 5713) will pick you up from your hotel and fly you by private plane to

The well-stocked Visitor Information Center

Yosemite National Park for around $250 per person.

Other tours, such as those to Alcatraz Island and the opportunity for a guided cavort around the city's nightclubs, are detailed at appropriate points in the A–Z section of this book.

Tourist offices

Find the time during your stay in San Francisco to drop by the Visitor Information Center, on the lower level of Hallidie Plaza by the junction of Market and Powell streets (open Monday–Friday 9–5:30, Saturday 9–3, Sunday 10–2; tel. 415/391 2000). The center carries a large number of hotel and restaurant leaflets (many of which qualify the holder for discounts) and free publications issued by the Convention and Visitors Bureau. The multilingual staff is ready to answer visitors' questions. You will also be able to pick up the two maps recommended under Maps, page 263.

For general information ahead of arrival, send $2 plus postage to San Francisco Convention and Visitors Bureau, PO Box 429097, San Francisco, California 94142-9097.

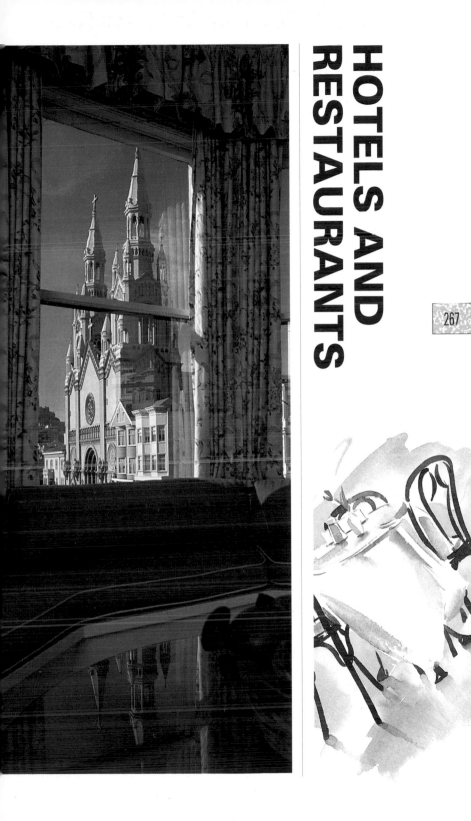

HOTELS AND RESTAURANTS

The following recommended hotels and restaurants have been divided by area and into three price categories:

- **budget ($)**
- **moderate ($$)**
- **expensive ($$$)**

Note that phone numbers prefixed 800 are toll-free numbers accessed by first dialling "1." These numbers can be usually dialed from anywhere in the U.S. or Canada, though in some cases there is an additional toll-free number for calls made within California. Omit the 415 area code if dialing from within San Francisco.

ACCOMMODATIONS

CHINATOWN

Astoria ($) 510 Bush Street (tel. 1-800/666 6696; 415/434 8889). Slightly pricier than Chinatown's other budget-rate options but the Astoria boasts a laundry and round-the-clock room service, and will pick up its guests from the airport.

Grant Plaza ($) 465 Grant Avenue (tel. in California 1-800/472 6805; elsewhere in U.S. 1-800/472 6899; 415/434 3883). Located in the bustling heart of Chinatown, the Grant Plaza offers small but nicely furnished rooms all with private bathrooms, TVs, and phones—and at an unbeatable price.

Holiday Inn Financial District ($$) 750 Kearny Street (tel. 1-800/424 4292; 415/433 6600). Despite its name, this branch of the well-known chain rises high above Chinatown and is by far the biggest and best-equipped hotel in the neighborhood, but its large size tends to make guests feel anonymous.

Obrero Hotel ($) 1208 Stockton Street (tel. 415/989 3960). On a perennially crowded section of Stockton Street with compact rooms lacking private bathrooms and TVs, this nevertheless offers accommodations which will barely dent your budget—and breakfast is included.

Temple Hotel ($) 469 Pine Street (tel. 415/781 2565). Somewhat shabby and unappealing but the rooms, while spartan, are clean and generally quiet, and are offered with or without private bathroom.

CIVIC CENTER & TENDERLOIN

Abigail Hotel ($$) 246 McAllister Street (tel. 1-800/553 5575; 415/861 9728). In 1926, the Abigail opened to host visiting theatrical performers and still, in greatly renovated and updated form, exudes a home-away-from-home charm enhanced by its European antiques and furnishings. Breakfast is included.

Albion House Inn ($$) 135 Gough Street (tel. 415/621 0896). An inviting bed-and-breakfast alternative in an area dominated by run-of-the-mill hotels, with nine cozy rooms and a relaxing lounge dominated by a colossal fireplace.

The Atherton ($) 685 Ellis Street (tel. 415/474 5720). Not the least expensive but certainly among the area's better buys; the rooms are attractively furnished and the on-site bar and restaurant is a welcome standby if the surrounding streets feel frightening after dark.

Friendship Inn ($) 860 Eddy Street (tel. in California 1-800/300 4511; elsewhere in U.S. 1-800/453 4511; 415/474 4374). This recently renovated budget-priced hotel now has a few more expensive rooms boasting jacuzzis; the regular rooms are not large but are clean and tidy.

Gates Hotel ($) 140 Ellis Street (tel. 415/781 0430). Plain but clean, this makes an adequate very low-cost base for a night or two.

Grand Central Hotel/Hostel ($) 1412 Market Street (tel. 415/703 9988). Provides competitively priced single and double rooms, and an even less costly option of small, shared dorms. Free tea and coffee are offered throughout the day and complimentary breakfast is included. Also has a few shelves of books on San Francisco and its environs for guests to browse through.

Hotel One ($) 587 Eddy Street (tel. 415/775 5934). Reliable option for well-maintained and reasonably sized rooms with private bathrooms. The location is central although the immediate streets tend to be seedy. Discount deals sometimes reduce the already low rates.

Inn at the Opera ($$$) 333 Fulton Street (tel. in California 1-800/423 9610; elsewhere in U.S. 1-800/325 2708 or 415/863 8400). Opera and ballet stars, classical musicians, and top-billed thespians are among the fellow guests with whom you might be sharing the breakfast buffet at this extremely cozy and tastefully decorated hotel. Along with vases of fresh flowers, each room has a microwave oven for after-theater feasts.

Mary Elizabeth Inn ($) 1040 Bush Street (tel. 415/673 6768). A church-linked inn which has been offering women-only accommodations since 1914, this still makes a friendly and low-key base.

Pensione San Francisco ($) 1668 Market Street (tel. 415/864 1271). A popular spot for its prime location; no TVs, no fridges, shared bathrooms and bargain rates.

Phoenix Inn ($$) 601 Eddy Street (tel. 1-800/CITYINN; 415/776 1380). While other hotels stuff themselves with antiques, the Phoenix uses contemporary Bay Area artwork and a bright color scheme to make guests—many of them are visiting rock musicians — feel welcome and relaxed. Facilities include in-room massage, outdoor heated swimming pool, and a modest complimentary breakfast.

YMCA Central ($) 220 Golden Gate Avenue (tel. 415/885 0460). With plain and simple single and double rooms with shared bathrooms, and a TV room, this makes a reasonable budget option and is available to men and women.

FINANCIAL DISTRICT & EMBARCADERO

Galleria Park ($$) 191 Sutter Street (tel. in California 1-800/792 9855; elsewhere in U S 1-800/792 9030, 415/781 3060). Adjacent to the shops of Crocker Galleria, this is among the boot of the city's boutique hotels—establishments which pride themselves on attentive service and congenial surroundings—offering a choice of nicely furnished regular rooms and exceptionally attractive suites.

Hyatt Regency ($$$) 5 Embarcadero Center (tel. 1-800/233 1234; 415/788 1234). Design themes of open space and crisp contours become apparent as soon as you enter the enormous glass-ceilinged lobby and continue into the guest rooms—efficiently furnished and with first-run movies on the TV—and up to the revolving rooftop restaurant.

Mandarin Oriental ($$$) 222 Sansome Street (tel. 415/885 0999). Occupying the top 11 floors of a towering modern high-rise, the Mandarin spares no effort in pampering its predominantly business-traveler guests. All the rooms are quiet and extremely comfortable and some of the rooms, including bathrooms, have fabulous views across the city.

Park Hyatt ($$$) 333 Battery Street (tel. 1-800/323 PARK; 415/392 1234). Squarely aimed at the high-flying business traveler, with complimentary Mercedes service to Financial District addresses and a fax machine and photocopier available. When they eventually finish working, guests can gaze from their windows across the city or the bay.

YMCA Embarcadero ($) 169 Steuart Street (tel. 415/957 9622). The nicest of the city's two YMCA's, with a choice of single and double private rooms or small shared dormitories; open to men and women.

FISHERMAN'S WHARF & FORT MASON

Comfort Inn by the Bay ($$) 2775 Van Ness Avenue (tel. 415/928 5000). Slightly better than average motel rooms at lower than average prices are the main reasons for choosing this over its neighborhood rivals; set on a busy street but within easy reach of the main tourist areas. A buffet breakfast is included.

Holiday Inn Fisherman's Wharf ($$) 1300 Columbus Avenue (tel. 1-800/465 4329; 415/771 9000). A high-quality and very up-to-date link in the worldwide chain within easy walking distance of North Beach as well as the tourist spots of Fisherman's Wharf. If you are hungry but too lazy to go out, the restaurant serves a very good buffet three times a day.

Ramada at Fisherman's Wharf ($$) 590 Bay Street (tel. 1-800/228 8408; 415/885 4700). Another branch of a nationally known midrange chain, the Ramada easily holds its own with its neighborhood rivals; for a family of four or more vacationing together, the unusually spacious and well-equipped suites can be a good option.

San Francisco International Hostel ($) Building 24, Fort Mason (tel. 415/771 7277). The largest youth hostel in the U.S. has small dormitories, laundry facilities, and a maximum stay of three nights in summer (five nights in winter), though these restrictions are likely to be waived if space is available.

San Francisco Marriott at Fisherman's Wharf ($$$) 1250 Columbus Avenue (tel. 1-800/228 9290; 415/775 7555). Well-to-do tourists and on-the-road Financial District dealers have both taken a shine to this efficient and well-presented hotel. Besides large, well-furnished, and generously equipped rooms, the price includes maid service twice a day, free morning newspaper, early evening snacks, and a light breakfast of pastries and coffee.

Sheraton at Fisherman's Wharf ($$$) 2500 Mason Street (tel. 1-800/325 3535; 415/362 5500). Everything you would expect to find in a hotel run by this competent upscale chain is provided in this recently built 500-room property, which is a very easy walk to the area's main stores and attractions.

269

Travelodge near Ghirardelli Square ($$) 1201 Columbus Avenue (tel. 1-800/255 3050; 415/776 7070). Not the most luxurious of the area's accommodations but an attractively priced base for exploring the neighborhood and nearby North Beach. Only 25 rooms so be sure to reserve early. There is a second, much larger and more expensive Travelodge in Fisherman's Wharf, at 250 Beach Street (tel. 1-800/255 3050; 415/392 6700).

Tuscan Inn at Fisherman's Wharf ($$$) 425 North Point (tel. 1-800/648 4626; 415/561 1100). Probably the most attractive lodging in Fisherman's Wharf, with cheerfully furnished rooms and an armchair-filled lobby where complimentary sherry can be sipped beside the fireplace.

The Wharf Inn ($$) 2601 Mason Street (tel. 1-800/548 9918; 415/673 7411). Redecorated to create relaxing rooms and a two-bedroom penthouse suite, the Wharf also presents guests with complimentary tea, coffee, and morning newspaper.

HAIGHT-ASHBURY & WESTERN ADDITION

Alamo Square Inn ($$) 719 Scott Street (tel. 415/922 2055). Located on the west side of scenic Alamo Square a few blocks from the heart of Haight-Ashbury, this rambling Victorian house offers bed-and-breakfast in a choice of 13 rooms decorated in widely varying but always appealing styles.

Archbishop's Mansion ($$$) 1000 Fulton Street (tel. 415/563 7872). From 1904, this sprawling home really was an archbishop's residence. Transformed into an antique-filled bed-and-breakfast inn, it now has 15 rooms individually decorated with themes pertaining to particular 19th-century French operas.

Grove Inn ($) 890 Grove Street (tel. 1-800/829 0780; 415/929 0780). An inexpensive bed-and-breakfast where the cheaper rooms have shared bathrooms; set within easy reach of Haight-Ashbury but in a dreary and sometimes intimidating section of the Western Addition.

Metro Hotel ($) 319 Divisadero Street (tel. 415/861 5364). Small, simple and suitably-priced, this friendly hotel is just two blocks from Buena Vista Park and a short walk from Haight Street.

The Red Victorian ($$) 1665 Haight Street (tel. 415/864 1978). There can be few more quintessentially Californian experiences than spending a night in this bed-and-breakfast inn, directly above a gallery of Meditative Art and a health-food café. Some of the variously themed rooms are decorated with original 1960s psychedelic posters and some of the four-poster beds are draped with tie-dyed canopies.

Stanyan Park Hotel ($$) 750 Stanyan Street (tel. 415/751 1000). The staff of this characterful 36-room Edwardian hotel, which faces Golden Gate Park, strive to create an intimate atmosphere similar to that of a small bed-and-breakfast inn; another contributing factor to the B&B ambience is indeed the breakfast: rolls, muffins, and fruit laid out in a spacious dining room.

Victorian Inn on the Park ($$) 301 Lyon Street (tel. 415/931 1830). Wind your way up the staircase—lined with historic posters and photos of San Francisco—of this imposing 1897 house and you will find 12 cozy rooms decorated with antiques; some have original, working fireplaces. Fruit, croissants, and fresh-brewed coffee are served for breakfast.

JAPANTOWN

Hotel Majestic ($$$) 1500 Sutter Street (tel. 1-800/869 8966; 415/441 1100). Dating from 1888 and said to be the city's oldest hotel, the five-story Majestic helped house the homeless following the 1906 earthquake; a thorough renovation and modernization has created a stylish and relaxing place, filled with French and English antiques and period furnishings.

The Miyako ($$$) 1625 Post Street (tel. 1-800/528 1234; 415/922 3200). Rock star David Bowie is just one former guest who has appreciated the luxury-class Miyako's clever fusing of Western and Japanese ideas; all rooms have sliding shoji screens and marble bathrooms with furo tubs, while the traditional Japanese rooms have tatami mats and futons.

Miyako Inn ($$) 1800 Sutter Street (tel. 1-800/528 1234; 415/921 4000). Not to be confused with the similarly named—and more expensive—hotel (see previous entry), the Best Western-owned Miyako Inn offers fairly standard accommodation except for steam baths and a few other Japanese touches.

The Queen Anne ($$) 1590 Sutter Street (tel. 1-800/227 3970; 415/441 2828). This handsome and extremely spacious 1890 Victorian building, which now offers reposeful nights in elegantly furnished rooms with high ceilings, originally served as a girls' school. Breakfast is included, as is afternoon tea and sherry which are served in the drawing room.

MARINA DISTRICT

Marina Inn ($$) 3110 Octavia Street (tel. 415/928 1000). If the comparative calm of the Marina District appeals, this modestly sized and attractively priced inn is a wise choice. A light breakfast is included.

Marina Motel ($) 2576 Lombard Street (tel. 415/921 9406). A budget priced option in a busy street in the largely residential Marina District, with a choice of regular and kitchen-equipped rooms.

MISSION DISTRICT & THE CASTRO

El Capitan ($) 2361 Mission Street (tel. 1-800/325 4116; 415/695 1597). Small, no-frills hotel in the heart of the Mission District; unmatched for price but do not expect peace and quiet on the neighborhood's lively main thoroughfare, which can feel intimidating after dark.

Haus Kleebauer ($) 225 Clipper Street (tel. 415/821 3866). This fine example of Victorian architecture, complete with stained-glass windows, offers bed-and-breakfast accommodations on the edge of the Castro in rooms where brass beds stand alongside microwave ovens and VCRs.

24 Henry ($) 24 Henry Street (tel. 415/864 5686). Five-room guest house on a tree-lined Castro side street; a small, friendly, and affordable base for gay men.

Willows Inn ($$) 710 Fourteenth Street (tel. 415/431 4770). Rooms may lack private bathrooms but the friendly atmosphere and the warm furnishings of this 1904 house do much to win the admiration of its guests, many of whom are gay or lesbian visitors to the city.

NOB HILL

Fairmont Hotel & Tower ($$$) 950 Mason Street (tel. 1-800/527 4727; 415/772 5000). A home-away-from-home for rich and famous visitors since 1907, the Fairmont still has sky-high standards of service and decadently decorated rooms large enough to swing several cats; the best of them also offer stunning city views.

Mark Hopkins Hotel ($$$) 1 Nob Hill (tel. 1-800/327 0200; 415/392 3434). Another long-serving Nob Hill landmark and treated to a $10-million facelift in the late 1980s, the Mark Hopkins offers a choice of "traditional" or "contemporary" rooms—neither of which should ever give cause for complaint—or a penthouse suite complete with grand piano.

Ritz-Carlton ($$$) 600 Stockton Street (tel. 1-800/241 3333; 415/296 7465). A new arrival on the Nob Hill hotel scene and occupying an architecturally distinguished building, the Ritz-Carlton has sumptuously furnished rooms with minibars and TVs with a range of movies; other features include a fully equipped fitness center and swimming pool, and an impressive art collection lining the corridors.

Stanford Court ($$$) 905 California Street (tel. 1-800/227 4726; 415/989 3500). The epitome of understated elegance, the Stanford Court's mix of good-sized rooms with tasteful and traditional furnishings, and friendly and ultraefficient service, has won it many friends among jet-setting aristocrats.

NORTH BEACH

Millefiori Inn ($$) 444 Columbus Avenue (tel. 415/433 9111). Tidy and welcoming bed-and-breakfast in the pulsating heart of North Beach with each of the comfortable rooms themed on a particular flower.

San Remo Hotel ($) 2237 Mason Street (tel. 415/776 8688). Located on the borders of North Beach and Fisherman's Wharf, the impressively priced San Remo is a fully renovated 1906 Italianate villa with small but serviceable rooms—bathrooms are shared—grouped around a central atrium.

Washington Square Inn ($$) 1660 Stockton Street (tel. within California 1-800/388 0200; 415/981 4220). Facing Washington Square, the inn's simple furnishings do their best to recreate the mood of a rural French *pension,* and the less expensive rooms have shared bathrooms. Breakfast is included, as is early evening tea, wine, and snacks.

PACIFIC HEIGHTS

Cathedral Hill Hotel ($$) 1101 Van Ness Avenue (tel. in California 1-800/622 0855; elsewhere in U.S. 1-800/227 4730; 415/776 8200). A massive 1980s renovation created this big, bold, and fully equipped modern hotel with dependable service and comfortable—if not particularly inspiring—rooms.

Days Inn near Fisherman's Wharf ($$) 2358 Lombard Street (tel. within California 1-800/556 2667; elsewhere in U.S. 1-800/325 2525; 415/922 2010). An inexpensive chain option, certainly within striking distance of Fisherman's Wharf but also a convenient and affordable base for the rest of the city.

HOTELS AND RESTAURANTS

Edward II Suites & Pub ($) 3155 Scott Street (tel. 1-800/473 2846; 415/922 3000). Four-poster beds and whirlpool baths are a feature of the pricier rooms at this bed-and-breakfast inn which is combined with an English-themed bar.

Laurel Motor Inn ($) 444 Presidio Avenue (tel. 1-800/552 8753; 415/567 8467). Unspectacular but good value, located in an out-of-the-way section of the city.

Lombard Hotel ($$) 1015 Geary Street (tel. 415/673 5232). On the southern fringes of Pacific Heights and just a few blocks from Japantown, and Civic Center, the Lombard is neatly furnished and boasts splendid views from its rooftop terrace.

The Mansions ($$) 2220 Sacramento Street (tel. 1-800/826 9398; 415/929 9444). Two side-by-side 19th-century mansions—one a twin-towered Queen Anne, the other a Greek Revival—were combined to create the Mansions, a rambling and delightful bed-and-breakfast inn with more than a few touches of engaging eccentricity.

Pacific Heights Inn ($) 1555 Union Street (tel. 1-800/523 1801; 415/776 3310). A reasonably-priced inn close to the neighborhood's premier shopping and dining strip, and offering adequate if unelaborate motel rooms.

Richelieu ($$) 1050 Van Ness Avenue (tel. 1-800/227 3608; 415/673 4711). Located close to the Lombard (see above), the Richelieu has been successfully restored to its early 1900s appearance with historical knickknacks and photographs lining the walls; the rooms are fully up-to-date, however, and include coffee makers

and minibars.

The Sherman House ($$$) 2160 Green Street (tel. 415/563 3600). A French-Italianate mansion of the 1870s set in an exclusive residential area, the Sherman House makes a happy hideaway for those who value privacy and outstanding service; wine tasting and classical music evenings sometimes take place in the drawing room, and another reason to stay is the excellent restaurant.

Union Street Inn ($$) 2229 Union Street (tel. 415/346 0424). With just six guest rooms in this beautifully maintained and decorated Edwardian home, you can be sure of getting the personal attention of the host, whose homemade jams can be used to top your breakfast muffin.

SOMA

European Guest House ($) 761 Minna Street (tel. 415/861 6634). A backpacker-aimed hostel with four-bed dormitories and an easygoing atmosphere; within a few minutes' walk of lively Folsom Street and, convenient for the long-distance bus links from the Transbay Terminal.

Harbor Court ($$) 165 Steuart Street (tel. 1-800/346 0555; 415/882 1300). Occupying a characterful 90-year-old building just south of Market Street, this is a cozy and stylish niche offering all the usual top-notch facilities—plus use of the neighboring YMCA's Olympic-sized swimming pool—and some fine bay views.

Hotel Griffon ($$) 155 Steuart Street (tel. 1-800/321 2201; 415/495 2100). A luxurious small hotel a few steps from Market Street, many of the guests are Financial District brokers

enjoying the well-stocked minibars and views across the bay. Guests have free use of the adjoining fitness center.

Inter Club Globe Hostel ($) 10 Hallam Place (tel. 415/431 0540). Aimed at globetrotting backpackers (everyone must show proof of recent travel overseas), this is a homely hostel just off the nightlife strip of Folsom Street with a number of attractive features—such as safety deposit boxes, free coffee, and no curfew.

Mosser Victorian Hotel of Arts and Music ($) 54 Fourth Street (tel. 1-800/227 3804; 415/986 4400). Skimps on the luxuries but with excellent rates and a great location—a short walk from Yerba Buena Gardens and just south of Market Street—this is one of the area's good value choices.

The Pickwick ($$) 85 Fifth Street (tel. 415/421 7500). Unpretentious lodgings at a very reasonable price close to Market Street and within a few blocks of Yerba Buena Gardens.

San Francisco Marriott ($$$) 55 Fourth Street (tel. 1-800/228 9290; 415/896 1600). Locally derided as the "Jukebox Marriott" because of its architecture, there is no denying that this distinctive high-rise offers top-class accommodations chiefly for convention-goers and business travelers; all the facilities you would want, and a health club for unwinding after stress-filled days.

Sheraton Palace ($$$) 2 New Montgomery Street (tel. 1-800/325 3535; 415/392 8600). Long before the fine hotels of Nob Hill were pampering the great and good, the Palace was firmly established as the city's most luxurious place to stay. Following a $60-

ACCOMMODATIONS

million renovation, the hotel reopened in 1991, and once again sets a high standard for comfort, service, and decor; stop by, if only to stare at the sumptuous Garden Court.

UNION SQUARE

Adelaide Inn ($) 5 Isadora Duncan Lane (tel. 415/441 2261). Unmatched for price, the Adelaide offers small but cozy rooms with shared bathrooms and a pleasant atmosphere in a quiet cul-de-sac off Taylor Street.
Alexander Inn ($$) 415 O'Farrell Street (tel. 1-800/253 9263; 415/928 6800). With sturdy dark-wood fixtures and vases of flowers brightening every corner, this is a welcoming and relaxing place to stay—fresh-baked pastries are served for breakfast.
Amsterdam Hotel ($) 749 Taylor Street (tel. 415/673 3277). Great value just below the crest of Nob Hill, with pleasantly furnished rooms (the cheaper ones lack bathrooms) and a complimentary breakfast-with views served on the rooftop patio.
Andrews Hotel ($$) 624 Post Street (tel. 1-800/926 3739; 415/563 6877). The pastel peach color scheme here will enliven the most fog-shrouded San Francisco morning, as will the fresh-brewed coffee, croissants, and fruit waiting outside your room.
Bedford ($$) 761 Post Street (tel. 1-800/227 5642; 415/673 6040). Slightly shabby corridors conceal impressively decorated rooms all with VCRs; from the higher floors there are excellent city views. No breakfast, but there is a complimentary early evening wine hour, and a free morning shuttle bus to the Financial District.
Brady Acres ($) 649 Jones Street (tel. 415/929 8033).

This should be every bargain-seeker's first stop in the neighborhood; the remarkably inexpensive rooms, painted in bold and joyful shades, are fitted with microwave ovens and coffee makers, and local phone calls are free.
Californian ($$) 405 Taylor Street (tel. 1-800/227 3346; 415/885 2500). A wealth of traditional fixtures and fittings, an impressive wood-beamed lobby, and the most appealing rates in its price category, conspire to make this a wise choice.
Campton Place Kempinski ($$$) 340 Stockton Street (tel. in California 1-800/235 4300; elsewhere in U.S. 1-800/426 3135; 415/781 5555). Travelers accustomed to luxury living but weary of large, impersonal hotels will love this medium-sized, ideally located place where the rooms are stylishly laid-out and where the staff embody professional and personal service.
Cartwright Hotel ($$) 524 Sutter Street (tel. 1-800/227 3844, 415/421 2865). The rooms can be small but are comfortable and very competitively priced for this central neighborhood; complimentary afternoon tea and cakes are offered in the book-lined study.
Four Seasons Clift ($$$) 495 Geary Street (tel. 1-800/332 3442; 415/775 4700). Large and luxurious, this caters to the whims and fancies of the rich and powerful, and accommodates them in spacious, gracefully furnished rooms—the higher the floor, the more impressive the view.
Handlery Union Square ($$) 351 Geary Street (tel. 1-800/223 0888; 415/781 7800). One of the area's most dependable boutique hotels, with all the usual facilities and comforts, plus in-room safes.

Hotel David ($) 480 Geary Street (tel. 1-800/524 1888; 415/771 1600). An all-you-can-eat breakfast and a discounted dinner from the ground-floor deli are both included in the room rate, and make the small but clean rooms temptingly good value for the budget-minded visitor.
Hotel Diva ($$) 440 Geary Street (tel. 1-800/533 1900; 415/885 0200). Sculptured in chrome and stainless steel, the Diva's high-tech design style sets it well apart from most San Francisco hotels. The futuristic fittings continue in the rooms where virtually everything electrical is remote-controlled, including the VCRs.
Hotel Nikko ($$$) 222 Mason Street (tel. 1-800/645 5687; 415/394 1111). The two-story marble lobby complete with waterfall is just the start; ascend on the ultrasmooth elevators and you will find your room tastefully furnished and fitted with a fully stocked minibar. From the higher floors, the views can be exceptional.
Hotel Union Square ($$) 114 Powell Street (tel. 1-800/553 1900; 415/397 3000). Cable cars rumble evocatively past the entrance to this affordable and well-run boutique hotel; the complimentary breakfast features croissants and a choice of herbal teas.
Juliana ($$) 590 Bush Street (tel. 1-800/382 8800; 415/392 2540). Muted pastel colors enhance the appeal of the smallish rooms in this completely renovated 1903 building; complimentary wine is served each evening in the lobby.
Kensington Park ($$) 450 Post Street (tel. 1-800/553 1900; 415/788 6400). An

273

impressively presented boutique hotel with many stylish furnishings and decorations; breakfast is included and complimentary afternoon sherry is served to the sound of the resident pianist.

King George ($$) 334 Mason Street (tel. 1-800/288 6005; 415/781 5050). This mid-sized hotel offers functional if unspectacular rooms and competent service in the heart of the theater area.

Monticello Inn ($$) 127 Ellis Street (tel. 1-800/669 7777; 415/392 8800). An enterprising and entertaining attempt to recreate a Deep South plantation home, complete with replica Federal-period furnishings and book-lined parlor.

The Olympic ($) 140 Mason Street (tel. 415/982 5010). A front-runner among the area's budget-priced possibilities, offering compact but clean rooms with a choice of shared or private bathroom.

Pan Pacific Hotel ($$$) 500 Post Street (tel. 1-800/553 6465; 415/771 8600). From the massive open-plan entrance court and its glass-sided elevators, the Pan Pacific is a strikingly designed hotel offering all the usual first-rate facilities.

Prescott ($$) 545 Post Street (tel. 1-800/283 7322; 415/563 0303). The airy lobby decorated with Native American artifacts sets a relaxing mood of low-key comfort which the guest rooms—and the jacuzzi-equipped suites—continue.

The Raphael ($$) 386 Geary Street (tel. 1-800/821 5343; 415/986 2000). Conveniently located for the mainstream theaters, the Raphael's rooms can be slightly small but most are luxuriously furnished, and the TV offers a wide selection of cable channels.

Savoy ($$) 580 Geary Street (tel. 1-800/227 4223; 415/441 2700). One of the many aging hotels in the area completely refurbished during the late 1980s, the reposeful Savoy is designed to suggest a small hotel in rural France. Breakfast is included, as is late afternoon sherry and tea.

Shannon Court ($$) 550 Geary Street (tel. 1-800/821 0493; 415/775 5000). Decorated in warm and relaxing pastel shades, the sizeable rooms also boast fresh flowers; breakfast is included, as is afternoon tea served with gourmet cookies. If money is no object, choose one of the suites which opens onto a rooftop terrace.

Sheehan ($) 620 Sutter Street (tel. 1-800/848 1529; 415/775 6500). Formerly a YWCA, the Sheehan has transformed into a very good-value hotel; the tidy, if sometimes slightly spartan, rooms are available with or without private bathrooms; an Olympic-sized swimming pool and a gymnasium are further draws, as is the complimentary coffee and muffin breakfast.

Sir Francis Drake ($$) 450 Powell Street (tel. in California 1-800/625 1668; elsewhere in U.S. 1-800/227 5480; 415/392 7755). No more than a skip and a jump from Union Square with would-be Tower of London Beefeaters greeting new arrivals as they enter, the Sir Francis Drake provides a taste of Old World grandeur at an affordable price.

Triton ($$) 342 Grant Avenue (tel. 1-800/433 6611; 415/394 0500). Custom-made designer furnishings, pastel shades, and art work by contemporary Bay Area artists help make this the hippest place to stay in the city; the rooms feature CD players (selections available from a CD library).

Villa Florence ($$) 225 Powell Street (tel. 1-800/553 4411; 415/397 7700). Extremely well-located for Union Square shopping, the Villa Florence's public areas are dotted with Italian art and antiques, and the guest rooms are tastefully furnished and are provided with coffee makers.

Vintage Court ($$) 650 Bush Street (tel. 1-800/654 1100; 415/392 4666). Classy and comfortable, the Vintage Court identifies its rooms not with numbers but with names of selected wine country wineries. The oenological theme continues in the lobby, where complimentary early evening wine is offered beside the fireplace with a copious pile of magazines.

Westin St. Francis ($$$) Powell Street at Union Square (tel. 1-800/228 3000; 415/397 7000). A much-loved San Francisco landmark, the St. Francis has been a prestige hotel since it opened in 1904 and became the city's first hotel to put sheets on its beds. The addition of a modern tower wing and the computerization of the check-in desk have done nothing to deter from its elegant and sophisticated ambience.

White Swan Inn ($$) 845 Bush Street (tel. 415/775 1755). Filled with English antiques, furnishings, and paintings, the White Swan strives to create a traditional atmosphere while providing comfortable bed-and-breakfast accommodations with a full range of services. The English theme includes a complimentary afternoon tea, complete with scones.

RESTAURANTS

BERKELEY

Blue Nile ($) 2525 Telegraph Avenue (tel. 510/540 6777). Delicious Ethiopian food served in a tastefully decorated room which has been a favorite eating spot of Berkeley's students—and many locals—for years.

Café Siena ($) 2490 Bancroft Way (tel. 510/644 0946). Sandwiches, salads, and other low-cost snacks, coffee in numerous styles, and a campus-side location make this a great snack stop while exploring the university.

Chez Panisse ($$$) 1517 Shattuck Avenue (tel. 510/548 5525). Credited with being the mid-1970s birthplace of California cuisine, Chez Panisse is still a pivotal part of Berkeley's so-called gourmet ghetto, and its cultured culinary presentations change daily; reservations are essential. Less costly, less formal, and, for most people, just as good, is the upstairs Chez Panisse Café.

THE CASTRO

La Méditerranée ($) 288 Noe Street (tel. 415/431 7210). Enjoyable spot for tasty, filling Middle Eastern and Greek food, none of it liable to harm your budget.

Thailand Restaurant ($$) 438A Castro Street (tel. 415/863 6868). Cozy upper-floor restaurant offering a long and impressive menu of Thai favorites including fiery red and green curries.

Welcome Home ($) 464 Castro Street (tel. 415/626 3600). One of a number of dependable coffee shops in the vicinity, this one serves filling breakfast omelettes and great-value lunches.

CHINATOWN

Bow Hon ($) 850 Grant Avenue (tel. 415/362 0601). For the price, there is no better place to sample Cantonese clay-pot stews; also features noodle soups and stir-fried dishes.

Brandy Ho's ($$) 217 Columbus Avenue (tel. 415/788 7527) and 450 Broadway (tel. 415/362 3268). On the border with North Beach, both branches of Brandy Ho's are popular for their outstanding Hunan cuisine; diners with delicate palates might find some of the dishes too hot to handle.

House of Nanking ($) 919 Kearny Street (tel. 415/421 1429). You will almost certainly need to line up outside before being seated at a table at this tiny but highly regarded restaurant, which was among the first to bring quality Shanghai and northern regional Chinese cooking to Chinatown.

Kowloon Vegetarian Restaurant ($) 909 Grant Avenue (tel. 415/362 9888). Vegetarians pining for duck's gizzard or chicken feet can feast on meat-free versions of such dishes here, though the extensive menu also features many excellent meal-in-themselves soups, and rice, and noodle dishes; take-out dim sum is available from the counter.

Lotus Garden ($) 532 Grant Avenue (tel. 415/397 0707). Slightly more expensive and with a much smaller menu than the Kowloon (see above), the Lotus Garden nonetheless offers delicious vegetarian Chinese fare.

Pot Sticker ($) 150 Waverly Place (tel. 415/397 9985). Located on a temple-laden side-street just off Grant Avenue, this enjoyable spot specializes in steamed and pan-fried dumplings filled with meat or, less commonly, seafood or vegetables.

Royal Jade ($$) 675 Jackson Street (tel. 415/392 2929). Cantonese seafood is the house specialty, though excellent dim sum is served at lunchtime when there is also a low-cost buffet offered on the top floor.

Sam Woh ($) 813 Washington Street (tel. 415/982 0596). An infamously rude headwaiter made this an essential Chinatown stop for many years; presently, however, only the very low prices and lively atmosphere—the kitchen occupies the entire ground floor and diners usually have to share the upstairs tables—make this a worthwhile local visit.

CIVIC CENTER & TENDERLOIN

Ananda Fuara ($) 1298 Market Street (tel. 415/621 1994). A serene atmosphere prevails at this informal and exclusively vegetarian restaurant, where "neatloaf" served with gravy and potatoes is one popular option, and where the chef creates a daily "Peace Special."

California Culinary Academy ($$) 625 Polk Street (tel. 415/771 3500). The student chefs who may—or may not—become the culinary stars of the future, create the quality lunches and dinners (timed seatings only) served here.

Miss Pearl's Jam House ($$) 601 Eddy Street (tel. 415/775 5267). A strong selection of inventive Caribbean-style lunches and dinners served amid exotic decor and Jamaican music delights the predominantly young, hip, and affluent diners.

101 Restaurant ($) 101 Eddy Street (tel. 415/928 4490). One of the best of the neighborhood's growing band of no-frills Southeast Asian restaurants, offering a mouthwatering array of Vietnamese dishes at a price to please the tightest budget.

Pag Asa Kitchen Express ($) 350 Golden Gate Avenue (tel. 415/776 8082). Delightful Filipino fare, served cafeteria-style for breakfast and lunch, draws a devoted band of regulars to this extremely inexpensive hole-in-the-wall.

Salud! ($$) 500 Van Ness Avenue (tel. 415/864 8500). A cut above most of the city's Mexican restaurants, with artistically presented regional specialities offered in a bright and airy room.

Sorndang Café ($) 472 Turk Street (tel. 415/931 9433). Cheap and cheerful place in which to enjoy a good-value Thai lunch or dinner.

Spuntino ($) 524 Van Ness Avenue (tel. 415/861 7772). Impressive range of modest-sized Italian meals and snacks—and wickedly good gelato—which appeals to the area's opera- and ballet-goers, and passersby, alike.

Stars ($$$) 150 Redwood Alley (tel. 415/861 7827). Currently the hottest spot for the city's leading socialites to be seen grazing on the usually (though not always) delectable creations of a celebrity chef; gossip columnists occupy bar-side vantage points.

Stars Café ($$) 500 Van Ness Avenue (tel. 415/861 4344). A less costly and less socially intimidating offshoot of Stars, but with food to thrill the most jaded tastebuds.

Zuni Café ($$) 1658 Market Street (tel. 415/552 2522). A noted spot for classy northern California cuisine, the Zuni offers gourmet hamburgers and a selection of seasonal dishes bearing the influence of French and American regional cookery.

FINANCIAL DISTRICT & UNION SQUARE

Aqua ($$$) 252 California Street (tel. 415/956 9662). Painstakingly selected and prepared—and then carefully presented—seafood draws a style-conscious crowd to one of the city's most modernistically designed dining places.

Café 222 ($$) inside the Nikko Hotel, 222 Mason Street (tel. 415/394 1111). Though not always successful in its efforts to mate Asian and Californian cuisines, Café 222's evening buffet of soup, salad, and fish and meat main courses, can be very satisfying.

Corona Bar & Grill ($$) 88 Cyril Magnin Street (tel. 415/392 5500). Inspired by the cuisines of Mexico and the American southwest, the Corona draws an expectant and trendy crowd; the paella is the house speciality and is seldom less than excellent.

Dottie's True Blue Café ($) 522 Jones Street (tel. 415/885 2767). This small and friendly diner offers great start-the-day omelettes—breakfast also includes fruit and cereal options—and a variety of health-conscious lunches.

Dutch Kitchen ($$) inside the St Francis Hotel, Union Square (tel. 415/397 7000). Ordering à la carte can be disappointing but the breakfast buffet, with its bacon, eggs, cereals, fresh fruits, and more, can be a good way to start the day and to see some of this landmark hotel.

Fog City Diner ($$) 1300 Battery Street (tel. 415/982 2000). The abundant chrome and neon evoke the 1950s but the food is resolutely 1990s California, with a host of innovative appetizers and main courses based on regional American cooking. It aims to delight the predominantly well-dressed and affluent Financial District diners.

Indonesia Restaurant & Cafeteria ($) 678 Post Street (tel. 415/474 4026). A glorious selection of Indonesian dishes—available in mild as well as ultra-spicy forms—all at inexpensive prices and served in a no-frills setting.

John's Grill ($$) 63 Ellis Street (tel. 415/986 1133). It may overdo its mention in Dashiell Hammett's *The Maltese Falcon* (a replica of the sought-after bird sits in the upstairs dining room), but John's Grill also serves some exceptionally good steak, seafood, and pasta dishes for lunch and dinner.

Lefty O'Douls ($) 333 Geary Street (tel. 415/982 8900). Named for a baseball legend and decorated with sporting memorabilia, this cafeteria-style restaurant serves inexpensive American fare throughout the day.

Lori's Diner ($) 336 Mason Street (tel. 415/392 8646) and 500 Sutter Street (tel. 415/981 1950). Both branches of this 1950s-style diner are dependable places to significantly boost your calorie intake: heavyweight breakfasts, sandwiches, burgers, and creamy milkshakes are served around the clock.

Masa's ($$$) at the Vintage Court Hotel, 648 Bush Street (tel. 415/989 7154). Praise has been lavishly heaped upon Masa's since its 1983 opening, and the acclaim continues to be justified: the city's finest French restaurant by far, and one which complements its tremendous food with top-rate service.

276

The Pine Crest ($) 401 Geary Street (tel. 415/885 6407). Lovers of traditional coffee shops will enjoy lingering over a cholesterol-intensive meal in one of the red-vinyl booths; for anyone else, the Pine Crest's most appealing feature is that it stays open around the clock.

Postrio ($$$) inside the Prescott Hotel, 545 Post Street (tel. 415/776 7825). Celebrity chef Wolfgang Puck opened this shrine to California-style gourmet eating—his first restaurant outside Los Angeles—in 1989, and San Franciscans have yet to stop raving about it; reservations are essential.

Sol y Luna ($$) 475 Sacramento Street (tel. 415/296 8696). A variety of tapas—many familiar items and others which reflect the creativity of the Spanish chefs—and eye-catching decor are two good reasons for lunching here; dinner is served to the accompaniment of live music.

Splendido's ($$) 4 Embarcadero Center (tel. 415/986 3222). The predominantly southern French and Italian food is excellent, but even more striking is the setting: a would-be Mediterranean village complete with Moorish arches and Spanish tiles.

Thai Stick ($) 698 Post Street (tel. 415/928 7730). It is far too easy to order more than you can eat—and still spend less than you think—in this enjoyable, good-quality Thai restaurant; be sure to leave space for the delicious tapioca pudding dessert.

Tommy Toy's ($$$) 655 Montgomery Street (tel. 415/397 4888). The city's premier upscale Chinese restaurant serves winning French-influenced fare in an ornate setting, attracting the city's most famous faces and its fussiest eaters in similar numbers.

Yank Sing ($$) 427 Battery Street (tel. 415/362 1640) and 49 Stevenson Street (tel. 415/541 4949). Though pricier than their equivalents in nearby Chinatown, both branches of Yank Sing offer some of the finest dim sum in San Francisco.

FISHERMAN'S WHARF & FORT MASON

Alioto's No.8 ($$) 8 Fisherman's Wharf (tel. 415/673 0183). The seafood is of variable quality, but the fact that this is the neighborhood's oldest restaurant—founded in the early 1900s by a Sicilian settler whose son later became city mayor—might be sufficient justification to eat here.

Big Sky Ranch ($$) Ghirardelli Square (tel. 415/441 1223). Be it campfire chili, Yankee pot roast, or berry cobbler dessert, this restaurant overlooking Fisherman's Wharf promises "American heritage" fare served in a "true ranch style" setting.

Buena Vista Café ($) 2765 Hyde Street (tel. 415/474 5044). A good bet for simple inexpensive food in this pricey area, though best known for its punch-packing Irish coffee, a drink claimed to have been served for the first time in the U.S. here in 1952.

Chowders Seafood Diner ($) Pier 39 (tel. 415/391 4737). A fast-seafood diner amid Pier 39's plethora of over-priced restaurants and a commendable place to enjoy clam chowder in a sourdough bowl.

Eagle Café ($) Pier 39 (tel. 415/433 3689). Satiating the ample appetites of longshoremen since the 1920s, the Eagle Café was shifted by crane to its current position in 1978. It maintains its culinary traditions by serving well-filled omelettes and substantial sandwiches at rock-bottom prices to a mix of wharf workers and tourists, who relish this authentic slice of local life.

Gaylords ($$) Ghirardelli Square (tel. 415/771 8822). Boasting stunning views across the Golden Gate, Gaylords is a branch of a mid-range chain which specializes in serving Northern Indian fare in attractive settings; neither service nor food should disappoint.

Ghirardelli Soda Fountain ($) Ghirardelli Square (tel. 415/771 4903). Milkshakes, ice cream, and decadent sundaes are all on offer in this outlet of the locally revered chocolate manufacturer; specialties include the mighty "earthquake sundae", which serves four.

Greens ($$$) Building A, Fort Mason (tel. 415/771 6222). An outstanding vegetarian restaurant where gourmet-pleasing dishes are created using the produce of an organic farm run by a Zen Buddhist retreat. The bay views are as stunning as the food; reservations are essential.

HAIGHT-ASHBURY

Blue Front Café ($) 1430 Haight Street (tel. 415/252 5917). Inviting spot for Middle Eastern snacks and good-sized American sandwiches.

Cha Cha Cha ($) 1805 Haight Street (tel. 415/386 5758). Delicious Cuban and Caribbean dishes served in a tropically decorated—and frequently packed—room, where the serving staff leave diners in no doubt as to who is in charge.

Coffee Zone ($) 1409 Haight Street (tel. 415/863 2443),

An extremely diverse clientele and a great range of snacks—as well as usually excellent coffee—make this a fine place for a pick-me-up while exploring the area.
Dish ($$) 1398 Haight Street (tel. 415/431 3534). The eclectic and ever-changing lunch and dinner options reflect the seasons and the mood of the chef; whatever you order, you can expect a meal of good quality and can eat it surrounded by wall-hung dishes of every shape and size.
Escape from New York Pizza ($) 1737 Haight Street (tel. 415/668 5577). Local branch of an increasingly popular outlet for thick, chewy pizza served whole or by the slice with a variety of toppings.
Ironwood Café ($$) 901 Cole Street (tel. 415/664 0224). Classy Californian cuisine served to diners seated in comfortable booths.
Jammin' Java ($) 701 Cole Street (tel. 415/668 5282). Another highly recommended neighborhood coffee house offering great refreshments and a chance to observe local life.
Kan Zaman ($) 1793 Haight Street (tel. 415/751 9656). Middle Eastern food, strong coffee, and exotic ambience: diners sit on cushions surrounded by hookahs and entertained by belly dancers.
Pork Store Café ($) 1451 Haight Street (tel. 415/864 6981). Dependable purveyor of wholesome American breakfasts—the side dishes include Deep Southern favorites such as grits—and lunchtime fare that features delicious soups, sandwiches, and thick burgers.
Tassajara Café & Bakery ($) 1000 Cole Street (tel. 415/664 8947). Some San Franciscans come to Haight-Ashbury solely to enjoy the wondrous fresh bread and pastries baked and served here.
Thep Phanom ($) 400 Waller Street (tel. 415/431 2526). Top-notch Thai food for dinner only, at a price to suit even the most threadbare of budgets; be sure to arrive early or make a reservation.

JAPANTOWN

Elka ($$$) 1625 Post Street (tel. 415/922 3200). A traditional-style setting for tremendous Japanese dishes reflecting the flair and creativity of Californian cuisine; serves lunch and dinner, and a mighty Japanese breakfast.
The Good Earth ($) 1865 Post Street (tel. 415/771 0151). Specializes in using only fresh, all-natural ingredients—chosen for their flavors—in breakfast, lunch, and dinner dishes which are offered at reasonable cost to health-conscious eaters.
Isobune ($$) Japan Center (tel. 415/563 1030). Watch the chef prepare sushi and then make your selection from little sushi-laden boats which float past the counter-seated diners.
Korea House ($$) 1640 Post Street (tel. 415/563 1388). Eating Korean food in the heart of Japantown may seem perverse, but this is a reliable outlet for popular Korean dishes such as spicy barbecued meat, and numerous varieties of soup and noodles.
Neecha ($) 2100 Sutter Street (tel. 415/922 9419). Unexciting but dependable range of Thai favorites offered at tempting prices.
Sanppo ($$) 1702 Post Street (tel. 415/346 3486). Among the best-priced and best-decorated Japanese restaurants in the area, serving food which seldom fails to please.

MISSION DISTRICT

Angkor Borei ($$) 3471 Mission Street (tel. 415/550 8417). Excellent Cambodian food served in inventive and stylish ways; distance from the city's fashionable areas helps keep the prices lower than they might otherwise be.
El Toro Taqueria ($) 598 Valencia Street (tel. 415/431 3351). Popular with locals for down-to-earth Mexican food costing just a few dollars per huge plateful.
La Cumbre ($) 515 Valencia Street (tel. 415/863 8205). Cafeteria-style outlet for simple but tasty low-cost Mexican favorites.
New Dawn ($) 3174 16th Street (tel. 415/553 8888). A contemporary bohemian twist on the traditional coffee shop, with crazy decor and anything-goes ambience but offering no-nonsense breakfasts and lunches.
Nicaragua ($) 3015 Mission Street (tel. 415/826 3672). An extremely cost-effective and friendly place to sample the traditional fare of the Central American country.
Pauline's Pizza Pie ($$) 260 Valencia Street (tel. 415/552 2050). Dinner-only spot serving thin-crust gourmet pizzas with a choice of organic toppings.
Saigon Saigon ($$) 1132 Valencia Street (tel. 415/206 9635). Black-pepper catfish and coconut chicken are among the specialties of this highly rated and fairly priced Vietnamese restaurant.
Salvadoreno ($) 535 Valencia Street (tel. 415/431 6554). A Salvadorean bakery with many inviting shelves of cakes and pastries.
St. Francis Candy Store & Soda Fountain ($) 2801 24th Street (tel. 415/826 4200). The last remaining soda fountain in San

278

Francisco, the family-run St. Francis has been offering simple sandwiches, ice-cream, and frothy milkshakes to its customers since 1918. **Scenic India** ($) 532 Valencia Street (tel. 415/621 7226). Unexciting but well-priced selection of curries and tandoori dishes.

NOB HILL

Big Four ($$$) in the Huntington Hotel, 1075 California Street (tel. 415/771 1140). Californian reworkings of classic French dishes are the staples of this ultra-elegant, very traditional dining place, where the city's rich and powerful regularly indulge themselves.
Crown Room ($$$) in the Fairmont Hotel, 950 Mason Street (tel. 415/772 5131). An enormous buffet and panoramic views are the features of this 24th-floor restaurant, though the dizzying elevator ride to reach ground level does nothing to aid digestion.

NORTH BEACH

Basta Pasta ($$) 1268 Grant Avenue (tel. 415/434 2248). Enjoyable Italian eating—including fine pastas and succulent wood-fired pizzas—with large windows giving views of the people-packed street outside; another plus is the unusually late opening hours: service continues until 1:45am.
Bohemian Cigar Store ($) 566 Columbus Avenue (tel. 415/362 0536). Long-established North Beach café with excellent focaccia bread snacks and great potential for people watching.
Buca Giovanni ($$$) 800 Greenwich Street (tel. 415/776 7766). Not many out-of-towners know about this basement restaurant which serves some of the

best Tuscan-style food in the neighborhood; dinner only, reservations essential.
Caff e Trieste ($) 601 Vallejo Street (tel. 415/392 6739). From the 1950s to the present day, the family-run Trieste has drawn writers, poets, artists, and anyone seeking a flavorful cup of coffee and a variety of tempting cakes and snacks. The amateur opera performances staged here on Saturday afternoons have become a neighborhood institution.
Calzone's ($$) 430 Columbus Avenue (tel. 415/397 3600). Large, busy, and somewhat overrated spot for pasta, seafood, and pizzas; stick to the simpler dishes and aim to arrive early enough to grab a prime window table.
Campo Santo ($) 240 Columbus Avenue (tel. 415/433 9623). The high-kitsch Mexican Day of the Dead decor, and classy—sometimes fiery—south-of the-border food, make this one of North Beach's most appealing newcomers.
Capp's Corner ($$) 1600 Powell Street (tel. 415/989 2589). Owned by a former boxing champion, Capp's has delicious pasta lunches and serves five-course set dinners—as well as à la carte options—to satiate the most ravenous of appetites.
Fior d'Italia ($$) 601 Union Street (tel. 415/986 1886). Among San Francisco's oldest Italian restaurants and undoubtedly one of the best, Fior d'Italia offers wonderfully fresh pasta dishes either in the elegant backroom or at the less formal tables overlooking Washington Square.
Gold Spike ($) 527 Columbus Avenue (tel. 415/421 4591). Filled to bursting point almost every night for unbeatable North

Beach atmosphere and wonderful six-course Italian dinners.
La Bodega ($) 1337 Grant Avenue (tel. 415/433 0439). Long-established and much admired Spanish restaurant which serves a ridiculously inexpensive paella special every night except Friday and Saturday; live flamenco music often accompanies the eating.
The New San Remo Restaurant ($) 2237 Mason Street (tel. 415/673 9090). Being located a few minutes' walk from the busiest North Beach streets helps this intimate northern Italian restaurant keep down the cost of its alluring fixed-price five-course dinners.
North Beach Pizza ($) 1499 Grant Avenue (tel. 415/433 2444). Famous throughout the city for its thick, chewy pizzas served with a host of toppings, North Beach Pizza is a great late-night stop, and the lines which were once a perennial feature have been reduced to the opening of a second branch just down the hill at 1310 Grant Avenue.
North Beach Restaurant ($$) 1512 Stockton Street (tel. 415/392 1700). Among the neighborhood's more elegant and formal Italian restaurants, the choices include a fixed-price seven-course dinner, and there is an extensive wine list.
The Stinking Rose ($$) 325 Columbus Avenue (tel. 415/781 7673). The food is predominantly Italian but the unique element is the fact that every dish—and many of the drinks—make liberal use of garlic.
Susie Kate's ($$) 655 Union Street (tel. 415/981 KATE). Stylish interpretations of downhome Southern U.S. fare, such as hush puppies, cheese grits, fried chicken, and sweet potatoes, attract plenty of curious diners.

Viva's ($$) 1224 Grant Avenue (tel. 415/989 8482). Frequently crowded due to its tremendous northern Italian specialities and some excellent seafood dishes; the daily specials are always a good bet.

Washington Square Bar & Grill ($$$) 1707 Powell Street (tel. 415/982 8123). Though no longer the premier hangout of city journalists and influential politicians, you are still likely to spot a few (locally) famous faces among the crowd digging into pricey Italian food.

PACIFIC HEIGHTS, RUSSIAN HILL & MARINA DISTRICT

Angkor Palace ($$) 1769 Lombard Street (tel. 415/931 2830). There are many less-costly places to enjoy high-quality Cambodian food in San Francisco, but this one of the few where diners remove their shoes on entering and are seated on floor cushions.

Art Institute Café ($) 800 Chestnut Street (tel. 415/749 4567). Part of San Francisco Art Institute but open to the public, this café serves inexpensive lunches and snacks, and has a patio area with great views of Fisherman's Wharf and Telegraph Hill.

Blue Light Café ($$) 1979 Union Street (tel. 415/922 5510). Spicy and creative dishes based on the food of the American southwest; a reliable place to sample this increasingly chic cuisine.

Café Caravan ($) 1312 Chestnut Street (tel. 415/441 1168). This simple coffee shop, serving reliable breakfast omelettes and generous lunchtime sandwiches, is a welcome addition to an area dominated by fashion-conscious restaurants.

Café Marimba ($) 2317 Chestnut Street (tel. 415/776 1506). Draws plenty of regular visitors for its tasty variety of regional Mexican dishes, served amid a clutter of Latin American folk art.

Caravansary ($) 2257 Chestnut Street (tel. 415/922 2705). A dependable place for an inexpensive snack, the options include a promising array of Middle Eastern delights alongside the usual American fare.

Doidge's ($) 2217 Union Street (tel. 415/921 2149). Began as a tiny diner and rapidly evolved into a popular breakfast and lunch spot, largely because of its expertly prepared omelettes and other light dishes; reservations are required for the excellent Sunday brunch.

The Elite Café ($$) 2049 Fillmore Street (tel. 415/346 8668). Whether its red beans and rice or stuffed eggplant, this goumet-pleasing cajun/creole restaurant serves the spicy favorites of Louisiana in endlessly inventive and mouthwatering ways.

Judy's Homestyle Café ($) 2268 Chestnut Street (tel. 415/922 4588). Cereals, fresh fruit, and delicious muffins enliven the usual egg-based breakfast offerings, while the Sunday brunch has become a popular local rendezvous.

Kabul West ($$) 2800 Van Ness Avenue (tel. 415/931 9144). Sautéed pumpkin with yogurt is just one of the many delights in this increasingly well-respected Afghan restaurant.

La Follie ($$$) 2316 Polk Street (tel. 415/776 5577). First-class French food created and presented with imagination and style; reservations are essential. A rarely less than delightful fixed-price three-course meal is served Monday to Thursday, with an *à la carte* menu at other times.

Moghul India ($$) 1956 Lombard Street (tel. 415/928 3868). One of the best of the city's growing band of Indian restaurants, serving all the expected dishes plus several unusual and intriguing house specialties.

Perry's ($$) 1944 Union Street (tel. 415/922 9022). A wood-paneled New York-style restaurant and bar which offers ample portions of meat and seafood and has a long-standing reputation as Pacific Heights' premier singles' meeting spot.

Pheu Ang Thai ($) 2001 Union Street (tel. 415/775 4735). One of the most budget-friendly dining options on fashionable Union Street, this Thai restaurant carries a lengthy menu of soups, salads, and curry dishes, plus an enticing number of noodle and rice options.

Sushi Paradiso ($$) 1475 Polk Street (tel. 415/567 0184). An intimate and classy setting for top-quality sushi and other seafood dishes from around the world.

Tay Viet ($) 2034 Chestnut Street (tel. 415/567 8124). One of the area's least expensive ethnic restaurants, serving tremendous Vietnamese specialties.

Thai Spice ($) 1730 Polk Street (tel. 415/775 4777). Top-quality Thai food served in an airy setting puts this among the city's premier ethnic eating spots; an enormous menu includes an impressive number of vegetarian dishes.

Vlasta's ($$) 2420 Lombard Street (tel. 415/931 7533). A cozy, family-run restaurant with an intriguing variety of tasty, if sometimes slightly stodgy, dishes of central European origin.

RICHMOND DISTRICT

China House Bistro ($$) 501 Balboa Street (tel. 415/752 2802). The regional cuisines of northern China fill the menu and include many Shanghai specialties.

Eats ($) 50 Clement Street (tel. 415/752 8837). It may look like an eat-and-go fast-food restaurant, but here you will find sizeable, generously proportioned breakfasts and lunches of superior quality to take out or devour while lingering at a window table.

Hong Kong Flower Lounge ($$) 5322 Geary Boulevard (tel. 415/668 8998). Certainly not the cheapest local place to eat Chinese food but this unsurprizingly busy restaurant offers the finest Cantonese fare in San Francisco; it serves top-notch dim sum at lunchtime, too.

Khan Toke Thai House ($$) 5937 Geary Boulevard (tel. 415/668 6654). Lovers of Thai food bemoaning the fact that city restaurants usually serve only mild forms of their national dishes to appease American palates, will find plenty to stimulate their tastebuds among the authentic spicy options.

Little Russia Bakery ($) 5217 Geary Boulevard (tel. 415/751 9661). One of the popular haunts of the area's long-established Russian population, this likeable deli serves assorted Russian snacks, pastries, and cakes.

Mel's Drive-In ($) 3355 Geary Boulevard (tel. 415/386 2244). You really can make a drive-in order at this 1950s neighborhood landmark, though most customers take a seat and dig into classic coffee shop fare such as thick, cheese-coated burgers and enormous barbecued meat sandwiches.

Minh's Garden ($) 208 Clement Street (tel. 415/751 8211). Serves great-value Vietnamese food from 11a.m. to 11p.m.; anyone unfamiliar with this type of cuisine will find the friendly staff a great source of information when ordering.

Royal Thai ($$) 951 Clement Street (tel. 415/386 1795). More expensive and with a more formal ambience than many of the city's Thai restaurants, though widely regarded as among the best of its kind; no lunches are served on weekends.

Star of India ($$) 3721 Geary Boulevard (tel. 415/668 4466). A lengthy menu, which includes many mouthwatering vegetarian selections, helps make this low-key spot one of San Francisco's more appealing Indian restaurants; the weekday lunch buffet is a bargain.

Straits Café ($) 3300 Geary Boulevard (tel. 415/668 1783). Wonderful and inexpensive Singaporean food, with many vegetarian options and a particularly strong selection of seafood dishes.

SOMA

Café Rocco ($$) 1131 Folsom Street (tel. 415/554 0522). Good selection of northern Italian fare and a sun-filled patio (fog permitting) on which to eat it; serves breakfast and lunch daily, and dinner too from Thursday to Saturday.

The Fly Trap ($$) 606 Folsom Street (tel. 415/243 0580). In one form or another The Fly Trap has been around for a century. Although this is a new version, it evokes an old-style San Francisco ambience and serves commendable Italian-influenced meals.

Hamburger Mary's Organic Grill ($) 1582 Folsom Street (tel. 415/626 5767). Garishly decorated and often patronized by a nightclubbing clientele, Mary's generously sized burgers are generally the best picks from a menu which usually also includes soups, sandwiches, and salads.

Max's Diner ($$) 311 Third Street (tel. 415/546 6297). Meatloaf, turkey sandwiches, cheeseburgers, and hunks of fried fish all feature among the meals famously served in large portions in this New York-style diner, which is usually packed with local office workers.

Moshi Moshi ($) 2092 W. Third Street (tel. 415/861 8285). Very reasonably priced Japanese food served in a simple setting; the much-praised sushi is a reliable lunchtime choice; the dinner menu features a wider selection of seafood.

Ruby's ($$) 489 Third Street (tel. 415/541 0795). Informal and handily located, with a small menu which features salads, pastas, sandwiches, and inventively filled pizzas and calzone. The fresh soups and daily specials are also worth a try.

Sirtaj ($) 48 Fifth Street (tel. 415/957 0140). The 13-course lunch buffet is one cost-effective way to sample the Indian food served here, which also features good-value set dinners beside a lengthy menu of other Indian delights.

South Park Café ($$) 108 South Park Avenue (tel. 415/495 7275). Brings a touch of culinary sophistication to a section of SoMa still in the early throes of gentrification; the food—and the ambience— is modeled on that of a French bistro.

Index

INDEX

INDEX

INDEX

287

Picture credits

The Automobile Association would like to thank the following photographers, libraries and associations for their assistance in the preparation of this book.

ASSOCIATED PRESS/TOPHAM 21a Earthquake destruction
ALLSPORT UK LTD 164a Amp Lee SF 49ers, 165b T Rathman SF 49ers (Otto Greule)
BANCROFT LIBRARY 29a, 29b Miwok Indians, 77b Chinatown 1890
MARY EVANS PICTURE LIBRARY 30a Golden Hind, 32a Washing for gold, 32b, 33a, 33b Gold Prospectors, 34a Nob Hill, 34b Fire 1851, 35 Chinatown 1927, 36a First Trans-Continent link, 36c Norton I, 37a Samuel Brannon, 37b Ambrose Bierce, 39a Earthquake destruction
RONALD GRANT ARCHIVES 16a *The Maltese Falcon*, 16b Clint Eastwood, *Dirty Harry*, 17a *The Convention*, 17b *Vertigo*
MAGNUM PHOTOS 20a Buckled street (Eli Reed), 20b Earthquake destruction (M K Nichols), 111 Hippies
RAY 'SCOTTY' MORRIS 234a, 234b *Beach Blanket Babylon*
NATURE PHOTOGRAPHERS LTD 21b California gray whale (P R STERRY)
POPPERFOTTO 42a Hippie couple
DAN REST 232b San Francisco Opera
SAN FRANCISCO CHRONICLE 233b *Sleeping Beauty* (M Macor)
SAN FRANCISCO CONVENTION & VISITORS BUREAU 10c Chinese Market (Mark Snyder), 165a S. F. Giants Baseball Club (Kerrick James), 252 Cable car Gripman (Mark Gibson)
SAN FRANCISCO MUSEUM OF MODERN ART 160 *Woman with the hat*, Henri Matisse (Elise S Haas Collection), 161a *Guardians of the Secret*, Jackson Pollock
SAN FRANCISCO SYMPHONY 231b, 232a Herbert Blomstadt & Symphony (T McCarthy)
RON SCHEIL 241 Statue
SPECTRUM COLOUR LIBRARY 28a San Andreas Fault
THE MANSELL COLLECTION 30b Drake, 32c Record of gold discovery, 36b Claus Spreckels, 38a Fire, 38/9 Destruction
TOPHAM/PICTUREPOINT 40b General strike, 42c Ron Landberg & Rev Harris, 110b People Haight Street

The remaining photographs are held in the Automobile Association's own photo library (AA PHOTO LIBRARY) and were taken by Rob Holmes with the exception of page 217b, which was taken by H. Harris, the spine and pages 2, 3, 4, 5a, 9b, 12b, 18c, 19b, 47, 89a, 89b, 135, 151a, 215, 219, 220, 223, 240, 243, 256, which were taken by B. Smith, and page 12a, which was taken by W. Voysey.

Contributors

Series adviser: Christopher Catling   **Joint series editor**: Susi Bailey
Copy editor: Beth Ingpen   **Designer**: Tony Truscott Designs
Verifier: Christine Rickerby   **Indexer**: Marie Lorimer